THE
GLORY
YEARS

SCOTT WALKINSHAW

THE
GLORY
YEARS

The Rise of Oxford United
in the 1980s

pitch

First published by Pitch Publishing, 2025

pitch

Pitch Publishing
9 Donnington Park,
85 Birdham Road,
Chichester, West Sussex,
PO20 7AJ
www.pitchpublishing.co.uk
info@pitchpublishing.co.uk

A CIP catalogue record is available for this book
from the British Library.

ISBN 978 1 80150 935 0

Typesetting and origination by Pitch Publishing

FSC
www.fsc.org

MIX
Paper | Supporting
responsible forestry
FSC™ C016779

Printed and bound on FSC® certified paper in line with
our continuing commitment to ethical business practices,
sustainability and the environment.

Printed and bound in India by Replika Press Pvt. Ltd.

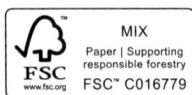

Contents

Dedication

For Emma,
Millie and Hamish.

Preface

FOR MORE than 40 years, when I've mentioned that I'm an Oxford United fan, the response has been familiar. 'Oh, I remember when they played in the First Division,' or even, 'I used to go to the Manor, back in the day.' More recently, the response has been, 'Weren't you in the Conference?' or, 'What division are you in now?'

Over time, the story of Oxford's rise through the divisions in the 1980s has become fragmented. The details have faded; the singular moment of winning the Milk Cup in 1986 has become stripped of its context.

The Glory Years sets out to re-establish the foundations of a story which deserves to be passed through the generations, from the arrival of Ian Greaves through the irrepressible Jim Smith and on to Maurice Evans and Mark Lawrenson.

Having lived through those years, I hadn't appreciated what a remarkable story it was: from near bankruptcy to a failed merger, from back-to-back titles and giant-killings right through to that day at Wembley. It all seemed so normal back then.

Nor did I appreciate the backdrop against which it happened. The crushing impact of hooliganism and the ban from Europe brought the English game to its knees and ultimately cleared the way for the Premier League, and the death of the flamboyant personality manager and the emergence of a raspy Scot who transformed Manchester United and with it English football.

Almost by accident, Oxford United were there throughout, playing an active part in a curious era. They humiliated Alex Ferguson on his debut and then again when his revolution spluttered; they were a direct victim of the European ban, and yet through it all they were a beacon of joy during a bleak time.

At the centre of the story is Robert Maxwell. Cruel and demonic, complex and ingenious, he foresaw the modern era and the domination of TV but he could never shake the perception that he was an outsider and the establishment resisted. His nemesis, Rupert Murdoch, would eventually benefit from his foresight.

But, Maxwell, Smith and Evans, along with John Aldridge, Ray Houghton, Malcolm Shotton, Gary Briggs and many more, brought magic to the eccentric Manor Ground and injected Oxford United with a history that lives on today. Their successes gave the club purpose and hope when it was drifting and hopeless; their achievements dragged fans through the harshest times.

But inevitably, while the feelings remain, the memories fade. *The Glory Years* aims to relive that time and bring it back to life.

Chapter 1

Me

A MONOCHROME despair wrapped everything in a film that suffocated the warmth from the atmosphere. This wasn't a Victorian winter with snow to playfully skip through or the warming glow of open fires: it was long, dank, featureless, and very British, a joyless cold that seeped through the skin and into the muscles. Even my mum's best efforts to wrap me up and protect me offered little defence; my cheeks glowed and my toes ached as I descended into a dense and inescapable numbness.

I looked out to the empty expanse of rutted turf as the public address system crackled persistently above. There was rhythm in its coughing and a faint melody through the unforgiving static hiss. At the far end, on the front of a box-like corner stand, behind a row of three-wheeled Invacars, cards were hung on a wooden board – A 0-0, B 1-0, C 2-1 – half-time scores tapped out in footballing Morse code.

The speakers spewed out their half-time entertainment: Abba and the Police. 'Another Brick in the Wall' by Pink Floyd had soundtracked Christmas at our grandparents' house. My aunt, 11 years younger than my dad and closer to my age than his, played it continuously. I found its sinister choir of children protesting against their captures a frightening insight into the mind of oppressed teenagers.

My dad's father was known as 'Granda' – a Gallic affectation that survived their journey south. As a scientist he'd been redeployed from Broxburn near Edinburgh to Harwell about 15 miles from Oxford to work at the Atomic Weapons Research Establishment. He had a useful disposition for a scientist; pragmatic, gentle and thoughtful, it afforded him and his family a comfortable life.

He and my gran were deposited on to a new-build estate for the growing scientific community on the edge of Abingdon, a rapidly expanding market town. Every day, the men would dutifully board the buses and head to the labs leaving the women to tend to tasks broadly categorised as 'other'. Lonely and homesick, Granny fell into periods of depression while looking after her three children.

Dad was born in Scotland as the war ended. His middle-class upbringing, through the optimism of the 1950s and 1960s, afforded him Italian suits and imported Elvis Presley singles. He combed his hair into a lacquered quiff. Despite the looming threat of the Cold War, the family remained in their comfortable bubble. One night, Granda was visited by mysterious foreign men for an earnest discussion at the dining room table. He never spoke of it, but it's assumed they were Russians encouraging him to defect, as some of his colleagues had previously.

Dad went to polytechnic in Wolverhampton to study maths and pursue his dream to follow Wolverhampton Wanderers home and away. He'd been dazzled by the glamour of Wolves' marquee friendly against Honvéd in 1954 when Molineux swarmed with over 55,000 fans, shimmering under the floodlights and broadcast live on television. The spectacle gripped his imagination and offered a glimpse into a bigger, more glamorous world.

He was ten years old, an impressionable age when new experiences are chiselled into you. He passed on the stories that lived in him, so they lived in me too. Football was about adventure.

The glamour of Wolves being declared world champions seemed far away, but he was just a bus ride from Headington United, a Southern League juggernaut on the outskirts of Oxford. He and his friends would finish school on a Saturday, make a pack of sandwiches and travel across the county to watch them play.

Headington United's successes drew crowds from around the area and their reputation was something the Football League couldn't ignore. In 1962, when Accrington Stanley resigned from the league, Headington – by this point Oxford United – were elected to replace them.

Seventeen years later, on 29 December 1979, we were standing on the sparse London Road terrace, the home end of Oxford's bijou stadium, the Manor Ground. We'd shivered our way through the opening half of a turgid battle against Hull City, the interval coming as blessed relief allowing people to duck behind the stand to salvage some warmth from a tray of chips, a cup of Bovril or the drag of a cigarette.

To a seven-year-old the narrow concourse behind the terrace was like the bubbling human cauldron of a Turkish bazaar, a hubbub of people. It was uncomfortably cramped and smelly, an assault on the senses.

If you could navigate the relentless torrent of people, you'd eventually find the club shop: a dimly lit curiosity of badges, programmes and scarves. In the corner was a wizened man in fingerless gloves. Nobody ever seemed to have the courage to buy anything.

I'd stare at it all in joyful wonderment and was particularly obsessed with the old programmes, each club offering an insight into a world beyond the Manor – Plymouth,

Colchester, Walsall. Dad would buy a programme from a street vendor outside the ground and I'd obsessively absorb its content; the teams on the back, the referee and linesmen, the season's results in an unreadable font. There were stories of reserve games, grainy pictures of a trip to Southend or Hartlepool, a tantalising advert for the next game; little clues of something beyond my reach. Over time I'd hone my geography skills through their colours, home grounds, rivals and league status.

We didn't venture behind the stand; we stayed where we'd been for the previous hour, frozen motionless. My dad was terrified of me disappearing into the throng to be sold to traffickers or vagabonds.

'Do you want to stay for the second half or shall we go home?' he said.

It was memorable only because the option of leaving a game early hadn't entered my vocabulary. Most of my experience of football was through the filter of television. Games were a tightly edited avalanche of thrills. I had little idea that football was boring or that it might be abandoned halfway through.

I was too young to make decisions. A few years earlier Dad had taken me to a sports shop to choose my first football kit. The shopkeeper presented two unbranded, heavy cotton football shirts, one in the old gold of Wolves and the other in the blue of Scotland.

I chose blue and matched it with white shorts and blue socks. If Dad was disappointed, he didn't show it. He said it could be an Everton or Ipswich kit, and so Ipswich became my team.

A few months later Ipswich played Arsenal in the 1978 FA Cup Final. Arsenal were my uncle's team, so the game became a friendly family feud. When Roger Osborne fired in from close range 15 minutes from time, not only had they won the cup on a sweltering hot day in front of 100,000 people, I seemed to have won it with them.

I'd been to the Manor before. My first game, when I was three, saw us lose 2-1 to Southampton. Dad said I spent most of it mesmerised by the floodlights, and an image of me staring up at the pylons is etched in my memory, though it can only be from what I've been told.

I didn't go to the Manor as a fan – it was just part of any visit to my grandparents at Christmas. Sometimes we'd go to Highbury to watch Arsenal, a short train journey from our home in Welwyn Garden City. Games at the Manor were small and straightforward whereas Highbury was complex and epic. The smells, the noise of street vendors, the vastness of the stadium felt complete.

Football could be boring with periods where nothing happened, and sometimes it lasted for the whole game. Even the best bits weren't always worth the wait. Back at the Manor, on that dank day in 1979, the prospect of another 45 minutes of nothingness was daunting, even to my dad.

To get a child's concession, I had to pass through a dedicated turnstile in the corner by the London Road terrace. Dad would give me money and pass me through – I'd hand it over and push on the giant iron gate which would resonate with a mechanical clunk. He'd race through another entrance and catch me as I was spat out on to the other side. That momentary loss of control triggered a deep illogical panic for him, but for me, that second of independence was part of the ceremony of a game: walking to the ground, merging with other fans until we became a crowd, the clanking turnstiles manned by people I assumed lived in the kiosk behind the grate.

The players would appear from the Beech Road tunnel and wave from the centre circle. I liked those who did things I couldn't. For a while, my favourite player was left-back John

Doyle because he could clear the ball beyond the halfway line with a satisfying 'schick' as his boot clipped the turf. Joe Cooke was another favourite because he was black and I wasn't.

But this game had dragged; Oxford had listlessly attacked the Cuckoo Lane End, the open concrete terrace housing a smattering of away supporters. From the covered London Road terrace, it was hard to make out what was happening as the ball ping-ponged between players. Narrow misses would prove to be wild hacks to the corner flag, dangerous crosses would drop hopelessly behind the goal. You read the game from the reaction of the crowd and players; the context rather than the action itself. It was an education in understanding the dynamics of football.

Leaving early had advantages: escaping the cold, and Granny would mollycoddle me with crisps and lemonade like I'd been tortured by an oppressive regime. I also had my Christmas presents – Subbuteo floodlights and a tiny presentation party with the Queen holding the FA Cup.

I looked around the Manor's five stands, built by the people of Oxford as the club evolved from a village team to a professional operation not yet 100 years in the making. I was struck by the novelty, the pitch, the scoreboard, the toxic odour of Bovril and cigarettes, the adultness. Did I really want to return to the safe, normal, warm world outside?

'Let's stay,' I said.

I now realise that if Dad wanted to stay, he probably wouldn't have asked. It must have been a terrible game for him to even contemplate going home that early.

The players returned; the stands filled, the floodlights illuminated, and the temperature dropped. The sun lowered like the house lights in a theatre, Oxford in their yellow Adidas shirts having the advantage of the Manor's notorious slope, a drop of seven feet from corner to corner.

The home side immediately burst into life; the sleepy crowd, over-indulged by Christmas and the drab performance, became animated. The noise melded into a singular roar. Five minutes after the break, in a rare moment of co-ordinated artistry, Peter Foley's free kick was met by Paul Berry to head the opening goal. Hull, hovering precariously above the Third Division relegation zone, with four wins all season, were broken. Nine minutes from time, Foley beat the offside trap on the left and guided in the second, then four minutes later Berry completed the rout as the drudgery of the first half evaporated into the darkening skies.

As the final whistle went, we headed for the exit and were swept down the steps from the terrace and along the long path back into the normal world outside. The adrenaline thawed my frozen bones.

I'd made the right decision. I'd stayed.

Chapter 2

Ian Greaves

IAN GREAVES looked out of the window of his cramped office under the Beech Road stand to see a playful squirrel scuttling along the wall. Something about the squirrel made him feel uneasy. It was Christmas Eve 1980, the first day at his new club. Despite spending the last few months in Hereford, helping his old mate Frank Lord, the tranquil countryside felt alien; what kind of stadium had trees hanging over the stands?

Born in Oldham, Greaves had grown up during the war in the shadows of the town's textile mills. Life in the north was visceral; he could see the factories, smell them, hear them, even taste them.

In Oxford, the offices and cloisters of the university were a far cry from the immediacy of the north. Privilege threaded through the city, future prime ministers and world leaders were moulded; aristocrats cemented their societal rites, their futures assured.

Greaves's experiences contrasted with the genteel Oxford suburbs and a city that felt somehow insulated from life's harsh realities. After being sacked by Bolton Wanderers, he'd been out of work for a year. He knew whether it was the next meal or the next day, nothing was guaranteed.

Greaves was a grafter; as a teenager he was a reliable all-rounder, and during national service he played cricket, hockey and football for the Lancashire Fusiliers, developing a reputation for hard work and steadfastness. His qualities attracted Matt Busby at Manchester United, who signed him in 1953. Busby styled him into a no-nonsense full-back and he played 15 times as a deputy to Bill Foulkes, winning the league title in 1956 as one of the fabled Busby Babes.

Five years later, as the Babes threatened to dominate club football for a generation, Greaves was due to fly with the squad to Yugoslavia for a European Cup tie against Red Star Belgrade. An injured elbow kept him at home as the team played out a 3-3 draw that eased them into the semi-finals after a 1-0 home-leg win.

The squad celebrated with a cocktail party at the British Embassy before departing for the airport. Leaving in sunshine, they landed in Munich to refuel. As they prepared to depart, the weather turned, and the temperature dropped. The pilot aborted his take-off twice, and on the third attempt the plane failed to gain height, clipped a fence and careered into trees, killing 23 passengers including eight of Greaves's Manchester United team-mates.

He was lucky, though it didn't feel like it; his injury had saved his life. With survival came guilt. 'Geoff [Bent] never came back – and he was my best mate,' Greaves recalled later. 'I now celebrate two birthdays every year, one on the day of the crash. But for the grace of God, it would have been me there.'

The grief of the city was projected on to the surviving players. Greaves, now 25, was thrust into the limelight, a senior squad member and first-choice full-back. He wore the number three shirt of skipper Roger Byrne, who'd perished in the crash. Two weeks after the disaster, Greaves lined up against Sheffield Wednesday in the FA Cup at Old Trafford. 'I can remember the dressing room was very quiet,' he said.

'I couldn't get Roger out of my mind; I was getting changed where he would have sat. I was wearing his shirt.'

Thirty years on, Greaves's misgivings at his bucolic surroundings were well placed. Oxford United were a club carelessly adrift. An accidental success, conceived to occupy local young men during the cricket off-season, had grown to be a Southern League powerhouse.

Headington was a village consumed by the city's polite urban sprawl. The Manor, their home since 1925, was stitched into the suburb's fabric, flanked by houses, a bowls club, the John Radcliffe Infirmary and London Road, a main artery into the city. The ground offered little opportunity to grow beyond its achievements. The centre of Oxford, a hive of ingenuity, was a two-mile freewheeling downhill bike ride away, but the club were a lifetime away from the dreaming spires and the hotbeds of English football.

Fans still talked about their heroic rise from non-league and the 1964 FA Cup campaign, the club's high-water mark which saw Oxford beat title-chasing Blackburn Rovers to reach the quarter-finals. Now, nearly two decades later, even the ghosts of the past were moving on.

To many, the Southern League days were a fresh memory, the Third Division an acceptable level of success. But, like many lower-league clubs, Oxford were heading into an abyss. Britain was an economic wasteland as recessionary pressures fuelled social unrest that channelled through to the decaying terraces of English football, which became a focus for restless, bored, disaffected young men.

Oxford's Cowley car plant, once the largest factory outside the US, lost nearly 80 per cent of its workforce. Manufacturing was replaced by a growing service sector, working-class people serving the elite.

Football's working-class romance was consumed by violence, halving crowds in less than a decade. Government, the police and the media, hardened by the experience of war, saw no excuses. The economic slump didn't compare to the horrors of the battlefield. Hooliganism was the insolence of a spoilt youth – an innate moral decline. Football had no political or social capital; there was no willingness to arrest the slide. With the sport starved of money and support, those who remained were overwhelmed.

Greaves could see the inertia, the gentle passing of time, the talented but featherweight Andy Thomas, the reliable but stale Peter Foley. Greaves called it a youth club, reliant on a flow of talent produced by mercurial scout Fred Ford.

You didn't need to be an insider to see the problem. Oxford were 22nd in the division with the worst home record in the country, they were lost and in desperate need of a story.

To Greaves, football was a privilege, something to be worked for and worked at, and at home in the north-west it was integral to cultural identity. Oxford was defined by its tension between town and gown, but few could deny the gown dominated. The football club was irrelevant.

'They held Second Division status for eight years,' Greaves said. 'But the locals didn't understand what a small miracle they were part of. Human nature being what it is, they've grown disgruntled by being relegated. Gratitude for being given so much in a short time. The public doesn't know the meaning of the word. Now they may have to face up to another spell in Division Four.'

Ambition and purpose ebbing away, Greaves knew complacency would be all-consuming. The squirrel on the wall, and its ambivalence towards its predators, spoke volumes about the club he'd inherited.

During his interview at director Bill Reeves's house, Greaves told the Oxford board he wanted to grab the club. 'I know more about football than you,' he said. 'More about selling and buying players, more about tactics, more about free kicks, corner kicks. So, no interference.'

Greaves's side had one win in 12 and four consecutive defeats. A 3-0 FA Cup exit to Plymouth Argyle had finally put paid to his predecessor, Bill Asprey, after 17 miserable months in which he failed to arrest the long-term slide.

The decay was having a wider effect – average crowds dipped under 4,000, a quarter down on the previous season. The club needed more than double that to break even. Their lottery kept them afloat, but the once healthy profits had fallen by two-thirds. Oxford were edging towards financial oblivion.

Greaves had little opportunity to meet his squad before the daunting Boxing Day home game against league leaders Charlton Athletic and their potent attacking force of the fearsome Derek Hales and youngster Paul Walsh. Charlton had been relegated the previous season and were impatient to return to the Second Division. They'd won 15 of their previous 16 games and hadn't lost for three months.

The Christmas holidays pushed the crowd over 5,700 – good for the season, but still only a third full. Greaves tucked himself into the tight, white brick dugout in front of the Beech Road stand with his assistant Roy Barry and 66-year-old authoritarian trainer Ken Fish, his tracksuit and hair presented to a military standard.

The starting line-up had one change from the previous defeat away at Millwall. Misfiring striker Keith Cassells was out with chickenpox and had been replaced by the disenchanted Peter Foley, a well-liked local boy who'd lost his way after missing out on a move to West Bromwich Albion, managed by former Oxford defender Ron Atkinson.

With the advantage of the slope, United took the early initiative and immediately looked more threatening. Inside 20 minutes, defender Malcolm McIntosh worked the ball to Mark Jones, who drove in a low cross. A deft touch from Joe Cooke diverted the ball into the path of Paul Barry, who lashed it beyond Charlton goalkeeper Nicky Johns for a shock opening goal.

The breakthrough strengthened Oxford's resolve, their aggression undermining their opponents' seemingly impenetrable confidence. Wingers Jones and Tim Smithers launched hopeful crosses into the box at every opportunity in an ugly and unexpected offensive barrage.

Oxford threatened after the break; Foley and skipper Billy Jeffrey had chances but as the game moved into its final act the shell-shocked league leaders woke from their stupor. Hales cannoned a shot off the bar and, as the final whistle approached, centre-back Malcolm Shotton heroically blocked what would have been a last-gasp equaliser.

Fate? A honeymoon victory? There was no time to dwell on the miraculous performance. The following day Oxford travelled the short distance to mid-table local rivals Reading. Cooke's near-post header from Jones's cross with 18 minutes to go secured their first consecutive league wins for eight months. A third clean sheet in a goalless draw with third-placed Rotherham a fortnight later sparked the team into life.

Greaves was a realist. 'I'm not kidding myself,' he said. 'Mickey Mouse could come in and get players going for a while. But ultimately a team, like water, finds its own level and I know I'll have to improve the standard with new players.'

His first move, at the end of January, showed the constraints he was working within. An approach for Aston Villa's Scottish international Alex Cropley failed when the midfielder dithered, and Greaves walked away. Unable to change the players, Greaves needed to change the philosophy of the ones he had.

He called it 'northern football'; fair play and skill was replaced by a focus on shape and discipline. Training sessions were tightly controlled, sometimes lasting no more than 20 minutes. The team delighted in frustrating their opponents as much as entertaining the fans. For Greaves, wins made supporters happy and that resulted from a hard-working team. It mirrored his playing days.

He found his bedrock at the centre of defence: Shotton, a 23-year-old Geordie with a wide jaw and sergeant major moustache, and his partner, the stern-faced 21-year-old Yorkshireman Gary Briggs, who'd been with the club for two and a half years after joining from Middlesbrough. Greaves gave the duo licence to explore the boundary between intimidation and ill discipline.

Greaves tightened the bolts of his playing unit. His front two, Peter Foley and Keith Cassells, buffered the prodigiously talented teenager Andy Thomas, giving him space to influence the game. On the wings, the defensive-minded Jones and Smithers were preferred to the expansive Kevin Brock. In mid-February, Greaves added the experience of 34-year-old former Welsh international Malcolm Page from Birmingham.

The impact was immediate; Oxford became hard to beat, losing three of their remaining 21 games, only revealing their vulnerabilities when the centre-back partnership was broken by an injury to Shotton.

As solid as their defence was, they'd only scored more than once on four occasions and Shotton was top scorer with five goals. By March, Oxford were still just a point above the relegation zone and facing a visit to Walsall.

Oxford led with three minutes to go after Jones scored his first goal for the club. Searching for a second, the ball dropped and appeared to hit Cassells on the arm. There was a pause as the shrill of a whistle pierced the noise of the crowd.

Walsall's keeper, Ron Green, picked the ball up and rolled it to Colin Harrison to take a free kick. Unaware of the pause in play, Cassells darted in and prodded it into the empty net. To everyone's astonishment, the referee Allan Banks awarded the goal. The whistle the players had heard wasn't his; the free kick was a phantom. The angry protests forced Banks to run to the other end of the pitch to consult a policeman, who hadn't heard anything, and Cassells' first goal for the club was confirmed. In the dying seconds, with Walsall still fuming, Foley made it 3-0.

The flash of good fortune catapulted Cassells forward, and ten days later he scored again in a 2-0 home win to Barnsley. The following Sunday, Oxford headed to Fratton Park to face promotion-chasing Portsmouth, whose experiment to stimulate crowds backfired when the gate fell 2,000 short of the season's average.

Pompey led when David Gregory's mishit shot after two minutes deflected past keeper Roy Burton off Briggs. Eight minutes later Cassells headed his third goal in four games to equalise. Foley had a second-half goal disallowed for offside before Peter Mellor saved Shotton's penalty after a foul by Steve Aizlewood on the increasingly dangerous Cassells. The point was the least they deserved.

In the penultimate game of the season, Oxford confirmed their survival when Smithers dispossessed Millwall's 16-year-old Keith Stevens 30 seconds into his debut and scored off the post. Having inherited a team lacking in purpose and staring at relegation, Greaves had engineered a remarkable turnaround, steering the team to 14th.

Oxford's looming financial predicament meant Greaves was forced to reduce his playing budget, losing the versatile Joe Cooke to Exeter City and replacing him with Reading striker Ollie Kearns, who'd phoned the club asking for a job.

Perversely, in just over three years, the British record transfer fee had tripled from £516,000, paid by West Brom for Middlesbrough's David Mills, to £1.5m when Bryan Robson signed for Manchester United. Both signings involved new United manager Ron Atkinson.

Oxford chairman Bill Reeves proposed a transfer levy to be shared across the 92 clubs to redistribute wealth more equally. The idea was rejected, and as the financial scramble intensified, Oxford had no money and no voice.

The players sensed the problems; overnight stays before away games became vanishingly rare, pre-match meals were downgraded to soup and sandwiches and the team coach carrying the players became smaller. There was talk of players driving themselves to games to save money.

To encourage a more positive approach, the Football League voted to introduce three points for a win for the start of the 1981/82 season. They reasoned that more attacking meant more goals and larger crowds.

Greaves's success and outgoing personality meant he was briefly linked with a job at Plymouth and the vacancy at West Brom left by Atkinson's move to Old Trafford.

The season started promisingly with four wins in Oxford's opening five games, including a 3-0 aggregate victory against Brentford in the Milk Cup, the rebranded League Cup following a lucrative sponsorship agreement with the Milk Marketing Board.

Cassells continued to thrive; the mild-mannered former postal worker was signed from Watford as part of a £100,000 deal which took Les Taylor to Vicarage Road in 1980. He and Greaves became close, the work they put in together improving Cassells' game was starting to pay dividends.

He matched his previous season's goals total before the opening month was over. The miserly defence led by Shotton and Briggs kept three clean sheets in four games – only succumbing to a 3-2 defeat at Newport County, whose goals came from promising Liverpudlian striker John Aldridge and two from Alan Waddle, the cousin of Newcastle United's Chris.

With transfer fees spiralling, the pressure to unearth new talent was growing. An early season league win over Millwall saw the stands packed with scouts watching Andy Thomas, one of a batch of teenagers being tipped to play for England, including Charlton's Paul Walsh and Carlisle's former Oxford triallist Peter Beardsley.

Although form wavered in September and October, Cassells reached double figures in a 1-0 win over Millwall in the second round of the Milk Cup – more than any Oxford player had achieved in the whole of the previous season. The reward was a tie with Everton at Goodison Park.

Immediately before the game, Oxford adopted a notable new look. For their home game against Lincoln City they carried on their shirts the name *The Sunday Journal*, a rare commercial innovation, as the FA and media grappled with the moral panic of logos featuring on team kits.

The *Journal* was owned by Eynsham-based entrepreneur Tony Rosser who'd owned the club during the 1970s to feed his fledgling newspaper group with exclusive stories. Working with Rosser was his distribution manager Nick Harris, a mainstay of BBC Radio Oxford's coverage of the club.

Oxford went into their first visit to Goodison Park in good spirits but with little expectation of coming away with a result. Everton had appointed former player Howard Kendall as their new manager at the start of the season but despite an aggressive recruitment drive, his team were mid-table and had just suffered a 3-1 defeat in the Merseyside derby.

Oxford maintained a stubborn resistance with Cassells missing two clear chances. They held out until the 70th minute when Irish striker Eamonn O'Keefe – who'd been sent off against Liverpool – redeemed himself with the opening goal.

With two minutes to go, Cassells beat Mike Lyons and loomed down on Jim Arnold's goal. Arnold's faint touch on Cassells' shot allowed Mark Higgins to clear off the line. In the dressing room, Cassells hurled his boots at the door in frustration, but Oxford left with renewed confidence as Everton fans remained to applaud their efforts.

The following month, Oxford drew Southern League side Dover away in the FA Cup. Greaves was confident of a routine win, relaxing the night before the game with an appearance on the BBC2 chat show *Friday Night... Saturday Morning* hosted by Oxford board member Desmond Morris and featuring guest Susanna Kubelka, an advocate for sex for the over-40s.

He joined the players from London the following morning and was surprised to find that the mood was tense. He hadn't accounted for Oxford's dismal record against non-league clubs. They hadn't beaten part-time opponents for 15 years, losing to Barking, Nuneaton Borough, Kettering Town, Chelmsford Town and Bedford Town.

Greaves's confidence was well placed as Foley stretched the part-timers, setting up Smithers to open the scoring. Despite dominating, a second goal didn't come. Dover had treated their players to a special pre-match steak lunch, departing from their usual poached eggs, which helped power them towards a second-half fightback. Greaves only relaxed when Thomas converted Foley's pass four minutes from time.

Oxford moved up to sixth with a 3-0 win over relegation-threatened Preston, Cassells' brace taking his total for the season to 12. Greaves had unearthed an unexpected talent and other clubs were starting to take notice.

As momentum built, freezing temperatures and heavy snow in December 1981 played havoc with the fixture list. The worst weather in a century meant the next round at Aldershot had to be postponed to the following Tuesday.

With only two fixtures in the second round reaching a conclusion, the third-round draw on the following Monday contained 82 clubs. Oxford and Aldershot were drawn away to Fourth Division Bournemouth or non-league Dorchester Town.

In the rescheduled game, Oxford looked set for a comfortable evening when Cassells started and finished a move to make it 1-0 after five minutes. A disallowed goal three minutes later just delayed the second which he nodded in after 11 minutes, seemingly putting Oxford in control.

Twelve minutes later it was 2-1 when Murray Brodie retaliated for Aldershot. Another from Ian McDonald with 20 minutes left forced a replay. 'I don't know what Len [Walker, Aldershot's manager] did to them at half-time,' Greaves said. 'But it worked. They were fantastic.'

The weather had more severe consequences as between the end of October and the start of February Oxford played at the Manor just three times. They were already haemorrhaging £2,000 to £3,000 a week; their debts mounted and their creditors grew concerned.

The players' November wages pushed the club beyond their overdraft – they now owed the bank £162,000 with a limit of £150,000. The Oxford board approached Barclays Bank seeking an extension to their facility, but the bank responded by saying they would only honour the club's cheques until the end of the year. Rather than giving the club more leeway, they'd placed a noose around its neck. With other creditors looking on, Oxford had been given two weeks to find the money or close.

The board frantically sought a solution, contacting publishing tycoon Robert Maxwell, who promised to underwrite the immediate debts to buy some time to find a long-term solution to their problems.

The sustained period of bad weather meant the FA Cup replay with Aldershot was delayed for two weeks until five days after Christmas. Despite the turmoil, Oxford felt confident of progressing but fell behind when Stuart Robinson scored for the Fourth Division side after 11 minutes. Cassells equalised 15 minutes later with a far-post header and grabbed his second just before half-time from a penalty after being fouled by Joe Jopling.

Twenty-five minutes from time, Andy Thomas put the game beyond doubt following a mazy solo run. Cassells completed his first professional hat-trick with two minutes remaining, heading in David Fogg's cross, before Aldershot narrowed the gap to 4-2 in injury time.

The fixture backlog meant the next round against Bournemouth was just three days later. Cassells and Thomas took their good form into the game, both scoring to complete a comfortable 2-0 win.

The fourth-round draw was kinder with a trip to First Division Brighton & Hove Albion. A large crowd and half the gate receipts would keep Oxford afloat for a while longer.

After weeks of uncertainty, Maxwell committed to the club and was elected chairman. He wanted to attend the game, but when Brighton refused him permission to land his helicopter on the Goldstone Ground's pitch, he remained at home. An early sign that he and football were not the most natural bedfellows.

Over 3,000 Oxford fans travelled to the south coast on specially commissioned coaches and trains. Ninth in the First Division, Brighton, managed by Mike Bailey,

Charlton's manager for Greaves's first game at the Manor a year earlier, were beginning to lift their sights towards a first trip to Wembley.

Oxford opened brightly with eight players who'd faced Charlton for Greaves's debut, an indication of how much they'd developed as a team. After just 30 seconds, Thomas troubled keeper Graham Moseley with a 25-yard shot and seven minutes later Jones fired narrowly over. Cassells rattled the Brighton defence with his pace moments before Gordon Smith nearly broke through but Briggs and Shotton combined to tidy up.

It was a frenetic opening; Jones grazed the bar before Tony Grealish's volley went close for the hosts. Then Oxford started to take control; Cassells nearly gave them the lead before Steve Foster cleared a Smithers shot, then Jones nearly made a breakthrough with Moseley happy to cling on to the ball on the line.

After 19 minutes, Cassells pushed the ball past defender Steve Gatting, who tripped as the striker accelerated, offering a free run on goal. Cassells approached Moseley as he had Jim Arnold against Everton, and this time he struck it cleanly into the net for 1-0.

Oxford's relentless pressure gave them momentum and five minutes later Moseley pushed the ball on to the post from Jones's shot. Thomas released Cassells to test Moseley again, but the ball was cleared off the line by Garry Nelson.

Just before half-time, Jones worked the ball out to Billy Jeffrey on the right. Jeffrey's cross found Foley, who volleyed home for 2-0. It had been a blistering first half of forceful attacking from the Third Division side. Mike Bailey thought his team had been 'murdered'.

Moments into the second half Gordon Smith nearly pulled a goal back, forcing Roy Burton into his first meaningful save. Any hope of a Brighton comeback was extinguished five minutes later as a short corner from Jones was played to John Doyle, whose cross found Foley to guide a looping header beyond the keeper for the third.

The win was the result of the round and one of the club's greatest FA Cup giant-killings. It was the biggest winning margin for a lower-league club at a top-flight team for 20 years, a new high-water mark for a team Greaves had transformed in little over a year. 'This is probably the greatest day in my career,' he said. Oxford supporters, packed into the corner terrace, celebrated as Cassells ran a solo lap of honour. Mike Bailey, having witnessed the start of Greaves's revolution, couldn't explain what he'd seen at its peak. For Greaves, it was a fairy story.

Match of the Day chose Watford's win over West Ham, Tottenham's home victory over Leeds and Coventry's defeat of Manchester City as their featured games, but Greaves was the guest of honour.

Afterwards, he headed back to Oxford, passing a billboard for a local newspaper advertising the day's headlines. The local media were leading with news about university places in the city. Despite Greaves's efforts, the transformation of his team's fortunes and a historic giant-killing, the club still hadn't penetrated the city's consciousness. The sense of unease that Greaves felt on his first day returned.

Chapter 3

Robert Maxwell

ALTHOUGH EASY to miss, on the unassuming New High Street, just off London Road in Headington, opposite where the Manor Ground once stood, there's a giant fibreglass shark embedded into the roof of a house.

Commissioned in 1986 by eccentric radio producer Bill Heine, and the creation of artist John Buckley, it's a commentary on impotence and the desperation of a nuclear threat. To most people, it's a giant fibreglass shark embedded in the roof of a terraced house.

Headington is full of eccentricities: continue towards Oxford city centre and on the opposite side to the shark, there's a large stone gateway marking the entrance to Headington Hill Hall, the one-time home of Robert Maxwell.

Headington Hill Hall is a grand Italianate mansion built by the Morrell brewing family in 1824 which had a reputation for lavish parties. The Morrell family sold the hall to the city council in 1953 after it was used as a military hospital during the war. The council planned to demolish it and build offices, but when they ran out of money, they offered a 21-year lease to the highest bidder. With few people able to maintain the estate, publishing tycoon Maxwell took up the offer at a discounted rate.

Maxwell moved his scientific publishing empire, Pergamon Press, into the stables and made the main house his family home. His relentless work ethic, his son Michael's brain damage after an accident, and the death of daughter Karine from leukaemia shook the family unit. Betty, Maxwell's wife, committed to re-establish the family's roots, restoring the house to its former glory. He called it the best council house in the country.

The family lived in the house in what historian Ben Macintyre described as a place of luxury and cruelty. Maxwell rekindled its reputation for extravagant parties, which would run late into the night and attract politicians and industrialists, deepening his influence in British society. During the day, he would rule the family with the same fearsome discipline he ran his businesses. He insisted that Betty lived by a set of six rules of marriage while the children would be drilled with facts they were expected to regale at family dinners each evening.

Maxwell's reputation stretched across the sedate world of academic publishing. Oxford was awash with stories of working for Pergamon and his volcanic temper.

He was born Ján Ludvík Hyman Binyamin Hoch, into extreme poverty in Carpathian Ruthenia, a region straddling what is now Ukraine, Romania, Slovakia and Poland. Despite holding Czech passports, Ruthenians considered themselves independent, often resulting in persecution and marginalisation.

Maxwell was part of a large Jewish minority within the region and lost most of his family to the Nazis in Auschwitz during the Second World War. Maxwell had escaped to France and joined the Allies, winning a Military Cross for bravery.

Stateless, orphaned and persecuted, Maxwell seemed unbridled from convention; he felt he'd earned the right to make a life of his choosing, vowing never to be under anyone's control again.

After the war, he reinvented himself, adopting the name Robert Maxwell and speaking in a deep, clipped English accent. Using the survivalist entrepreneurship from his brutal upbringing, he exploited the vacuum left by the collapse of the Nazis, setting up a business to sell abandoned academic literature via the connections and informal supply chains he'd established in the army. Multilingual, his mastery of Russian gave him access to valuable Soviet research as the Cold War developed. His business grew rapidly, amassing him a fortune.

His limitless pursuit for power and, perhaps most importantly, legitimacy saw him stand for election as a Labour MP in 1959. An unconventional socialist, he targeted the marginal seat of Buckingham but failed in his first attempt. Five years later, his brash campaigning and election promises rode roughshod over the dour English political establishment, mobilising the poorly educated rural constituency to effect a three-point swing in his favour, allowing him to take his seat in the House of Commons.

Maxwell admitted politics didn't suit his temperament; compromise and collaboration were not his preferred methods. His maiden speech was jeered by the opposition and, to his horror, ignored by his party. Although styled as an English gentleman, he was still a foreigner and a Jew. Despite the war, antisemitism still cast a shadow.

Sensing an attack on its socialist ideals, the Parliamentary Labour Party closed ranks, blocking Maxwell from the prime minister, Harold Wilson. Political legitimacy prevented, he was defeated in the 1970 election and censured for undue interference in local constituency affairs.

His attention turned to his labyrinthine business empire. A year earlier, he lost control of Pergamon and was expelled from its board after over-inflating its profit forecast. Share trading was suspended and the Board of Trade labelled him unfit to act as a director of a company. The police took no action but newspaper coverage was damning.

The scandal awakened Maxwell to the power of a media who'd shredded his reputation and controlled the narrative. Newspapers could be more influential than the government. In 1969 he'd tried to buy the *News of the World* but was gazumped by another outsider, Australian Rupert Murdoch, sparking a deep resentment which would resonate for decades.

In 1974, with Pergamon ailing, Maxwell regained control of the company. A huge physical presence – six feet tall and weighing over 20 stone – he was feared and admired in equal measure. His bullying gave him a cache in the febrile materialistic society that was emerging during the 1980s, a blowback from the previous decade's bleak austerity. To many he was an innovator in a country lacking ingenuity.

Maxwell was on holiday in Jamaica when he received a call from Jim Hunt, Oxford United's urbane club secretary. It was serendipitous that a flamboyant millionaire with an unquenched desire for profile and legitimacy lived next door to a club offering both those qualities.

Maxwell showed a passing interest in Arsenal, but his extensive *Who's Who* profile listed his hobbies as chess and mountain climbing – incongruous, except as a metaphor.

Despite reservations, Oxford were desperate, and all opportunities had to be investigated. Fortuitously, working in the club offices was Hunt's assistant Bob Oakes whose father, Nick, was managing director of Illustrated Manuals Ltd, a company he'd sold to Pergamon. When Bob told his father about the club's predicament and their hunt for investment, Nick set about briefing Maxwell about the club's problems.

Some suggested Maxwell's interest was to rekindle his political ambitions, but he saw football as a failed institution, rife with corruption and violence. Revitalising bankrupt businesses was how he'd made his money; he called the club a turnaround opportunity.

On the other hand, he may simply have been bored. Close associates thought he'd become restless despite the enormous profits reported by his businesses. He'd embarked on a flurry of investments in failing companies; Oxford United seemed to offer him an adventure he craved.

Maxwell could see that American sports offered a vision of a future he could benefit from. Like Tony Rosser years earlier, he could see the opportunities of marrying up compelling content with the media that distributed it. Maxwell was a cartographer; only he knew how his interlocking businesses mapped together and how the money flows allowed him to report eye-watering profits. He could see significant rewards from plotting a path from his media empire to professional football.

At first, he seemed ambivalent to the club's plight, suggesting that Hunt call him again when he was back in the country. Hunt persisted, insisting that Oxford wouldn't survive as the bank planned to stop honouring cheques in a matter of days. Maxwell told Hunt he'd underwrite the debts to buy more time.

With the immediate crisis averted, the club and Maxwell embarked on a breakneck courtship. There were reservations; the directors raised Maxwell's censure by the Board of Trade and the turmoil at Pergamon. Maxwell's advisors told him not to touch the investment given his lack of knowledge about the game.

The Manor offered lucrative real estate, but the prospect of it growing as a stadium was remote. The council had little motivation to help due to football's reputation and the ambivalence of the Oxford people towards its club. Maxwell was undeterred, enlisting Edmund Gibbs, the club's long-time secretary, to help navigate the mess.

Maxwell paid £120,000 to meet the club's commitments, claiming the role of chairman had been thrust on him 'like a bed of nails'.

A condition of the sale was absolute fealty to Maxwell's plan, euphemistically framed as 'total commitment from the Oxford public'. He centralised power, reducing the frequency of board meetings from fortnightly to quarterly, and insisted that the Independent Supporters' Club chairman Les Town, vice-chairman Bill Black and secretary Gary Whiting join the board.

It was politically astute; Maxwell was well versed in handling self-interested groups as unions were a thorn in the side of all publishers. Bringing fans on board while retaining absolute power over decision-making would neuter supporter opposition.

His main target was the city council who held the key to the club's survival. They would decide where the club's new stadium would be located. They'd earmarked a site in March 1980 for a £15m leisure complex, 30,000-seater stadium, and Asda superstore on the border of the River Cherwell and the city's northern bypass. Maxwell pushed for planning permission to be granted without delay.

With football impoverished and embattled, it sought inspiration from across the Atlantic; labelled 'Soccer City', the new facility included a synthetic pitch. But, located on a floodplain and green belt, if the application went to a planning inquiry, it would be placed in the hands of South Oxfordshire's Conservative MP Michael Heseltine. Maxwell, as a former Labour MP, would have no influence.

While momentum was building on the pitch, Ian Greaves's confidence was slipping away. In the year since his appointment, he'd transformed Oxford with virtually the same players he'd inherited. He'd turned the club from being one staring at relegation to giant-killers seeking promotion.

Maxwell was as brash as Greaves was pragmatic; running the club along commercial lines could sweep away everything Greaves had achieved, including perhaps the manager himself. With an ambivalent media and public, he started to question his future.

His mind was made up the night he picked up the *Oxford Mail* to read Maxwell saying he had a target of promotion in the next 18 months. Greaves was blown away by his chairman's ambition; there'd been no discussion about what was achievable or how. Greaves felt he was being set up to fail. He headed to Headington Hill Hall. Standing at his enormous desk, Maxwell brushed the comments off. 'Licence, dear boy,' he laughed. 'Licence.'

Maxwell manipulated the media like he did his shareholders and investors. Outlandish claims grabbed headlines that washed over logic and analysis, but Greaves wanted honesty and didn't appreciate media games being played in his name. If he couldn't rely on his chairman, he came to the painful conclusion it was time to go. Just over a year after taking charge at Oxford and ten days after his greatest triumph, Ian Greaves walked out of the Manor for the last time.

Wolverhampton Wanderers, with the rich history Greaves craved, had just sacked their manager John Barnwell. Their past glories were long faded and crippled with debt, they sat at the foot of the First Division. They needed a realist who wouldn't fear their inevitable relegation.

Greaves applied for the Wolves job on Monday, 1 February 1982, completing the deal the next day before contacting Maxwell to resign. By that evening, he was watching his new team fall to a bleak 2-1 defeat at Arsenal in front of their lowest crowd since 1974.

While Greaves prepared his next steps, Maxwell told his board he'd rejected the resignation and appealed to Harry Marshall, the Wolves chairman, to uphold a gentlemen's agreement that managers wouldn't be poached during the season.

But Greaves didn't have a contract – Marshall insisted he'd applied for the job and not been poached. Greaves matched the Wolves brief and was announced as their new manager on the eve of Oxford's derby at home to Reading. Maxwell, undeterred, announced legal action against Greaves and Wolves.

The following day, Oxford fans, sensing a lost opportunity from Greaves's departure, queued down the lane leading up to the London Road terrace in the fading hope that he may have performed a U-turn. When they finally got into the ground for the delayed kick-off, it was caretaker manager Roy Barry in the dugout. Above him in the Beech Road stand, for the first time since the takeover, was Maxwell.

With the offer of vouchers for the upcoming FA Cup tie at Coventry City, the crowd ballooned to nearly 10,000, the biggest in five years. But Oxford, without Malcolm Shotton, seemed disjointed and Reading took charge.

The visitors' striker, Kerry Dixon, spurned several chances, Lawrie Sanchez struck a post and Pat Earles hit the bar. The breakthrough, though, came after 35 minutes as Mark Jones connected with David Fogg's cross at the far post to score in his first league game since November.

Reading pushed for an equaliser and with 13 minutes remaining, Dixon prodded the ball home after a ricochet off the post. The celebrations were short-lived as the linesman flagged for offside. The referee waved away the visitors' wild protests, sending off Alan Lewis for a second caution after a first-half foul on Keith Cassells. Fired by indignation, Earles cannoned a shot off the bar but the breakthrough wouldn't come, giving Oxford an undeserved derby win.

The protests continued after the whistle with players surrounding the referee as he made his way to the tunnel. Through the throng pushed the Reading manager, the mild-mannered Maurice Evans, who received a booking for the confrontation. 'The referee had an absolute stinker and I'm sure he knows it,' he said, unrepentant.

While attention turned to who would replace Greaves, his legacy echoed as Oxford headed into their FA Cup fifth round tie at Coventry with promising teenager Mark Wright playing in place of the influential Shotton.

Having cruised past Brighton, expectation of another upset against First Division opposition was high and 5,000 Oxford fans meandered their way through the countryside by car and coach to Highfield Road.

On arrival, it was clear something wasn't right. Coventry were the first English club to adopt an all-seated stadium to civilise the toxic culture. Many Oxford fans saw this as a target, while the home fans saw their noisy and confident lower-league opposition as an invasion to be repelled.

Before the game fans clashed in a series of skirmishes. The police couldn't contain the trouble through the maze of streets surrounding the ground. By the time the teams came on to the pitch, the atmosphere was tense.

Oxford, all in yellow, defended stoutly against the Coventry attack which included ex-England midfielder Gerry Francis and future international Mark Hateley. But they looked a shadow of the team that destroyed Brighton, almost dragging Coventry down to their level in a turgid affair.

With the game goalless, Oxford fans were calling for half-time when Garry Thompson broke the deadlock, pouncing on a loose ball in the box. As drab as the half had been, Oxford didn't deserve to be behind.

Five minutes after the break Coventry sealed the tie as Hateley headed in Peter Bodak's cross, before Thompson finished a five-man move, heading in at the back post for number three. Oxford's exit was confirmed when Wright was hustled by Hateley, who cut inside to blast the ball into the top corner for an emphatic fourth.

Having been full of expectation, anger in the stands boiled over. Seats were ripped from their moorings and thrown on to the pitch. Families scurried for cover, the helpless police advising them to hide their scarves to ensure their safety outside the ground. Thirty-five fans were arrested in a grisly end to a glorious run. The deep cultural problems within the game percolated to the surface.

Maxwell's immediate issue was to find a successor to Ian Greaves, someone who could propel Oxford forward, meet his ambitions and cope with his excesses. He wasn't going to financially support the club forever; profit came from success. There was no prospect of achieving that within the confines of the Manor – he needed to scale the business.

Chapter 4

Jim Smith

IT WAS an unusual pre-Valentine's Day sight. Among the tables for two and flickering candlelight were eight people, including some of the most recognisable faces in the country.

Ron Atkinson was a household name; nicknamed 'Mr Bojangles', a larger-than-life character with angular features, extravagant jewellery and a sculptured receding hairline defiantly resisting his slide towards middle age. He was Oxford United's record appearance-maker and the current manager of Manchester United.

Atkinson and his wife Maggie were joined by his brother Graham, Oxford's record goalscorer. They were with Oxford director Paul Reeves, an old friend of Atkinson's from his days at the Manor. With them was Birmingham City manager Jim Smith and his wife Yvonne. At just 41 his distinctive bald head surrounded by a nest of hair led Atkinson to nickname him the 'Bald Eagle'.

The pair bonded as managers of two giants of Midlands football, sharing expensive tastes in drink and cigars. Smith had a reputation at St Andrew's for spending big and delivering little. In 1978 he signed Argentinian World Cup winner Alberto Tarantini, whose career in England ended with him punching a fan. A year later Smith sensationally sold England international Trevor Francis to Nottingham Forest for £1m.

Reeves was reeling after Oxford's FA Cup mauling against Coventry. Smith's Birmingham had scraped a 2-2 draw with West Ham, while Atkinson's Manchester United secured a 1-0 win at Ian Greaves's Wolves, putting them second in the table and building the anticipation they might secure their first league title since 1968.

The opportunity to take a moment out with their wives for a dinner in Stratford-upon-Avon offered a welcome break and an opportunity to catch up. The main gossip of the evening would have been the upheaval at Aston Villa, the champions of England. Ron Saunders, who the Atkinson brothers had played under during his brief spell as Oxford manager in 1969, had steered Villa to the title using only 14 players. Their championship defence had been lacklustre, but their mid-table position had given them space to progress to the quarter-finals of the European Cup.

Saunders was frustrated at his board's lack of ambition in building on his title-winning squad. Villa chairman Ron Bendell resisted the urge to match the spending of his rivals, adding just one player to the roster. The tension simmered into the new season, Bendell became infuriated at what he thought was Saunders briefing the local press about Villa's financial problems. The animosity drew focus on Saunders' rolling contract which meant that, if he was sacked, he would be owed a full three-year term in compensation. Replacing him, even if Villa wanted to, would be very expensive.

On 5 February, the board announced their decision to change Saunders' contract to a conventional fixed term. The following day, with the manager seething, he took the champions to Old Trafford to play Atkinson's Manchester United, slumping to a 4-1 defeat.

With the power shifting in favour of the board, the team's poor form left Saunders isolated and, as he clambered to re-assert himself, open warfare broke out, forcing Saunders to resign.

Two miles away, Birmingham City chairman Keith Coombs sensed an opportunity. As Smith and Atkinson dined with their wives, he was plotting. If he offered Saunders a similar contract to the one he had at Villa, he could poach one of the leading managers in the country from the champions of England and their greatest rivals. It would cause a sensation.

First, he needed to remove Jim Smith. Having suffered relegation in Smith's first full season in 1978/79, Birmingham bounced back the following year and secured a mid-table finish. After the draw at West Ham, they sat above the relegation zone, but Smith felt his investments in the squad were showing signs of progress, although the lack of success compared to Villa meant the pressure was building.

The Tuesday following the dinner, Smith headed into training preparing for Birmingham's evening fixture against Sunderland. Coombs called and asked to see Smith at the stadium. On arrival, they passed the chairman's office and entered the boardroom. Smith felt a sense of unease. As confusion clouded his senses, he quickly got the gist; he was about to be fired.

Ron Saunders was unveiled the next day.

Although interested in the vacancy at Villa, Smith needed a break. Villa's owner, Doug Ellis, offered him his villa in Son Vida in Majorca to recharge his batteries. Smith had negotiated a good financial package with Coombs but needed to refocus and get back into the game quickly.

While plotting his next steps, the phone rang. It was Paul Reeves, and just four days after their dinner he had an unexpected proposition: 'Do you want the Oxford job?'

Ten days after Greaves's resignation, Roy Barry told Maxwell he should accelerate his search for a new manager. Barry was confident of his chances having overseen an unbeaten run in the league. Maxwell considered former Watford and Blackburn manager Ken Furphy, who'd been managing in the North American Soccer League for six years. When Reeves heard the news of Smith's departure from Birmingham, he'd contacted Maxwell. A First Division manager at the Manor suited the chairman's ambition and aspiration.

Smith was less sure; dropping to the Third Division felt like a setback. He'd established himself in the top flight and just been replaced by the manager of the First Division champions. He wanted to emulate his old friend Atkinson. Despite Ian Greaves's FA Cup success, he might be forgotten at Oxford.

But Smith's needs were practical more than aspirational – he needed money. As he contemplated the offer, Robert Maxwell called. In his booming voice, he introduced himself and announced the purpose of his call with a directness that Smith would become familiar with. Maxwell invited Smith to Headington Hill Hall to iron out the details. His persistence dominated everything he did, filling every space, offering no escape.

Doug Ellis's Spanish villa was waiting and a few days with Yvonne would have given them some space to think. The meeting with Maxwell presented a practical problem; they were due to fly to Spain from Manchester that evening, meaning he'd need to travel north immediately afterwards to make their flight.

His first problem was recalling who Maxwell was. He'd heard the name, but confused him with Rupert Murdoch. Maxwell's antipathy towards Murdoch was obsessional and had tripped him up more than once. Smith would do well to avoid that mistake.

The following afternoon, Smith arrived in Oxford hoping Maxwell might meet him early so that he could return to Manchester to catch his flight. He was ushered into a small room and left to wait for three hours with only the occasional visit of Maxwell's PA, Jean Baddeley, to break up the time.

Eventually, Maxwell's imposing frame burst through the door. He shook Smith's hand vigorously and apologised for making him wait before escorting him into his huge oval office. He offered Smith a drink, suggesting he'd been tipped off by a Birmingham director about his preferences for Scotch and wine. Smith bristled, feeling someone was trying to undermine him.

The two men, their ambition and directness, seemed to complement each other immediately. Then, as they closed on a deal, Maxwell announced he needed to leave.

Smith needed to catch his flight, but Maxwell phoned Yvonne and asked if she'd rather travel to Spain alone or wait until the following day. She deferred to her husband, who said he'd prefer her to wait. Maxwell put the phone down before arranging a morning flight from Heathrow on the condition Smith would shorten his holiday from two weeks to one.

There was something impressive about Maxwell; there was no problem he couldn't fix. Just after Smith's appointment, Malcolm Shotton confronted his new manager asking for the £750 Maxwell had promised the team for winning at Brighton. When Smith approached Maxwell, the chairman reached for his briefcase, counting the cash out in £50 notes. When two notes fell on the floor, he picked them up and shoved them in Smith's pocket.

Days later, after a whistle-stop trip to the US, Maxwell arrived in Heathrow and called a board meeting for 8.30pm to announced Smith's two-year contract, a period he insisted would be sufficient to gain promotion. He then told Jim Hunt to arrange a press conference at Maxwell House in

London to reveal the appointment. When Hunt reached Maxwell's headquarters, he found Smith looking bemused.

Smith's arrival brought about a convenient amnesia that characterised many of Maxwell's dealings. Having threatened both Wolves and Ian Greaves with litigation, he announced, 'I have decided to abandon legal action. They richly deserved to be sued and I would have expected to win but now that we have Jim, I cannot claim we have been damaged.'

Despite their FA Cup exit, Oxford were fifth, five points off third with at least one game in hand over their rivals. Keith Cassells was the division's in-form striker, Andy Thomas and Kevin Brock were flourishing, and they had a rock-solid defence. Smith's instinct was to attack; Greaves's defensive legacy was his parting gift.

Smith's first move was to relieve Roy Barry of his duties and head to Bristol for a scouting mission with trainer Ken Fish. He knew he had to build relations with key people around the club and none were more important than the man everyone called Mr Fish.

Smith's first game was away at relegation-threatened Bristol City, and although losing Tim Smithers to a freak tennis injury and Mark Wright to illness, he welcomed back Malcolm Shotton, who'd recovered from the broken nose which had kept him out of the previous seven games. Shotton celebrated with a goal in a 2-0 win that put Oxford fourth.

Three days later they headed across town to face Bristol Rovers, who posed a bigger threat than their rivals. In treacherous conditions, Oxford battled their way to 1-1 with 25 minutes to go before the referee abruptly abandoned the game due to a waterlogged pitch.

Smith's first game at the Manor came on 13 March against mid-table Southend United nearly two weeks after his appointment. Despite the anticipation, the match unravelled with Cassells adding to Smith's injury problems as Oxford conceded twice to register their first home defeat for four months.

Captain Billy Jeffrey missed a frustrating goalless draw with Exeter four days later. It was followed by a 2-1 defeat to Lincoln which required Smith to field a near scratch team featuring Paul Berry, Phil Lythgoe and Andy Kingston, none of whom had started more than five games all season, plus Mark Wright and Ollie Kearns, who'd started less than ten. A draw at Doncaster the following Tuesday compounded the sense of frustration. Oxford dropped to eighth, five points behind Reading in third, but with five games in hand.

Smith's competitive, combative squad were falling apart. Maybe Greaves's instinct about Maxwell's involvement had been right and he'd got out before the rot set in. And it wasn't just injuries Smith had to deal with – the transfer window was closing and teams were making their final adjustments for the run-in.

As March ended, Maxwell's ambition to build a club to compete at the top was tested for the first time when First Division title-chasers Southampton offered £150,000 for Cassells and Wright.

Maxwell accepted, depriving Smith of the club's leading prospect and its top goalscorer – two goals short of Oxford's scoring record for the season. Fans and some directors questioned whether the experiment had been worth it. If they'd known an offer for their players was coming, they might not have even needed Maxwell's money.

In return, Smith signed powerful 19-year-old winger George Lawrence on loan alongside versatile midfielder Trevor Hebberd, who'd become surplus to requirements as Saints boss Lawrie McMenemy built a star-studded team around England captain Kevin Keegan.

Both players debuted at home to Chesterfield. Lawrence's impressive pace was rewarded with a goal, but Hebberd seemed nervous, too timid and lightweight for the division. As an early test of Smith's ability to bring quality players to the club, it fell short of expectations as the game petered out to a frustrating 1-1 draw.

There was also a debut for Ray Train, another deadline-day signing from Watford, who manager Graham Taylor described as 'a ratter, a sniffer and a passer'. Smith hoped he'd bind the team together and handed him the captaincy.

The faltering form dropped Oxford to seventh, six points off the promotion places with just a game in hand over their rivals. Promotion – in their hands a month earlier – was growing more unlikely. After they registered their sixth game without a win in a draw at home to Gillingham, the promises of their new manager and owner started to have a hollow ring.

The following week against Brentford, after conceding early, Train's marshalling in midfield gave Hebberd the freedom to head Oxford's equaliser on 16 minutes. Peter Foley, returning after five games, gave a renewed attacking focus that had been missing since Cassells' departure. Just before half-time, he connected with Train's free kick to secure Smith's second win.

It was a timely victory as the divisive Maxwell, the sale of Cassells and Wright, Smith's limited impact and his underwhelming signings had left fans suspicious. This was tinder to a potential forest fire of problems with Oxford's bitterest rivals, Swindon Town, visiting the Manor the following Wednesday.

Injuries receding, Smith fielded a full-strength side for the derby with Shotton and Briggs securing the back line, Train ratting in midfield and Hebberd freeing Brock and Lawrence down the flanks to feed Foley.

Oxford swarmed over the relegation-threatened Robins and it wasn't long before the ever-reliable left-back David Fogg opened the scoring from the spot after 15 minutes.

Shotton doubled the lead five minutes later, making it 2-0 by the break. The cushion allowed Smith to introduce Andy Thomas from the bench to provide a glimpse of the team he wanted Oxford to be. The substitute extended the advantage on the hour before Lawrence made it four 11 minutes from time with Foley completing the rout moments later.

It was the biggest winning margin in the history of the derby and Oxford's first victory against Swindon for nine years. Fans poured on to the pitch first in celebration, then confrontation as the rivals squared up to each other.

Trust in the system and the availability of players allowed Smith to follow up with a second derby annihilation at injury-ravaged Reading three days later. The morning kick-off, Maurice Evans's brainwave to curb pre-match drinking, saw two goals from Kevin Brock and a third from Billy Jeffrey secure a 3-0 win. They were now a point behind Fulham with games in hand over Carlisle and Lincoln; promotion was back in Oxford's hands.

Over the Easter weekend, a 3-1 win against Doncaster Rovers on the bank holiday Monday meant Oxford had won four games in nine days, beaten two local rivals, scoring 13 goals, and conceding two. Now fully in control of promotion, Jim Smith had arrived.

The slew of goals overhauled the goal difference of fourth-placed Burnley, their opponents at the Manor the following Saturday. A surge of confidence and the warm spring weather meant the ground pulsated with over 10,000 fans for the first time in six years.

In-form Burnley were driven by the goals of Northern Ireland international Billy Hamilton. The combative striker had spent an unhappy period at Queens Park Rangers before moving to Turf Moor, where the homely stability suited his character. Hamilton's physicality, a stark contrast to his gentle off-field temperament, matched Shotton and Briggs, and perhaps inevitably, the titanic battle resulted in a goalless stalemate that helped neither side.

Three days later Oxford returned to form with a 3-2 win over Wimbledon and followed it up with a useful draw against Preston. Equal on points with Lincoln with a game in hand, the season was pivoting, and its gaze was resting on the County Ground, Swindon.

A rare Ollie Kearns goal against Plymouth helped Oxford jump to second but a frustrating goalless draw against Millwall saw six teams separated by four points with four games to go. With Burnley and Fulham having games in hand, Oxford couldn't afford to slip up.

To grasp their promotion opportunity, Oxford needed to break a nine-year sequence and win at the County Ground. There was no better time to do it; mired in financial problems, Swindon were pinned into a relegation fight as tight as Oxford's promotion race. The problems had created a toxic brew that regularly boiled over on the terraces.

In a thunderous derby atmosphere both teams probed for an opening. After a bruising first half, within a minute of the restart, Swindon struck when striker Paul Rideout put the ball beyond Roy Burton for 1-0.

Oxford pressed for an equaliser, their growing desperation stretching the game and leaving opportunities for a counter-attack. On the hour, Swindon extended their lead through Roy Carter. Promotion was slipping away until six minutes from time when Billy Jeffrey pulled a goal back in front of chaotic scenes in the Oxford end.

Needing a point at least, the stands seethed with frustration and anger. Swindon were homing in on a famous win, a boost to their survival hopes and a blow to their rivals' promotion dream.

With three minutes to go, two smoke bombs were launched from the Swindon end into Roy Burton's penalty box. Smoke billowed across the pitch, engulfing Burton in a blinding fog. The players paused, waiting for referee Eric Read to stop the game and allow the pitch to be cleared. But, with Swindon attacking, Read allowed play to carry on. The Oxford players screamed for a whistle; surely the game couldn't continue? Burton waved at the fog while looking for the official. The ball dropped to Rideout, who put it in the back of the net. Read awarded the goal, claiming he hadn't seen any smoke until after the ball had gone in.

The stadium descended into chaos; Oxford fans, players and management were incandescent. Read was unmoved and the goal stood. Oxford fans tore at the fences that were penning them in. Police moved to quell the disorder and were met with a hail of missiles.

The linesman called Read over to the side of the pitch, and while consulting, a coin hit him in the eye, knocking him to the ground. 'I thought at first I'd been blinded,' he said afterwards. 'I could hear voices, but not see anything.' The injury caused an eight-minute delay as the police encouraged Read to go to hospital. After treatment from Ken Fish, he insisted on continuing in defiance of the hooligans.

The game restarted and within seconds, Kevin Brock attacked and was brought down by full-back Charlie Henry. Oxford fans appealed for a penalty but Read, believing the foul was outside the box, awarded a free kick. Minutes later, unmoved by the chaos around him, he poured more oil on the flames, finally awarding Oxford a penalty for a handball by Mike Graham which David Fogg converted for 3-2.

The long and ugly night ended before Swindon faced another Football League inquiry and announced they were contemplating painting the County Ground with indelible anti-vandal paint to deter trouble. Smith was disgusted by Read's performance. Oxford's hopes had been given a hammer blow; promotion was out of their hands.

The manner of defeat crushed Oxford's spirit and the following Saturday a George Lawrence goal was a consolation as they fell to defeat against Gillingham. Three days later they went down again, 1-0 to Bristol Rovers in the rearranged fixture from the abandonment in the early days of Smith's reign. The defeat effectively consigned the club to another year in the Third Division.

Oxford concluded their season with a 3-0 home defeat to relegated Wimbledon, an ignominious end to a tumultuous period. The fans, though, seemed content – the club had nearly gone bankrupt, been bought by an ambitious millionaire, become FA Cup giant-killers, lost their manager, sold their brightest prospect and star striker and missed out on promotion by a whisker. The season had gone up in smoke. Swindon's relegation was scant compensation; Oxford's ambitions were no longer local.

Smith had been at the Manor for just ten weeks and hoped the summer would give him the opportunity to start fulfilling Maxwell's burning ambition of promotion.

The following Monday, George Lawrence returned to Southampton, and six players were released including captain Billy Jeffrey, whose ten-year Oxford career ended when he signed for Blackpool. Smith handed the captaincy to Shotton, who combined with Briggs to create a commanding presence in the Oxford back four.

After a shaky start, Trevor Hebberd had settled well with Ray Train in midfield but only contributed two goals. Despite finishing fifth, Oxford were the division's 12th-highest scorers. Smith's instinct was that goals were essential to his survival as manager because they would get people through the turnstiles and please his chairman. He needed a replacement for Keith Cassells, signing Gary Barnett from Coventry City, Mick Vinter from Wrexham and Steve Biggins for £8,000 from Shrewsbury Town.

Oxford's refreshed team adopted a fresh look from Bradford-based firm Spall Sports. Their new shirt featured a fine royal blue pinstripe and across the chest was the club's new sponsor BPCC – Maxwell stamping his authority on the club.

Smith's striking problems seemed to be resolved as the team travelled to Gillingham on the opening day of the new campaign. Barnett opened his account with the only goal of the game and scored again, after a David Fogg penalty, in a 2-0 win over Reading in the Milk Cup.

The home campaign opened with a 2-0 win over Bournemouth and 3-0 over Doncaster with Vinter and Biggins opening their accounts. Goals from Hebberd and Thomas registered their fifth consecutive win at Preston before another 2-0 victory over Reading in the second leg of the Milk Cup completed a perfect start to the season.

Sitting at the top of the table, Oxford faced their biggest test yet with the visit of second-placed Portsmouth to the Manor. The sunshine and the team's form meant the upbeat mood attracted nearly 10,000 people through the turnstiles; Maxwell's influence was paying dividends. As kick-off approached, a sense of unease grew. The area behind the London Road terrace became crowded. There were unfamiliar faces and shouts of frustration that the turnstiles weren't turning quickly enough. Order disintegrated until the dam burst as fans in Portsmouth colours vaulted the barriers to get into the stadium and raced into the terrace before the police could stop them.

The volatile cocktail descended into chaos as rival fans clashed, scattering people into the safety of the Osler Road terrace. The police tried to intervene but controlling the mob was impossible in such an enclosed space.

As the players emerged, with Portsmouth fans remaining in the London Road terrace, an uneasy truce was called. After 17 minutes, former Oxford player Mick Tait was brought down in the box by Hebberd and the referee pointed to the spot in front of the Pompey supporters. Bobby Doyle stepped up and buried the penalty. The goal sparked the renewal of hostilities; the game was paused as fighting grew fiercer until it became a full-scale riot that stretched across the whole stand. Fans watched in disbelief until, from the tunnel, the huge figure of Robert Maxwell appeared, sprinting across the pitch followed by a phalanx of eager photographers he'd corralled on his way down from the directors' box. With his jacket and tie removed, Maxwell called for calm, climbing across the moat separating the London Road terrace from the pitch and laying his hands out messianically.

With the crowd calmed, a policeman's helmet tossed around in the melee was retrieved, and order was restored. Maxwell made his way into the crowd and stood with them briefly for the photographers to find their perfect shot; a man of the people, first among equals.

The headlines were written long before Briggs's goal secured a point. 'What had been high spirits became pitched battles,' Maxwell said afterwards. 'I was worried because children could have been hurt. It was very ugly – they were attacking each other, and coins were being thrown. The police don't relish this kind of battle and were grateful for my help.'

The chairman had claimed his first PR coup.

Chapter 5

Desmond Morris

FOOTBALL WAS at a crossroads; financial collapse and hooliganism had left it a decaying edifice of what it once was. Modernisers, like TV presenter Jimmy Hill, saw its future as a branch of the entertainment industry. Anthropologist Dr Desmond Morris took a different view.

Dr Morris had gained international fame with his book *The Naked Ape*, a study of humans as evolving animals, casting back to their ancestral origins to shape their response to the evolving world. He was a prolific writer, a lecturer in fine arts within the Army Education Corps and had a first-class honours degree from Birmingham University. He was also a director of Oxford United, using his privileged access to the club for much of his primary research.

Football bored him; he only attended games because of his son Jason's obsession. They'd once been at a match in Malta where the referee had made a disastrously wrong decision. A riot ensued, blood was let, and Morris was entranced. His observations became the basis for his new book, *The Soccer Tribe*.

Published in 1981, it characterised football as a series of tribal rituals that bonded people together. Confrontation and aggression, he believed, was necessary for groups to develop an identity. He concluded that football had to be tribal and that attempts at making it more civil, more 'feminine', would destroy it.

The more he watched matches at the Manor, the more he sensed football re-connecting people to the primeval hunting patterns of their ancestors. The unpredictability, speed and intensity stimulated the crowd, inducing a level of collective anxiety.

Tribes had rituals, costumes, superstitions and taboos. Violence, he argued, wasn't essential, but ritualised aggression was. It was a shared ordeal, a suffering in the hope of achieving an ecstatic moment of victory. What he would observe in the coming months would confirm his fears about the game.

The Portsmouth riot resulted in 61 arrests including 44 Oxford fans. Six policemen were injured – one hit by a dart, another knocked unconscious and a third carried off on a stretcher. Robert Maxwell appointed himself as the club's moral guardian, opening an inquiry into the trouble. The previous March, he'd installed CCTV around the Manor, allowing the disturbances to be caught on camera. The absolutist role suited Maxwell, who was used to writing, adapting, and ignoring rules in his business life. He was happy to tear them up if they didn't suit him.

When taking over the club he demanded complete compliance to his plan, but he'd been frustrated by the council's attitude towards the stadium development. There was little political consensus towards Oxford United; the preferences of each council ward determined the support or otherwise of the club's ambitions. There was support in the working-class south of the city, where the Rover car plant was, but less so in the wealthier northern suburbs, where the academic classes lived. Then there was Maxwell, a divisive presence who split the city between awe and anger.

The divisions meant the stadium remained a constant and unresolved issue, much to Maxwell's frustration.

The riot seemed to derail the team on the pitch, and after the Portsmouth draw, they lost for the first time that season, at Huddersfield, triggering a five-game run with just a win against Chesterfield, followed by a draw at home to Cardiff, a Milk Cup defeat at Huddersfield and another league defeat to Millwall.

Dropping to third, four points behind leaders Lincoln City, injury and the unconvincing form of the new strike partnership of Steve Biggins and Mick Vinter forced Jim Smith to seek more firepower. He returned to his old club Birmingham City to sign striker Neil Whatmore on loan; Whatmore had played under Ian Greaves at Bolton Wanderers as a foil for their playboy striker Frank Worthington, who Greaves labelled 'the working man's George Best'.

Smith reunited the pair, paying £350,000 to bring Whatmore to Birmingham, but Worthington's off-field antics meant Whatmore struggled and he was perceived as another expensive flop. Smith's successor, Ron Saunders, was happy to let the striker go, although Maxwell was unwilling to meet the £100,000 price tag to make the deal permanent.

Whatmore's debut came at home to Walsall. In the opening minutes, attacking the London Road terrace, he linked up with Trevor Hebberd, whose cross was met by Malcolm Shotton's bullet header to open the scoring. Minutes later, David Linney fed the ball to Gary Barnett, who found Whatmore at the near post to clip in for a debut goal. A foul on Foley allowed David Fogg to make it three from the spot. Oxford were back to their rampant best.

Walsall responded before half-time with a rifling shot from Kenny Beech, but Whatmore and Barnett linked up early in the second half to release Brock to drive the ball beyond the Walsall keeper for 4-1. Alan Buckley's freak looping overhead kick pulled a goal back but the result, and Whatmore's performance, was a timely reminder of the team's potential.

The win returned Oxford to second in the table, but despite another Whatmore goal four days later, a 2-2 draw with Brentford saw them drop to third.

Smith was beginning to see what he might be able to achieve at Oxford. With Maxwell's support the job could be more than just a bridge back to better things. He needed to think longer term and address difficult issues.

Roy Burton had been Oxford's first choice in the number one shirt since his debut in 1971. Short for a goalkeeper, he was an agile stopper who'd made nearly 450 appearances. He wouldn't have looked out of place on the terraces, his drooping moustache and ill-fitting kit making him a favourite of the London Road fans. When launching the ball upfield, it was customary for his shorts to expose his bare backside. Like Briggs and Shotton, he represented the heart of the club, although at 32 his career was reaching its end.

For the visit to Wrexham, Smith made the seismic decision to replace Burton with John Butcher, a summer signing from Blackburn Rovers. It was the first league game Burton had missed for over two years. The disruption doubled inside five minutes when Briggs was sent off for scything down John Muldoon as he raced in on goal. Within a minute Gary Barnett hit the post before Mick Vinter, returning for the first time in three weeks, scored against his old club just before the half-hour mark. Oxford held out until 20 minutes from time when Rob Savage equalised for 1-1.

Butcher's home debut came the following Wednesday against Huddersfield in the Milk Cup. Trailing to a two-goal deficit from the first leg, Steve Biggins started for the first time in a month, scoring the only goal in an unconvincing victory. In injury time, with Oxford chasing the game,

Huddersfield striker Mark Lillis broke free. Gary Briggs barged him out of the way, giving the referee no option but to send the centre-back off for the second time in four days.

Briggs believed he was a victim of the game's modernisers. At the start of the season, Jimmy Hill, leading a panel of Matt Busby and Bobby Charlton, recommended that 'professional fouls' should be punished with a red card. Briggs had to re-calibrate his aggression although Smith defended him, saying, 'Both Briggs's sendings-off have been harsh. Referees don't seem to be using common sense any more.'

Briggs's extended suspension meant Oxford's patchy form continued into November. Whatmore was a consistent goalscoring threat but draws with Exeter and Sheffield United were sandwiched between defeats to Bradford and Plymouth. Oxford drifted back to tenth place, seven points behind the promotion places, their early form a distant memory.

There was a further blow as Whatmore's loan ended and Ron Saunders sent him back out to his old club Bolton. With no place for the striker at St Andrew's, Smith sensed an opportunity.

Form was the least of Oxford's troubles; they were also facing an FA inquiry. Following the trouble at Portsmouth, the Sheffield United game was marred when missiles were thrown from the London Road terrace. A fine or points deduction wouldn't be viewed favourably by those considering the club's application for a new stadium; nobody would invite these problems into their neighbourhood.

The FA Cup offered a welcome break from the league, with Oxford hoping for another run deep into the competition. They were pleased to get a home tie against Southern League South side Folkestone Town. Immediately before the match, Smith revealed a familiar face to bolster his faltering team, with George Lawrence returning on a £45,000 permanent deal from Southampton.

The powerful, unpredictable winger had found opportunities limited since returning to The Dell and jumped at the chance of first-team football. Described by Smith as a 'big softie', a fan favourite, he was also Maxwell's favourite player, although many suspected it was because he was the only black player in the side, so the easiest for Maxwell to recognise.

Lawrence missed the game against Folkestone, but Fogg, Shotton, Vinter and two goals from Foley secured a 5-2 win, breaking the non-leaguers' 22-game unbeaten run and easing Oxford into the next round.

The following week, they faced Lincoln at home in thick fog. By half-time, despite failing visibility, the referee persisted as Oxford pressed for an opening goal.

The game was briefly paused when Oxford fans pelted Lincoln's goalkeeper David Felgate with coins, but the hosts were unlucky not to be awarded a penalty minutes later when Vinter was brought down. On 63 minutes, with darkness falling and no prospect of the fog clearing, the referee finally abandoned the game. Neither manager had any complaints, though Maxwell threatened to close sections of the London Road terrace if trouble continued.

Lawrence made a scoring return two weeks later when Oxford travelled to Orient as their form burst into life with Foley scoring his second brace in two games, and Vinter and Tim Smithers chipping in for a 5-1 victory. The win celebrated Maxwell's first anniversary and a remarkable financial turnaround. From near bankruptcy, the club achieved profits of £101,542. It was a familiar story – all Maxwell's businesses seemed to benefit from his golden touch.

Maxwell attributed the success to his prodigious business acumen, but behind the headlines, there were concerns. Jim Smith had cut playing costs by reducing the squad from 24 to 17 players. Other savings had come from backroom redundancies. The FA Cup run and encouraging league form had increased matchday revenue by 45 per cent, but without the sale of Keith Cassells and Mark Wright to Southampton, Oxford were still operating at a loss.

Maxwell knew the club wasn't sustainable. He couldn't rely on FA Cup runs and player sales and, though he wasn't afraid to trim costs, they could only go so far before they would have a detrimental effect on the pitch. He warned that the club was viable only for a couple of years and that a new stadium was essential.

Smith allowed Andy Thomas to go on a month's loan to Fulham as Gary Briggs returned from his four-match suspension for the FA Cup second round tie at home to Worthing. Despite a comfortable 4-0 win, Briggs's return was short-lived after fracturing his cheekbone in a clash with a Worthing attacker. Although he completed the game, the injury would keep him out for weeks.

The mood was improved a week before Christmas when Foley's fourth goal in as many matches saw a narrow win over Wigan Athletic. There was an early Christmas present when the FA commission into crowd trouble at Sheffield United found in favour of the club. Despite the decision, Jim Hunt was worried that Oxford were running out of chances and started making plans to address the problem.

Foley scored his eighth goal in five games as Oxford took their form into the Christmas period with a 4-2 win over Bristol Rovers at the Manor. The following day, Roy Burton returned for his final game for the club in a 2-1 win over Newport.

On New Year's Day, Mick Vinter's goal gave Oxford another win over Southend. A goal after 12 seconds then set up a 3-0 win over Reading two days later, with Lawrence scoring twice. Oxford's eighth win in a row pushed them up to fifth, a point off the promotion places.

Hoping for a big name in the FA Cup, the draw for the third round wasn't kind, but blistering form meant the prospect of Torquay United at the Manor held few concerns. Despite high expectations, the Fourth Division side proved awkward opponents and Oxford were thankful for a tenth-minute header from Foley to scrape a 1-1 draw.

The team travelled south-west for the replay the following Wednesday in the hope of securing a home tie against Jim Smith's boyhood team, Sheffield Wednesday. The journey was nothing compared to that of Torquay fan Rick Pudner, who flew from Oman as cup fever gripped the Devon club.

Oxford looked comfortable as half-time approached but were sucker-punched by Torquay striker Steve Cooper who latched on to a long ball, rounded Butcher and slotted home for 1-0.

After the break Oxford battered the Torquay goal looking for an equaliser, but against the run of play, just after an hour, Jackie Gallagher struck to make it 2-0. As fans celebrated, in the grandstand 63-year-old Torquay fan Norman Brooks collapsed, falling into the arms of Anne Wilson, the wife of the Gulls' captain Brian and member of the singing group the Nolans. She cradled him as he passed away as the game continued.

A David Fogg penalty reduced the deficit after Foley was fouled, but despite constant pressure and a fierce following wind, Oxford couldn't find an equaliser and bowed out of the competition.

For Robert Maxwell, the result highlighted the club's plight. With no prospect of a lucrative FA Cup run or to sell more players to make up the financial shortfalls, he needed to accelerate Oxford's move from a hand-to-mouth existence.

Smith's troubles were just beginning – a 1-1 draw with Gillingham was marred by a broken cheekbone for the influential Trevor Hebberd. When, a week later, Billy Rafferty waltzed through the Oxford defence to score

Portsmouth's only goal past a sluggish Butcher, Smith knew he had to act, covering the loss of Hebberd by signing Aston Villa forward Terry Donovan on loan.

A narrow 3-2 win over Preston at the Manor slowed the slide but when Smith dropped Briggs for the 2-0 defeat to Bournemouth, the normally mild-mannered character off the field angrily demanded a transfer.

Smith sensed the unrest and restored Briggs to the starting line-up for the 1-1 draw with Huddersfield. He then lost Donovan when the midfielder was sent off during Oxford's 3-0 defeat to Cardiff.

As Smith approached his first anniversary in charge, the team were fifth in the division, exactly where they'd been when he had taken over. He responded by signing Neil Whatmore permanently after persuading Ron Saunders to let him go for £25,000.

He then addressed his lingering goalkeeping problem.

Steve Hardwick was the product of a Chesterfield goalkeeping academy. He'd played over 130 games and was a former England youth international. Now at Newcastle, he'd become disillusioned with football and hadn't played a first-team game for nearly two years.

Scapegoated by Newcastle fans, his first-team place was taken by Kevin Carr. His prospects of a new contract were slim and he faced a season of midweek reserve football in the Central League.

When Carr walked through a glass door and cut his hands while on tour in Madeira it looked like Hardwick's opportunity had come. After a good start to the season, manager Arthur Cox lambasted him for an error in a defeat to Shrewsbury. 'As far as the first goal is concerned,' he said, 'our keeper Steve Hardwick made the wrong decision.' As soon as Carr regained fitness, Hardwick was relegated back to the reserves. His Newcastle career was over.

Smith knew Hardwick through Trevor Francis, who had played with him at Detroit Express. Like Roy Burton, Hardwick was a good shot-stopper, and he was also six years Burton's junior.

With struggling Millwall up next at the Manor, Smith was desperate to get a deal over the line but 260 miles between the clubs slowed progress. Smith took matters into his own hands, driving to Newcastle to finalise the paperwork with Hardwick before returning south to complete arrangements in Oxford. Once the deal had been confirmed between the two clubs, he drove to FA headquarters in London to register Hardwick in time to face Millwall.

Returning to Oxford he was called by the Manor's veteran groundsman, Len Bateman. A heavy frost covered the pitch and with little prospect of temperatures rising, the referee declared it unfit to play on. Despite Smith driving over 600 miles in a day to secure the deal, Hardwick's debut would have to wait.

With Trevor Hebberd recovering from his broken cheekbone, Terry Donovan returned to his parent club. Neil Whatmore joined the starting line-up and Hardwick finally made his debut in an inauspicious 1-0 defeat to Walsall. Oxford had taken one point in nine and were sitting in seventh, eight points off the promotion places.

Despite their vapid form, Smith could now field his strongest 11. The following Wednesday, at home to Bradford, the team burst into life. Whatmore scored a 19-minute hat-trick, with Thomas and Vinter adding two more in a comprehensive 5-1 win.

It was short-lived and without Fogg, Lawrence, Thomas, Brock or Vinter, Oxford suffered a 3-1 defeat at Exeter, causing Smith to unleash his fury at the team's inconsistency. There was a partial recovery following a narrow 1-0 win over promotion hopefuls Lincoln City with Whatmore scoring his fifth goal since signing permanently but then Oxford slipped into another of their customary slumps. A win over Bristol Rovers was their only success after defeats to Sheffield United and Newport County and draws with Brentford and Plymouth.

A 2-2 draw with Orient saw Oxford drifting in seventh place, ten points off promotion. The London Road terrace booed the team off with a loud chorus of 'What a load of rubbish'. Smith snapped, 'Any crowd can be like a 13th man to a side, but there are times when our crowd cut us down to ten players.' A rift between the manager and fans wasn't ideal; this timing couldn't have been worse.

Despite the problems, Whatmore and Vinter were still showing good form so Smith offered Peter Foley the opportunity to fly to Hong Kong for a three-month loan spell with leading side Bulova. A year into his tenure, with Billy Jeffrey, Keith Cassells, Mark Wright, Roy Burton and now Foley gone, what had Smith achieved? He'd been given two years to get promotion, but he knew his volatile chairman could change at any time. Indeed, Maxwell was already hatching a long-term solution.

Reading were in an even worse situation than Oxford. They too were stuck in a dilapidated stadium at Elm Park, but they didn't have a Greaves, Smith or Maxwell to propel them forward. Maxwell reasoned there was only one way the two failing clubs could survive.

In the US there weren't clubs, just franchises, and fans were consumers. Sport wasn't tribal as Desmond Morris saw it, but a Frankenstein's monster of Jimmy Hill's family friendly vision for football.

Maxwell concluded that if he could bring success, fans would put aside any misgivings of standing alongside those they'd previously considered rivals. If the assets of both clubs were sold off, he could invest in a single facility without the burden of history; his solution was a merger.

One Sunday in early 1983, Maxwell had phoned Jim Hunt asking for the number of the Reading chairman, Frank Waller. Much of Maxwell's Oxford United work was done at weekends and Hunt assumed his chairman was lining up a bid for Reading's striker Kerry Dixon.

In fact, Maxwell wanted to court Waller and other Reading directors, mopping up shares in the Berkshire club in preparation for a takeover. Waller assured him he would deliver the votes from his board, making the merger a foregone conclusion.

With Reading facing relegation and Oxford pushing for promotion, Jim Smith would become manager with Reading boss Maurice Evans his assistant. Dixon was Reading's only asset, so the rest of the Oxford squad could feel reasonably secure. The only assurance Maxwell offered was that Reading would retain their nickname, with the new club being known as Thames Valley Royals.

One element was missing from the plan: Maxwell hadn't told anyone. In mid-April, as Oxford prepared to face Doncaster Rovers, Rovers' club secretary called Hunt to the phone. It was Maxwell announcing that he planned to reveal the merger to the public the following day.

In the press box, *Oxford Mail* reporter John Ley was already taking calls from the national press about the rumour. Ley raced down to find Smith, who phoned Maxwell. As the players returned from their warm-up Smith broke the news.

By the time the whistle had blown on a 1-0 win, the rumour mill was out of control. As the vidi-printer chattered away announcing the day's final scores, the presenter of BBC's *Grandstand*, David Coleman, interjected with the news that would grab all the headlines; Oxford United planned to merge with Reading and play as a new club at the start of the following season. The coach on the way back from Doncaster was deathly quiet as the players contemplated their uncertain futures.

Dumbfounded, Smith knew he was vulnerable. Speaking out against Maxwell's scheme would see him out of a job; supporting it would put him in conflict with fans who were already restless. With a mortgage to pay and three children to support, Smith remained compliant to his owner. He said he was excited by the prospect, pleading with supporters to accept the plan. 'I think it's the way football will go in the future,' he said, unconvincingly.

In preparation for a board meeting to ratify the proposal, Maxwell went on the offensive, threatening to resign as chairman if his merger fell through. The real villain, he insisted, was the council; their prevarication over the stadium made the merger the only viable alternative to bankruptcy.

The new ground would be equidistant between Oxford and Reading. Wallingford, 20 miles south of the city, was one option but Didcot mayor Basil Pryor enthusiastically embraced the plan and promised to be a leading voice of support through the planning process. He earmarked a 150-acre plot and contacted Maxwell, who said he'd view it from his helicopter. While the stadium was built, the team would alternate between Elm Park and the Manor.

The Oxford board, in the grip of Maxwell, approved the plan on 20 April, only suggesting an amended name – Thames Valley United. Despite the approval, Maxwell already seemed to be wavering, saying he would call the merger off if the club's future could be guaranteed for the next five years. He warned that anyone willing to do that would face a bill of £750,000 to upgrade the Manor to new safety standards.

Things were less straightforward in Berkshire; intimidated by Maxwell's overbearing style, Frank Waller had oversold the control he was able to offer. He could only rely on the support of three of their six board members, a minority of the controlling interest.

Reading had been for sale all season, and Maxwell's move activated some long-term suitors – including Deep Purple lead singer Ian Gilmore and former Reading player Roger Smee. Immediately after Maxwell's announcement, Smee convened a meeting at his house.

Along with directors Jim Brooks and Roy Trantor, Smee planned a counter-offer. They were backed by Reading Council who'd debated the merger in an emergency motion, the town's mayor George Robinson saying, 'I will do all I can to support any move to keep league football alive in Reading.'

The Football League, floundering to find a solution to the crippling financial problems clubs were in, supported the merger in principle. President Jack Dunnet described it as 'a bold and imaginative move which I'll be watching with interest'. Secretary Graham Kelly mused about how he would bring the league back up to its full complement of 92 clubs. Even John Ley of the *Oxford Mail* chose to back it. The merger had momentum where it mattered.

The usually unassuming Reading manager Maurice Evans, interviewed on the Monday after the announcement, could barely contain his anger, echoing the response from football's establishment.

Maxwell's media juggernaut was already rolling; he portrayed an unstoppable force behind the idea. It was more likely, he said, that the Thames would run backwards.

The response was swift. Oxford fans rallied, organising a protest group – Save Oxford Soccer (SOS) – and a demonstration at their next home game against Wigan. While Oxford and Reading supporters fought the merger organically, attacking the ethics of the plan, Smee focussed on the technicalities of the deal itself. It was here he discovered its fatal weakness.

The following Friday, Maxwell called a press conference at Lancaster Gate to reveal his plans. Jim Smith sat uncomfortably at the end of the table with Maurice Evans. Despite the aim to offer a united front, Maxwell, in combative mood, ejected a dissenting Reading director from the room before laying out his case. With his usual bombast, he turned to Evans for a comment. Evans declined, neatly side-stepping the opportunity to put himself in the same divisive position as Smith. Maxwell, far from being annoyed by Evans's lack of commitment, was impressed by his diplomacy.

Leaving FA headquarters, Waller was issued with an injunction by Reading director Roy Tranter. Smee had discovered unusual movements of the club's unallocated shares and sought a court order to allow time to investigate. The shares appeared to have been offered to Maxwell by Waller without informing the board, in essence, selling shares he didn't own.

The following day, Oxford faced Wigan at the Manor. Graham Kelly banned TV cameras from the ground, so they perched in the trees outside the stadium poking through any vantage point.

Around 1,500 fans planned a sit-in, gathering outside the London Road entrance with banners opposing the move, highlighting Maxwell's greed. As kick-off approached, they walked on to the pitch and sat in the centre circle. It was good-natured and peaceful, and even Maxwell was sympathetic, a marked contrast to how fans were perceived up and down the country.

The SOS committee informed the referee and players that the protest would last for 15 minutes, and most left at the allotted time. By the time 20 police intervened to remove the last few, numbers had dwindled to a dozen.

Kick-off was delayed by half an hour, and ten minutes later Maxwell appeared in the directors' box and the mood shifted, the football providing a mere backdrop as fans barracked their chairman.

Maxwell retreated before half-time having been at the game for little more than half an hour. As Maxwell disappeared below the stand, George Lawrence opened the scoring and Andy Thomas added a second after 66 minutes to secure the points while the fans claimed their first victory in the battle for the club's survival.

The following day, Maxwell appeared on Radio Oxford. Arriving in his Rolls-Royce with his son Kevin, he was confronted by two Oxford fans. Maxwell seemed unmoved, recalling the incident on-air with a curious fondness.

The court hearing was set for 3 May, weakening the merger's viability. It was the day after Reading's scheduled visit to Oxford in the league. With both clubs needing to plan for the following season, the delay complicated the issue further.

A win at Millwall and a draw with Wigan maintained Oxford's solid form, but Reading's one win in 11 was proving more significant. As the clubs prepared to face each other in both the court and at the Manor, with three games remaining, the Royals were in danger of being relegated. Two teams in different divisions would make re-organising the leagues even more challenging.

There was another dimension; Oxford City Council offered the club a new stadium site in Botley in the west of the city for £6m. Maxwell insisted the merger would proceed but admitted the offer changed the complexion of the issue.

Fearing trouble at their bank holiday showdown, kick-off was moved to 11am. Reading fans' mood was sombre after conceding a three-goal lead against nine-man Millwall the previous Saturday. They arrived carrying a coffin to signify the imminent death of their club.

The media focus was more off the pitch than on it. Maxwell arrived late, meaning he and the following press pack missed the kick-off. When he did convene, he insisted that fans were coming round to the idea; the 400 Oxford supporters who'd marched to the game in protest suggested otherwise.

The game was billed as a trial for the following season's Thames Valley Royals squad, but the most notable moment of the first half was Reading's Stewart Henderson running into the referee and knocking him out, causing a long delay.

At half-time, Maxwell held court, insisting that the Botley scheme was no more than 'election promises' with council elections due the following Thursday.

Maxwell left with 15 minutes to go, drawing the game into focus and it sprung to life as though unconstrained from its yoke. Neil Whatmore put Oxford ahead from Kevin Brock's corner, but with five minutes to go Mark Jones diverted Kerry Dixon's cross into his own goal for the equaliser. With the game drifting towards a draw that neither club wanted, Tim Smithers upended Jerry Williams in the box and the referee pointed to the spot.

As Dixon blocked all distractions from his mind, an Oxford fan appeared from the stands and launched the ball high into the crowd before setting off on a weaving run to elude the comic pursuit of the police. It took several minutes to restore order before Dixon stepped up to fire firmly to his right where Steve Hardwick got his fingertips to the ball, but couldn't prevent it from going in. Oxford's promotion hopes were crushed.

To conclude a chaotic day, immediately after the game, Jim Hunt found Roger Smee holding his own impromptu press conference under the Beech Road stand; the battle to win hearts and minds was very much on.

On hearing Smee's case the following day, Mr Justice Harman's withering assessment was that Maxwell and

Waller had issued themselves a controlling interest in the club. The ruling delayed share trading at Reading until the middle of June, landing another fatal blow. Maurice Evans contacted the Football League to ask how he should plan for next season. Believing the merger was dead, they advised him to plan for a separate team.

The following Thursday, Didcot mayor Basil Pryor faced the embarrassment of losing his seat in the local elections. Despite sweeping Conservative gains, he surmised it was due to his vocal support for the merger. Labour strengthened their majority in Oxford, improving the chances of gaining planning permission for the new stadium and giving Maxwell the opportunity to withdraw his plans.

The day before the end of the season, after a five-hour meeting the Reading board ousted Frank Waller, who conceded he didn't have the shares to force the deal through. His supporting directors stood down, opening the door for Smee to take over.

Maurice Evans celebrated with a 1-0 win against Wrexham but with Orient beating Sheffield United, Reading were doomed to play the following season in the Fourth Division. For all the upheaval, upset and protests, the Royals had sacrificed their league position to save themselves and their great rivals in the process.

As Smee prepared to be confirmed as Reading chairman at an Extraordinary General Meeting, the defiant Maxwell offered £5 a share to the club's shareholders. Director Roy Tranter called for the Football League to step in and call off the attack.

Maxwell responded by going to the High Court to seek an injunction against the EGM. Mr Justice Vinelott refused the request, declaring it 'very close to being an abuse of the process of the court' in a damning verdict on Maxwell's tactics.

Maxwell raged to an increasingly disinterested public, insisting it was the only way for the clubs to survive, before turning his fire on the council and threatening to resign if the stadium situation wasn't resolved.

While the story withered away as a curious footnote in the club's history, the death of the deal left a smouldering bitterness in Maxwell. He resented the intervention of the fans and the lack of engagement from the council. Maxwell's unquenchable ambition had found a limit; it was not in his nature to allow that to happen.

Chapter 6

Bobby McDonald

STARING AT the wreckage of his car through an alcoholic haze, Peter Bodak knew he'd made a catastrophic mistake. The 22-year-old Manchester City winger thought he'd made his big move when he'd joined from Manchester United in 1982, but erratic form had left him on the margins of the squad. When City were relegated to the Second Division, Bodak was transfer-listed by new manager Billy McNeill with his career in tatters.

City were scheduled to play a pre-season friendly with Blackpool, but its meaninglessness tempted Bodak out for a night at a local casino. Driving home through south Manchester in the early hours, he crashed into two lamp-posts, a gatepost and a gate before abandoning his car. The police found him at home where his breathalyser test was positive, but at the police station he refused a second test. He didn't need one to know what was coming.

In court, it didn't take long for the judge to reach his conclusion. Bodak was fined £200 and banned from driving for 18 months, but this was just the start of his problems.

Billy McNeill's underperforming squad lacked discipline. Bodak's crash was symptomatic of their problems. The manager recommended to his board that Bodak be sacked for breaching a 48-hour curfew placed on players before games.

Bodak hadn't been alone. Scottish international full-back Bobby McDonald rarely missed an opportunity for a night out. As a passenger, he escaped a court appearance, but McNeill wasn't interested in details and McDonald was also shown the door. Bodak appealed his dismissal, but the older, wiser McDonald negotiated a settlement and headed to pastures new.

The battle with Roger Smee hadn't been Robert Maxwell's only legal wrangle that summer. He'd rebranded his British Printing Corporation as the British Printing and Communication Corporation (BPCC), putting him on a collision course with Hull-based shop owner Norman Lovett, whose British Programme Collectors Club had carried the name since 1972.

Maxwell's lawyers contacted Lovett, pressuring him to change his name, but Lovett stood firm. The dispute took a year to reach court, including one delay resulting from Maxwell being unable to provide evidence after a colleague collapsed at his office. In July 1984, Lovett won his right to use BPCC, leaving Maxwell unable to register the trademark. Lovett and his wife Marian celebrated with a meal in Bridlington. 'I'm going for his profits,' he said.

In December, Maxwell appealed, claiming his profits had plummeted since the dispute had begun. By May he'd beaten the little shop owner from Hull, proving there were few fights he'd back down from.

Back in the summer of 1983, following the disappointment of the previous season and the tumult of the Thames Valley Royals debacle, Jim Smith hoped the break would give him an opportunity to focus. He needed quality players who were willing to play at the cramped Manor for an unfashionable club. It would take a special kind of player to meet the ambitions of the chairman.

The only new face for the first game of the season, at home to Lincoln City, was full-back Paul Hinshelwood from Crystal Palace. Smith chose an attacking midfield of Andy Thomas and Trevor Hebberd in preference to Ray Train. The new combination could release the pace and flair of Kevin Brock and George Lawrence down the flanks, giving Oxford a prodigious attacking threat.

The team still lacked goals; despite a successful pre-season, including a tour of the Republic of Ireland with matches against Sligo and Shamrock Rovers, Mick Vinter and Neil Whatmore had been poor. Only Steve Biggins had shown any form and Smith was preparing to put him on the transfer list after an injury-plagued season.

Despite Smith's concerns, Oxford scorched to a 3-0 win with Biggins scoring one and making another for Whatmore before Lawrence completed the rout. This was followed by a 1-1 draw with Fourth Division Bristol City in the first round of the Milk Cup, only a last-minute equaliser from Glyn Riley preventing Brock's 16th-minute opener from giving Oxford a first-leg lead.

September opened with a convincing 2-0 win at Wigan despite glass in the Latics' main stand being blown out by a gale-force wind. The team dropped their first league points in a goalless draw with Scunthorpe, who employed five at the back to contain Oxford's attacking strength. Smith knew he'd need something else to overcome defensive teams.

After Bobby McDonald's very public sacking, Smith asked assistant Ray Graydon to invite his old Aston Villa team-mate for a trial. After watching him play for Oxford's reserves against Arsenal, despite a 4-0 defeat, Smith was convinced enough to offer McDonald a contract. Smith thought his sacking was a demonstration of McNeill's authority rather than a reflection of the player. He was a strong character with a reputation but at 28 and with 300 top-flight appearances, just two years after being part of Manchester City's team which narrowly lost the FA Cup Final to Tottenham, he had all the quality Smith needed.

Smith's philosophy was 'know footballers, rather than football'. Around the dressing room, he'd pinned upm signs saying 'Simplicity is genius', 'A good player does simple things and when necessary, something extra' and 'Failure is not to shoot, not failure to score'. It mirrored his personality; only performances on the pitch mattered. He would bellow and berate from the touchline for 90 minutes but was the first to serve drinks on the way home.

With McDonald adding authority to the back four, Kevin Brock had licence to take risks and mature his craft. When Brock was attacking through the midfield, McDonald marshalled any gaps left behind.

Three days after his trial, McDonald replaced David Fogg in a 2-2 draw with Burnley, who equalised in the last minute after a mistake by Steve Hardwick. He kept his place for the Milk Cup second leg against Bristol City, where Andy Thomas sealed the tie with a goal after 16 seconds.

The reward was a match with ambitious Second Division Newcastle United, featuring former England captain Kevin Keegan, European Cup winner Terry McDermott, and exciting young attackers Peter Beardsley and Chris Waddle.

Smith welcomed the financial benefits of the draw but would have been happier focussing on promotion. With Gary Briggs and Malcolm Shotton anchoring the back four alongside McDonald and Hinshelwood, he felt confident unleashing a tsunami of attacking flair.

Partnering Biggins and Gary Barnett up front instantly paid dividends in a blistering 11-day period. A 3-2 win at Gillingham came after Hebberd and Barnett scored quick-fire goals and Biggins added the third. A week later, George Lawrence made up for an early miss by rounding the keeper to open the scoring against Millwall at the Manor. The Londoners struck back three minutes later, but another goal from Barnett sent Oxford into the break with a 2-1 lead.

Biggins missed two good chances before David Stride equalised with 18 minutes left. Lawrence and Jones added two more late on to put Oxford second in the table. Millwall boss George Graham lamented that it should have been 7-6.

The following Wednesday, Oxford welcomed Walsall to the Manor. With Newcastle manager Arthur Cox watching from the Beech Road stand, they were quickly in command when Andy Thomas rattled home the opening goal after four minutes. Despite conceding four minutes later, Oxford were rampant and Barnett extended their lead after 16 minutes. George Lawrence made it three after 26 and Barnett added a fourth five minutes later.

Shortly after the break, Lawrence extended the lead further before Walsall briefly rallied, pulling it back to 5-3. Thomas's second seven minutes from time capped a sparkling performance.

With 13 goals in three games, and seven conceded, Oxford were the top scorers in England, even without Vinter and Whatmore, who'd contributed 23 goals the previous season. The salvo was recognised when Jim Smith picked up the season's first Bell's Manager of the Month award.

A relatively modest 2-1 win at Preston with goals from Thomas and Biggins at the beginning of October finally put Oxford two points clear at the top of the table and ready to face Newcastle.

The tie threatened to be like duelling with flamethrowers. Confidence was high but Jim Hunt still put tickets on sale before the first leg in case Oxford suffered a heavy defeat at St James' Park.

Smith had Ray Graydon watch Newcastle twice and Oxford headed north confident they'd spotted a weakness in their opponents. The team stayed at the Gosforth Park Hotel and mingled with snooker players Steve Davis and Terry Griffiths, who were playing in a tournament nearby, a departure from the austerity of recent years.

Just 350 Oxford fans saw Malcolm Shotton leading the team out into a stadium he'd frequented as a boy but it only took a few minutes to show the visitors' intent as Steve Biggins fired over from three yards out.

Newcastle had a goal ruled out for offside and struck the bar before Briggs fired narrowly over. Eight minutes before the break George Lawrence barrelled down the right flank and delivered a precise crossfield ball into the box for Biggins to slot home from six yards. It was a slick and clinical goal that silenced their opponents.

Newcastle attacked furiously through Keegan and Beardsley, but only Terry McDermott's equaliser three minutes from time prevented Oxford from returning home with a first-leg lead.

Oxford had landed a telling blow and Keegan, who'd seen everything in his long and distinguished career, looked stunned. Talking to the press afterwards he said, 'I can't believe there are any better sides in the Third Division. If there are, it's a hell of a division.' It was a performance he'd expect at the top of the Second Division, maybe higher.

Jim Smith was also in awe and beginning to get a sense of the power of the team he'd built. What he'd seen was exciting and a little frightening. Promotion became his minimum expectation. What his team could ultimately achieve, he couldn't dare envisage.

Maxwell had given the club financial stability, but the team was a clever blend of homegrown talents, free signings and shrewd finds from the higher divisions, each one complementing the other. With the ball at the feet of Lawrence or Brock the crowd rose in anticipation, and defences crumbled, fearing what was to come. The Manor morphed into a living, breathing entity; a lair ready to entrap the strongest victim.

A win over Brentford preceded Oxford's first defeat of the season, at Plymouth, but they remained a point clear at the top of the table. Then, immediately before two goals from Trevor Hebberd secured a 2-0 win over Bradford, Maxwell seized another opportunity to ratchet up pressure on the council.

With a £1m bill to upgrade the Manor to Second Division standards, Maxwell haughtily declared, 'The deadline has long passed and time is running out. If we don't reach a decisive settlement on the new ground by the end of the year, there is no reason why I should continue to spend any more money on the club.'

Oxford were up for sale.

The distraction disrupted Oxford's flow when facing managerless Bournemouth, who were buoyed by rumours that Tommy Docherty was about to take their reins. The home side raced into a two-goal lead and Gary Barnett's goal 12 minutes from time couldn't prevent a second defeat of the season. Only Hull's defeat to Plymouth prevented Oxford from losing top spot.

Night fell on 26 October, shrouding the Manor in darkness, the floodlights illuminating the stage like a theatre. The shadows of the trees waved gently in the breeze. Beyond the Osler Road terrace's patchwork of corrugated iron roofing, the silhouettes of those trapped outside poked over the top, benefitting from whatever ledge or foothold they could find.

It was incongruous and disconcerting; a quirky assortment of stands surrounding the sloping pitch. The Manor was as much an opponent as the team – those who didn't understand would be devoured. The team defied its status; too good for its surroundings, too good for its division and better than it was on paper. If you didn't believe in magic, the Manor at night made you think again.

The first leg should have given Newcastle fair warning of what they were about to face, but they were quickly overwhelmed. Even without Biggins or Vinter, from kick-off Oxford poured down the slope towards the London Road. A deft through ball from Andy Thomas released George Lawrence, who should have scored in the opening minutes. Lawrence, impulsive and unplayable, was rampant down the wing, and a half-cleared cross fell to Bobby McDonald to fire a 30-yard volley narrowly over. Oxford's threat was everywhere.

They finally broke the deadlock on 19 minutes; a slick interchange between McDonald, Brock, Barnett and Thomas sent Brock free down the left wing. With the Newcastle defence retreating, his drive into the box fed a near-post cross to Whatmore, who chipped the ball home on his first game back from injury.

Newcastle briefly threatened with Waddle firing over, but after half an hour Brock broke clear, releasing Thomas, who shrugged off a challenge from Keegan, skipped a lunging tackle and unleashed a blistering 25-yard drive into the top corner for 2-0. The Manor was alive, thundering with appreciation, the sound pounding off the roof of the stand and resonating every nook and cranny of the old ground.

With Maxwell looking on, in the second half Brock nearly made it three before Thomas chipped the ball on to the bar. There was no rest. In desperation Keegan flicked a long ball on, but his clever touch drew a lunging challenge from Gary Briggs. Keegan collapsed in a bundle on the floor, and with Briggs already booked, referee Clive Thomas sent him to the dressing room.

Newcastle capitalised on their advantage; Beardsley crossed for Keegan to volley in for 2-1. The tie was back on a knife-edge then a nervy ten minutes passed with Oxford defending stoically, before the final whistle signalled the conclusion of a famous night.

Keegan was gracious in defeat, 'The better side won on the night. If they'd lost it would have been a travesty.' Jim Smith boldly declared his side was First Division quality.

The draw paired Oxford with Leeds United at Elland Road, another famous name and formidable task. With the former giants sitting in mid-table in the Second Division, in-form Oxford could face them with confidence despite Briggs's suspension meaning he would miss playing his boyhood club.

Facing Hull City at the Manor three days later was a reminder that the Milk Cup couldn't distract from the main goal of promotion. Smith kept his team talk simple, 'Hold it up front, possession in midfield and no silly buggers at the back. If in doubt stroke it back to the keeper.' Hull scored when Billy Whitehurst nodded down Steve McClaren's cross to Brian Marwood before Lawrence converted Brock's cross into the roof of the net for 1-1.

The warning signs were clearer still the following Tuesday when Oxford were savaged by Wimbledon's physicality and set plays which lent heavily on United's defensive frailties. After 11 minutes Hardwick's poor clearance, under pressure from Stewart Evans, allowed Glyn Hodges to put the hosts ahead. Two Alan Cork headers from Hodges corners made it 3-0.

Wally Downes and Gary Peters nearly extended the lead further, while Oxford's normally ferocious attack was limited to long-range efforts with Andy Thomas hitting the post. With the game lost and time ebbing away, Thomas's header was just a last-minute consolation in a sobering 3-1 defeat.

The loss exposed the team's weaknesses, and it wouldn't be long before others caught on. Oxford had won one of their last five league games, the Newcastle victory glossing over fluctuating league form which had been their downfall in the previous season. Smith knew he had to stay level-headed and as winter set in and pitches became tougher to play on, he couldn't always rely on his wingers to overwhelm and bamboozle defences. He needed maturity and backbone to help control games.

With Leeds on the horizon, third-placed Sheffield United visited the Manor, equal on points and separated by a single goal. At home, Oxford had been free to attack with a furious onslaught but with Trevor Hebberd dropping into the back four covering the suspended Briggs, there was little control to their frenzy.

Thomas had already hit the bar when Kevin Brock's corner created chaos in the box as Neil Whatmore challenged the Sheffield United goalkeeper. The ball dropped to Gary Barnett to swivel and fire home from two yards.

Despite the lead, the Blades' counter-attacking was a constant threat. With half-time approaching, Colin Morris beat McDonald to a long through ball and cut it back to Keith Edwards to fire past Steve Hardwick for the equaliser.

Another long ball early in the second half left Morris one-on-one with Hardwick. With Shotton struggling to cover, Hardwick charged from his line, his momentum flooring the midfielder inside the box for a penalty. Morris got to his feet and placed the ball firmly to Hardwick's right for 2-1 and Oxford were heading for their second defeat in a row.

As desperation grew, in the last minute Biggins flicked a long ball into the box to Whatmore, who returned the pass. The Blades' defence fumbled the striker's weak shot, giving him a split second to pounce on the stray ball and fire into the bottom-right corner for a crucial draw. Despite the late disappointment, manager Ian Porterfield knew his team had been lucky.

As Oxford headed to Elland Road, the stadium was enveloped in a thick fog and many visiting fans missed the kick-off due to a redirected train. Despite this, their confidence was justified after two minutes when a corner on the left was headed home by Mick Vinter beyond veteran Leeds keeper David Harvey. Six minutes later, Andy Thomas had the ball in the back of the net only for his effort to be flagged offside. Just before half-time, Kenny Burns pushed Mick Vinter in the box, but Hebberd's penalty was well saved.

Happy to still be in the tie at the interval, Leeds responded after the break. George McCluskey connected with a pass from Peter Barnes inside the box for the equaliser, forcing a replay at the Manor. It was the least Oxford deserved.

The draw made after the game provided a tantalising incentive to finish the job with the winners facing FA Cup holders Manchester United at home, reuniting Oxford with Ron Atkinson and his assistant Mick Brown, who'd managed the club during the late 1970s and taken them to Old Trafford for an FA Cup tie in 1975.

Jim Smith's attacking machine had limited Ray Train's opportunities, so the midfielder was allowed to go on loan to Bournemouth. Oxford returned to league action the following weekend with a convincing 3-1 win at Port Vale and followed it with a comfortable 2-0 victory over Peterborough United in the first round of the FA Cup. The draw paired Oxford with Reading in the second round, two teams that would have been competing as one had Maxwell got his way.

On the morning of the replay, Oxford awoke to find temperatures in the region had plummeted. When the sun rose, the shadowed area in front of the London Road terrace stubbornly refused to thaw.

The game was in doubt even as Smith, concerned he'd spurned his best opportunity in the first game, watched the Leeds coach arrive. When he overheard veteran Scottish international Peter Lorimer complaining about the pitch, he sensed a chink in their armour, intensifying his desperation to play.

Referee Martin Bodenham delayed his decision until 5pm. With the rest of the pitch thawed, to the evident frustration of the Leeds players, he declared the game on.

Ron Atkinson watched in the Beech Road stand as the players came out to a raucous Manor crowd. Malcolm Shotton won the toss, choosing to kick down the slope in the first half, knowing that Leeds feared the state of the pitch at that end of the ground.

Although unbeaten in eight games, Leeds were already mentally broken and Oxford refused to let them settle. After four minutes, Mick Vinter knocked the ball down to Bobby McDonald, who crossed to Kevin Brock to fire home past the motionless Harvey for 1-0.

Twenty-two minutes later, Lawrence flicked on Hinshelwood's clearance, sending Vinter clear on the right. His bouncing cross into the six-yard box reached Biggins at the back post to double the lead.

Totally dominant, three minutes later Oxford won a free kick 30 yards out. Brock, integral to everything Oxford were doing, fired in a clever drive which dipped just in front of Harvey off the frozen turf, causing him to parry it into the path of Vinter for number three.

Oxford had crushed Leeds with barely a third of the game played and even Kenny Burns, twice a European Cup winner with Nottingham Forest, seemed more intent on complaining to the referee about his decision to let the game go ahead. A brilliant point-blank save by Steve Hardwick prevented Andy Ritchie from pulling a goal back. The home side went into the break 3-0 up and in full command; few could remember a better half of football by an Oxford team.

After such a scintillating display, Oxford consolidated as they attacked the Cuckoo Lane End. Leeds clawed their way back, Ritchie firing the first warning, drawing another save from Hardwick before a Peter Barnes cross found Burns at the back post to nod in for 3-1.

The goal sparked Oxford back to life as Vinter's drive from outside the box was tipped over, Lawrence and then Briggs should have scored with Harvey tipping the ball on to the post. Minutes later, Biggins drove through the Leeds defence and forced Harvey to parry his shot into the air, Lawrence reacting to head number four into the empty net.

Oxford had destroyed Leeds with an unrelenting attacking spirit. They were psychologically and physically stronger against a team they were supposed to fear.

Perhaps Jim Smith, who'd just moved his family from Solihull to Woodstock, had made the right decision to join this strange little club on the edge of Oxford. If he could keep Robert Maxwell focussed and unleash his financial might, the quirky project he'd joined because he needed money could end up defining his career.

Maxwell still knew little about the game he'd bought into, but the name of Manchester United cut through to even the most disinterested onlooker. There was no better opportunity for Smith to spark Maxwell's enthusiasm.

Ron Atkinson was defiant. 'As much as I like Oxford,' he said, 'we're not coming here next Wednesday just to fulfil a fixture. We're coming to do the business.'

It had been over five years since more than 13,000 fans had packed into the Manor, but now it'd happened three times in just over a month. Supporters queued down London Road scrambling for tickets, overwhelming the sleepy ticket office with its single window next to the turnstiles.

A confidence-boosting 2-0 win over Newport County the following Saturday put Oxford back on top of the table. The league leaders were ready to take on the mighty Manchester United.

Chapter 7

Steve Biggins

IT HAD been nearly two years since Robert Maxwell descended on the Manor. From day one, impatience had coursed through the club. There was a sense of urgency in Jim Smith too, as his peers, not least the imperial Ron Atkinson, were dominating the First Division while he languished in the lower leagues. Maxwell's volatility didn't help the mood and there was no telling what he might do next, so Smith couldn't afford to be complacent.

Steve Biggins' arrival in 1982 was viewed as an underwhelming replacement for the popular Keith Cassells. Although he'd enjoyed two seasons as Shrewsbury's top scorer, he'd been released at the end of his contract; it was hardly the record of a top-class striker.

Even Smith seemed indifferent to his new signing. In his eagerness to bring in more firepower, he'd offered Peter Foley to Reading in exchange for their striker Gary Heale. That deal was complicated by Smith's signing of Mick Vinter from Wrexham. When Sparta Rotterdam stepped in with a firm offer for Heale, Reading manager Maurice Evans was happy to accept, which left Smith with a gap in his squad.

Smith turned to Biggins, fighting off interest from Bolton and Oldham, but he never seemed comfortable with his decision. A former PE and maths teacher in Walsall, Biggins had played non-league football for Hednesford Town. A move to Shrewsbury in 1977 gave him an unexpected opportunity in the professional game.

His background seemed to put him at a disadvantage at the Manor. His first season was disastrous, with Vinter and Neil Whatmore ahead in Smith's thinking. An early injury and the disruption of living in rented accommodation above a shop saw him make just eight starts and score two goals. At one point, Smith even experimented with playing him at centre-back against Bournemouth in place of the injured Gary Briggs. His last game of the season had been in February, and when the summer came Smith put him on the transfer list.

The birth of Biggins' son the day before the first game of the season, and a goal at home to Lincoln offered a timely boost. An early run in the team and table-topping form had given him confidence, but despite the start, Smith seemed committed to looking elsewhere and was quick to bring in Vinter and Whatmore whenever he could.

There was one defence against Smith's bias: while Vinter and Whatmore struggled for form, as long as Biggins scored goals, he kept his place.

Biggins had benefitted from the raw pace and energy brought by George Lawrence and Kevin Brock. Tall and slender, he could use his physical advantages to benefit the whole team. It was the combination of Lawrence and Biggins that brought the opening goal at Newcastle. A goal in the rout of Leeds took his total for the season to nine. Begrudgingly, Smith had to accept who his first choice striker was. Smith's reject, standing at the exit door of the Manor for nearly five months, was lifting his sights to face the might of Manchester United.

The Manor was intoxicated; Nottingham Forest in 1978 had been the last First Division side to play there, but the 5-0 humiliation just proved to be a brief flirtation with another reality and a reminder of Oxford's place in the world.

They hadn't beaten a top-flight team since 1970, when they'd overcome Wolves in the League Cup. The visit of Manchester United was different, threatening to surpass the great cup runs of the 1960s. The game brought a wave of media interest with TV reporter and former Oxford loanee David Icke training with the team for the BBC's *Breakfast Time*.

Maxwell capitalised, charging a premium for advertising and auctioning tickets to the highest bidders. Arriving through the turnstiles, regulars were shocked to find the crowds three and four deep over an hour before kick-off. Usual spots were occupied by unfamiliar faces; queues for programmes and refreshments were prodigiously long. It was like Oxford had entered a different dimension.

As the city closed on a bleak November evening, the Manor awoke like a beacon drawing people in. Its inadequacies were its strengths: the lack of space and narrow walkways, the shallow terracing, the uncomfortable bench seats. The away fans had the awkward, disintegrating Osler Road and its tiny single entrance. Visiting players sat shoulder-to-shoulder in the low-ceilinged changing room feeling the vibrations from the stand above, each rumble weakening their resolve and whittling their confidence.

Manchester United had a day less to recover after a 1-1 draw with West Ham. Atkinson replaced Arthur Graham with Kevin Moran, while Norman Whiteside came in for the cup-tied Garth Crooks, and Arnold Mühren made way for 20-year-old Welsh debutant Mark Hughes. Smith confidently retained the side that had beaten Newport.

With the players arriving to a deafening welcome, within two minutes the Manor exploded into life when Bobby McDonald's fierce effort was blocked. Malcolm Shotton then landed a thunderous challenge on Frank Stapleton which earned him a booking; a reminder he wouldn't be intimidated.

Just as Manchester United's history threatened to vaporise into the night sky, after nine minutes and against the run of play, Stapleton won a free kick after being fouled by McDonald. The calm and cultured Ray Wilkins found clarity in the feverish atmosphere to play in Mike Duxbury, whose back post cross found Hughes to head home with virtually his first touch in professional football.

But the illusion didn't burst and the goal didn't dampen Oxford's fervour; they continued to threaten with Vinter a constant menace. Just after the half-hour mark, Oxford won another corner in front of the London Road terrace which swelled like an angry sea. Brock backed himself up against the wall, scattering the police and officials crowding the touchline. The winger chipped the ball to the near post. Biggins' flick-on found McDonald, the full-back shielding the ball with his midriff before prodding home the equaliser.

Fans cascaded down the terraces in an ecstatic melee as McDonald was surrounded by his team-mates. This was more than lower-league enthusiasm; it was technical and tactical mastery. Atkinson prayed he could get his players into the changing room at half-time before Smith's side could inflict more damage.

When the teams returned, United tried to regain control by containing their opponents. Unheeded, Oxford threatened as Paul Hinshelwood went close with a savage drive and Vinter's curling long-range shot dipped narrowly wide. In response, Stapleton and Bryan Robson both wasted good chances.

After 90 minutes of pulsating cup football, the referee called time. The teams would need to resolve their differences in a replay at Old Trafford. 'That should keep the bank manager happy,' Jim Smith said with a wry smile.

There was no time to absorb the achievement, as less than 48 hours later Oxford were back in league action. In their search to escape financial peril, Southend United were experimenting with hosting fixtures on a Friday night. But with just seven fit players and no goalkeeper, they sought a postponement to the following Sunday. Heading to Old Trafford three days later, Oxford refused the request and the Football League ruled the game should go ahead.

Friday night rush-hour traffic then forced the Oxford coach to make a detour of several miles and they arrived just half an hour before the game. Smith leapt off the coach and sprinted to the referee's room to hand in his line-up moments before the deadline. Thankfully, a tenth-minute goal from Biggins settled the nerves as Oxford consolidated their position at the top of the Third Division.

Despite their form and performance in the first game, most believed Oxford's Milk Cup adventure would end at Old Trafford. With their opponents stripped of the mythical advantages of the Manor, Manchester United seemed destined to restore the natural order.

Smith thought differently. His bold plan was to attack, banking on complacency among the home support and the backing of 3,000 vociferous Oxford fans filling their portion of the half-full Old Trafford.

A win would be dreaming but Smith believed a draw was within his reach. A second replay would test Maxwell's resolve. Jim Hunt contacted his chairman after the Southend game to ask whether he wanted a replay at a neutral venue like Villa Park or would he prefer another go at taking the giant down the Manor? Would he take the money or the glory?

Hunt explained the toss of a coin would determine where any second replay was held. Maxwell liked the odds of a coin toss and enigmatically declared he'd be available. Oxford flew into the replay like a tornado. The draw at the Manor had humiliated United, who'd followed it with a home defeat to Everton. Rattled, they faced the jaws of a team refusing to acknowledge their place in the world, and Old Trafford trembled.

Gary Briggs led the charge, dumping Arthur Graham on the floor with a crushing challenge in the opening minutes. Graham responded by shooting over, but Oxford threatened more with Lawrence dominating the right flank after declaring himself fit the day before the game.

Both teams were swinging wildly trying to gain an advantage, Hinshelwood clearing off his line before Biggins screwed a chance narrowly wide seconds later.

Oxford went into the break feeling assured, but the game started to turn in the second half. United hoped to catch Oxford with a quick attack early on, but with Brock and Lawrence as willing outlets, they were quickly able to turn the home defence.

Atkinson grew increasingly frustrated on the sidelines; another draw meant missing out on a lucrative exhibition match in Dubai due to take place on the date of any second replay. Wilkins responded and nearly scored from a free kick, forcing Hardwick to save brilliantly, a fitting way to celebrate the birth of his daughter two days earlier. Whiteside then missed a chance when it seemed easier to score.

Then, after 69 minutes, Oxford shredded the rule book again, laying waste to the natural order. As they pressed for an opening, Gordon McQueen conceded a free kick on the edge of the United box. As McDonald and Thomas debated who should take it, Lawrence jostled the United wall to create a small gap that allowed Manchester United fan Brock to curl his shot high and wide of Gary Bailey's left hand into the top corner for a majestic opener. Oxford had taken the lead at the home of the most famous club in the world, propelling them into a place they'd never been before.

United sensed Oxford's giddy distraction and restarted with visiting fans' delirium still reverberating around the stadium. Mike Duxbury drove down the wing and crossed for Stapleton to head an immediate equaliser. Smith fumed at his side's lack of professionalism, but nothing could separate the teams.

Full time came and Oxford now faced 30 minutes of extra time, but with United's frustrations growing, there was no way through. Jim Hunt sat nervously in the stand praying that Oxford would hold out; a draw would be a famous result, but the money would please Maxwell more.

In the last minute, Wilkins' fierce drive was spectacularly tipped over the bar by Hardwick to keep the scores level before the final whistle blew. Three and a half hours of football couldn't separate the teams and another replay was needed.

Smith's premonition was right: Maxwell had to choose between the money of a neutral venue and the glory of a night at the Manor. In the bar afterwards, officials from both clubs discussed the prospect of a coin toss to decide the venue. The United hierarchy assumed that Oxford, with two memorable nights behind them, would cash in on their success and agree to a neutral venue or even a return to Old Trafford. It was the only logical conclusion.

'No,' came the emphatic response. Maxwell didn't respect norms, nor would he concede power to others. He wanted fate to decide the venue. United officials, facing unexpected resistance, suggested a financial incentive to aid the decision. Maxwell refused again. Ron Atkinson claimed an impasse would force the tie to default to Villa Park. Maxwell sensed their fear.

Maxwell protested to the Football League that United couldn't unilaterally force a change of venue by refusing to engage with the coin toss. The following morning Jim Hunt received a call from George Readle, deputy secretary of the Football League, apologising; they were wrong, the tie would only default to a neutral venue if both teams refused. Maxwell had struck a diplomatic victory, forcing a humbling climb-down.

Finally, the Football League arranged for both sides to phone in to witness the coin toss by secretary Graham Kelly at Lancaster Gate.

'Tails,' Maxwell called, seething with indignation.

The coin dropped. 'Tails,' Kelly said. 'Mr Maxwell, where do you want to play?'

'We'll see you at the Manor,' he barked before the line went dead. He'd chosen glory.

Two days later, Oxford turned to their FA Cup tie at Reading. Normally it would have been one of the biggest games of the season, particularly after the tumult of the merger. In this extraordinary year, it was a distraction from the Milk Cup and the quest for promotion.

Despite unifying against Maxwell a few months earlier, the animosity between the clubs was unquenched. While Reading had ousted their conspirators, Oxford still kowtowed to theirs, and yet, against all-natural justice, it was they who were thriving.

With grinding predictability, trouble flared before the game, and a 16-year-old Oxford fan was stabbed. Inside the ground, *Reading Evening Post* reporter Kevin Connolly claimed to see 'one man openly carrying a knife in the crowd … [while] youngsters sniffed glue from crisp packets'.

With Mick Vinter missing due to a groin strain, Oxford laboured, conceding early before Steve Biggins equalised. Violence swirled around Elm Park, delaying the second half before order was restored. On resumption, Reading's prolific striker Trevor Senior missed a penalty. Though not at their best, Oxford battled their way to another replay.

The 11th cup game of the season came just four days later. This time the Manor consumed Reading with ease, McDonald and Brock terrorising the left flank with Brock scoring after 18 minutes, bending a free kick beyond the Reading keeper Alan Judge in a moment reminiscent of his goal at Old Trafford. Judge kept Oxford at bay but could do little more than parry Hebberd's shot for Vinter to tap in the second ten minutes later. McDonald completed a dominant display as Oxford eased into the next round to face Burnley.

With four cup games in nine days, the league was almost forgotten. Before playing Rotherham, Jim Hunt headed to Manchester to pick up tickets for the United replay and spent the night drinking with Ron Atkinson and Jimmy Hill until the early hours before joining up with the team. Coming from behind, Whatmore scored twice from the bench after replacing the injured Shotton, putting Oxford four points clear at the top of the Third Division.

Just 48 hours later, transcending their league and historical status, Oxford and Manchester United prepared to step into the ring once again. The city had never witnessed anything like it; black market tickets sold for six times their face value, fans watched from garden fences and the bowls club, and TV gantries were built. One Osler Road resident erected scaffolding to create an improvised stand, allowing 20 fans to watch for free.

Shotton returned from his back injury. An hour before kick-off Smith told top scorer Biggins, having missed one game in the previous 11, that he would be starting on the bench.

There was more drama in the United camp when their England international goalkeeper Gary Bailey injured knee ligaments in training, forcing Atkinson to call for his

22-year-old deputy, Jeff Wealands. Making the 160-mile taxi ride south, Wealands arrived just three and a half hours before kick-off for only his fifth senior game. He was still recovering from the three hours' sleep he'd had the night before after his wife had given birth to their first son.

Due to their contemptuous familiarity, both teams seemed determined to find a resolution and avoid another replay. Early attempts by United to put the game beyond Oxford's reach brought Hardwick into action, denying Wilkins, Whiteside and Robson in quick succession. The pressure grew until the 37th minute when United forced two quick corners. From the second, Dutch playmaker Arnold Muhren found Whiteside, whose low flick dropped to Arthur Graham to steer a deceptive shot through a mass of defenders and into the net.

Undeterred, Oxford rallied and four minutes before the break Wealands saved from Briggs for a corner. Brock flighted the ball to the near post and Hebberd flicked it on. Vinter rose highest to nod the ball against the bar. It dropped to Lawrence, who reacted first and headed the equaliser. Smith looked on impassively as the Manor rose in appreciation.

Having slowed in the second half in the first two games, Oxford took command after the break. Andy Thomas forced a save from Wealands and Brock struck the post, allowing Kevin Moran to clear. Manchester United's captain, Bryan Robson, limped off to be replaced by Lou Macari as Oxford switched Whatmore for the forlorn Steve Biggins.

Reinvigorated, Oxford attacked again with two drives by Hebberd, a snapshot by Vinter, and a header from Lawrence all repelled by Wealands, defying any tiredness from his dizzying 24 hours. There was little doubt, in a tie of epic scale, that the First Division side were beginning to buckle.

Once again, the game went into extra time and minds began to turn to another replay at Old Trafford the following Wednesday. This time Oxford were intent on smiting their opponents, battering them, chipping away at any remaining composure. With a minute of the first period to go, Brock put in yet another cross. Biggins leapt into the sky leaving Arthur Albiston rooted to the floor. Swivelling his head, he guided a looping header high into the sky and down beyond Wealand's despairing reach for 2-1.

Biggins swung round in disbelief, his arms thrust into the air, his team-mates piling on top. Amid the mayhem there was a sense of vindication, proof that Smith had been wrong, that he had the ability his manager seemed to doubt.

On the bench Smith looked pensive, his pupils dilating and straining to capture every essence of his greatest achievement. In the second period United pressed hard for an equaliser, but with Lawrence and Biggins as willing outlets they were always vulnerable to counter-attacks. A Biggins break and an intelligent pass nearly brought a third goal for Andy Thomas.

As injury time came, the Manor finally seemed to hush. Steve Hardwick launched the ball into the sky before racing to collect his gloves from the back of his goal, and the referee brought the game to an end before it landed. After five and a half hours of unrelenting action, Third Division Oxford had beaten Manchester United.

Fans flooded on to the pitch as Robert Maxwell surveyed the scene at the front of the Beech Road stand like a Roman emperor. They were unified for once. Even the long convention of barring women from the boardroom was relaxed; things really were changing. Jim Smith was dazed by what he'd achieved, the greatest win of his career and the first over his old mate. 'We've competed with one of the best teams in the country and outplayed them,' he reflected.

For Biggins, the victory was bittersweet. Thrust into the limelight, he was asked what Smith had said to him after his winner. 'He didn't say anything to me,' the striker replied. 'Our relationship's been like that for some time.'

For Ron Atkinson, at the home of so many memories, it was the worst night of his career. 'It was difficult to believe which club was second in the First Division,' he said. 'We can have no complaints; in the second half they overran us.' Smith consoled him by buying the drinks late into the night.

Chapter 8

Kevin Brock

FRED FORD created a talent factory at the Manor. After managing Swindon Town, Bristol Rovers and Bristol City, he joined Oxford in 1973 as chief scout and youth organiser under manager Gerry Summers.

He nurtured a steady flow of discoveries including Peter Foley, Mark Wright, Billy Jeffrey and Andy Thomas, fuelling the club through its barren years of the late 1970s and early '80s. Ian Greaves was in awe of him, 'He pulls 'em out from under trees – and they can all play.'

Born in Middleton Stoney, a village just outside Bicester, Kevin Brock was a Ford discovery with the potential to go further than anyone before him. It took 18 months to secure his signature. Brock's family insisted that Ford remained at the club to oversee his development.

A regular in the Beech Road stand, he represented England schoolboys at Wembley before making his debut under Bill Asprey in 1979. Four months later he turned down the opportunity to join Brighton & Hove Albion but most assumed he'd eventually outgrow the club and move on to bigger things.

When Greaves shifted the team's emphasis, Brock's natural attacking flair didn't suit the manager's new system and he was often overlooked in preference of the more assured Tim Smithers and Mark Jones.

Despite his obvious talents, Jim Smith could have ended Brock's Oxford career, perhaps even his time as a professional completely. Smith wasn't prepared to dwell in the lower leagues and had to deliver Maxwell's persistent dream of promotion. He had prejudices about the team he'd inherited and an enviable network of contacts. Brock could have slipped away with the tide of those being shown the door.

In reality, he fitted Smith's philosophy perfectly; he was quick and nimble with a low centre of gravity, meaning he could maintain close control on poor pitches. He scored and created chances, and with Steve Biggins as his target the goals flowed. Brock didn't need to move; a team was being created around him.

Stung by their Milk Cup defeat, Manchester United chairman Martin Edwards disputed the official gate receipts of £43,001. Maxwell snorted with derision, 'Instead of congratulating us, the chairman of Manchester United wants some of the extra money we raised by auctioning some of our tickets.' It was an old Maxwell trick, selling 700 tickets to the Independent Supporters' Club to auction off. Few doubted the money would find its way back to Maxwell somehow. 'If Martin Edwards wants to sue us, he can,' Maxwell sneered. 'But it is money to which he's not entitled.' Edwards retreated, saying, 'To pursue it would have looked like sour grapes.'

The draw for the quarter-final was made with Oxford coming out of the hat first, securing another home tie where they were paired with Everton. The Manor readied itself for another famous night.

Oxford couldn't hope to meet the demand of another certain sell-out. Terrace tickets increased in price from £3 to £4 and seats by 50p to £8 with 200 reserved for auction. The club insisted that it needed to maximise revenue for survival, though others saw it as Maxwell cashing in.

It wasn't just the Milk Cup and FA Cup that Oxford were fighting for. The Associate Members' Cup aimed to alleviate the financial pressures for lower-league clubs in the second half of the season. It was a side issue given their success, but as Third Division leaders, Oxford were favourites.

Jim Smith seemed unperturbed. 'You don't get jaded when you're winning,' he said despite the precarious balancing of league and cup ambitions. Any hope of resting players was put to rest when they drew Swindon Town for the first time since the smoke bomb incident that destroyed their promotion hopes in 1982.

Christmas, normally the busiest time of the year, offered an unexpected break, as with no Saturday fixture on Christmas Eve Oxford had a full seven days between the win over Manchester United and their Boxing Day game with Bristol Rovers. Jim Hunt, run ragged in recent weeks, hoped he could get back to business as usual.

For Smith, the league was crucial; selling out Newcastle, Leeds or Manchester United was easy. League games were not just important for promotion. With plans drawn up for a 15,000-capacity stadium with a retractable roof, to be sited on Botley Road, they needed to convince the council there was a sustained demand for a new home.

He wasn't disappointed; a mania had gripped the club. By 2.30pm Hunt ordered the Manor's gates to be shut, leaving 1,000 people outside as the home terraces sold out.

Two Mick Vinter goals in the opening 20 minutes put Oxford in control, but Rovers fought back to 2-2 with half an hour to play. Midway through the second half a wall collapsed, forcing the game to be suspended while a fan was taken away on a stretcher. With three minutes to go Rovers sweeper Tony Pulis fouled Vinter on the edge of the box and

Brock guided another majestic free kick beyond the wall and into the net, securing three points and the Football League's Young Player of the Month award for December, a first for a Third Division player.

The hangover came the following day as the fixture schedulers conspired to send Oxford 170 miles north to face Bolton Wanderers, where they suffered a 1-0 defeat.

There was even time for one more game before the turn of the year, their 34th of the season, against Orient at the Manor. After 32 minutes Andy Thomas was fouled in the box, allowing Trevor Hebberd to convert the penalty. Brock fired through the keeper's legs seven minutes later, before crossing for Vinter to score a third. Brock won a second spot kick after he was fouled by Pat Corbett, allowing Hebberd to score again. A minute later, Orient won a penalty when David Grant fouled Mark McNeil and Keith Houchen converted. Orient pulled it back to 4-2 but Vinter made it five with ten minutes to go, allowing Oxford to end the year two points clear at the top of the table and still in all cup competitions.

Despite nine games in December, including three against Manchester United, Oxford had lost once and were optimistic they could maintain their form, secure promotion, and perhaps even make a major cup final for the first time in their history.

On 2 January, the team had another long journey for their tired legs to endure, to relegation-threatened Exeter City. Things looked promising within a minute as Oxford had the ball in the back of the net when Andy Thomas connected with a cross before crashing into the Exeter keeper, Len Bond. The referee disallowed the goal for a foul. While Bond climbed to his feet, Thomas remained motionless on the floor. Minutes later he was stretchered off, his leg shattered, and his season was over.

Exeter shocked the leaders with goals from Steve McCewan, Steve Neville and Mark O'Connor, with only a Gary Barnett goal in response. It was a devastating blow; Thomas's nine goals and scintillating form had been critical in the success of the season so far.

Jim Smith needed reinforcements. In the main, Maxwell allowed him freedom in all football matters apart from finalising deals. His embarrassing blunders were a source of constant amusement for the players, but he knew the opportunity for promotion wasn't to be passed up.

The first name to surface was Asa Hartford, the Manchester City and Scotland international. Hartford had been diagnosed with a hole in his heart and at 34, teams were reluctant to commit to him. He had pedigree and fitted Smith's model perfectly.

Maxwell contacted Hartford to begin his idiosyncratic negotiations. Hartford listened, but rumours he'd heard left him uneasy about Maxwell's commitment to Oxford. He didn't want to move if they were to flounder in the Third Division. Maxwell walked away in frustration.

Five days later, Oxford headed to Turf Moor to face an experienced Burnley side in the third round of the FA Cup. The team stayed in Blackburn, 12 miles from the ground. As planned, they left the hotel at 1.30pm under police escort. En route, Jim Smith, familiar with the town from three years managing Rovers, realised they were taking a curious route. The police thought they were marshalling the Chelsea team, who were due to play at Ewood Park in their FA Cup tie. Smith leapt to his feet and insisted they change direction; embarrassment averted, they arrived only 15 minutes later than planned.

Burnley had been stubborn opponents earlier in the season when a goal from Billy Hamilton and last-minute equaliser from Brian Flynn had given them a 2-2 draw. With

Steve Biggins on the bench, Oxford ground out a goalless draw and forced a replay they barely needed. But with Burnley hitting the woodwork three times, they counted themselves lucky.

Four days later, they met again at the Manor to resolve the tie. Beforehand, Smith picked up another Bell's Manager of the Month award; Maxwell looked on with a mixture of pride and arrogance etched on his face.

Oxford seemed uncomfortable as cup tie favourites. After six minutes, Vinter's one-two with Biggins set the striker free. His shot was parried by Roger Hansbury into the path of Lawrence for his 11th goal of the season.

With the deadlock broken, Burnley's ageing midfield struggled to contain the movement of Hebberd, Barnett and Brock, but further damage was contained by their solid back five. Withstanding the pressure, Burnley pulled level three minutes into the second half as Brian Flynn's corner was flicked on by Reeves, giving Hamilton a simple header for 1-1.

On the hour, Hansbury went down in his box unchallenged having been struck on the back of the head by a coin thrown from the London Road terrace, raising the spectre of more negative headlines and damaging Oxford's prospects of a new stadium. Compounding the problem, eight minutes later Hebberd drove a shot that Wilson deflected high into the air. Hansbury, still dazed, stood transfixed as the ball dropped on to full-back Derek Scott's head and into his own net for Oxford's winner.

The following day, Burnley lodged a complaint and demanded a replay due to Hansbury's injury. 'Burnley have more chance of getting the game replayed than I have growing grass on my garden pond,' Maxwell said, poetically. The FA agreed, rejecting the appeal but condemning the incident.

It had been a tough, rugged display in a long and gruelling season. With Thomas injured, Smith was concerned that he was running out of options. With 13 fit players, he recalled Ray Train from his loan spell at Bournemouth, fresh from dumping more humiliation on Ron Atkinson after their FA Cup win over Manchester United.

The fixture pile-up finally had an effect the following weekend with a 2-2 draw at Lincoln City, which was completed despite a half-time pitch inspection after heavy snow. The dropped points knocked Oxford off the top of the table, albeit with a game in hand over new leaders Walsall.

Four days later, Everton arrived at the Manor for what Jim Smith said was the most important game in the club's history. With the First Division visitors sitting in 11th and with one win in their previous seven league games, many had the Third Division side as favourites.

Before the game, BBC Radio's Nick Harris asked Maxwell if he was nervous. Maxwell, in typically ebullient style, replied, 'The last time I was nervous, I was standing in front of a German tank without any shoes on.'

For Jim Hunt, it was a different story as the Burnley incident resulted in a visit from Les Mackay, the chairman of the FA Disciplinary Committee. Hunt assured Mackay that the club were being proactive in curbing their recent crowd problems, banning the culprits and extending the fencing behind the London Road goal to stretch across the full width of the penalty box.

The Manor crowd had changed in the preceding months and anticipation was replaced by expectation. But, on a half-frozen pitch, compared to previous rounds, the game was uneven and disjointed. Everton, struggling for goals all season, generated the first meaningful chance on 20 minutes when Peter Reid released Kevin Sheedy to draw Hardwick into a smart save.

Moments later, Hebberd mopped up the loose ball at the edge of the area before being brought to a shuddering halt by Alan Irvine. Players squared up to each other and Irvine was booked, while Hebberd remained on the floor nursing a deep gash on his leg. After treatment from Ken Fish, he was forced off on a stretcher and replaced by Neil Whatmore. Having lost Thomas against Exeter, Oxford were without their first-choice midfield.

Weakened, the onus was now on Brock and Lawrence to provide an attacking threat, and immediately they combined to release Biggins and force Southall to save at point-blank range, proving there was life in them yet.

In the second half, Biggins headed a free kick narrowly wide before forcing Neville Southall into two excellent saves, and with just over 20 minutes remaining Brock was fouled by Alan Harper. Sensing an opportunity, the London Road terrace pulsated. Brock got to his feet and floated a free kick to the far post. Briggs rose strongly to head back across the goal to McDonald, who prodded home on the line for 1-0.

Semi-final destiny was within reach. The Manor readied itself for another kill, rising to a singular crescendo. From all sides noise cascaded on to the pitch. 'They were so full of themselves after that goal,' Everton captain Kevin Ratcliffe reflected later. 'The crowd was so loud that I thought we might have had it.'

The Manor sang in full-throated unison 'The famous Oxford United are going to Wembley'. In the stands, supporter Bob Wyllie felt his decision to book a coach and hotel for the final was vindicated. They'd never been this confident.

But finding direction in uncharted waters was hard and without Hebberd's influence, Oxford sat back. Everton were beginning to run out of ideas with nine minutes remaining as Southall punted the ball downfield, but Shotton comfortably towered over Graeme Sharp to head the ball down to the feet of Kevin Brock. For once, Brock struggled to tame the ball on the frozen, winter-ravaged pitch. Peter Reid, closed in, harrying and cajoling, clouding Brock's thinking and forcing him to work quickly. Smith called for a foul from the bench.

Sensing Brock's vulnerability, Irvine blocked another way out. The winger withstood the pressure, crafting a brief corridor to the safety of Steve Hardwick.

With Reid beaten, Brock rolled the ball through the grateful Oxford back four towards his keeper. As he looked up, from behind Malcolm Shotton there was a flash of blue. The captain's enormous frame had obscured 5ft 5in striker Adrian Heath, who darted in front of Hardwick as he advanced to retrieve the ball.

The world stopped. Reid and Shotton looked on motionless, Neil Whatmore watched helplessly in horror. Brock froze, calculating what was happening. On a treacherous surface Heath couldn't risk bringing the ball under control. He touched it beyond Hardwick, chasing it away from goal before wrapping his boot around it and instinctively directing it into the empty net.

Everton had been outplayed, but that moment of fate, the briefest lapse from Oxford's most gifted player had given the top-flight side a lifeline they didn't deserve. Afterwards, Smith raged at Irvine's challenge on Hebberd, saying he should have been sent off. Kendall dismissed the brutality as competitiveness. His fury needing an outlet, Smith turned on Brock, who, uncharacteristically spoke up: 'Boss, I wasn't trying to be flash.'

The following day, the draw for the semi-final was made, meaning the winners would face Aston Villa. Oxford's league game against Gillingham was postponed, allowing Smith to bring in the first of his reinforcements, John Trewick on loan from Newcastle.

The following week, despite the setback of Heath's late equaliser, Smith was still confident. A pre-match storm dusted the Goodison pitch with snow, conditions, he hoped, that would play to their advantage.

But things quickly turned sour. In front of their biggest crowd of the season, Everton opened the scoring after just seven minutes when Kevin Richardson drove past Hardwick from the edge of the area. After half an hour Kevin Sheedy fired through a crowded box into the right-hand corner for 2-0; Oxford's Milk Cup adventure was crumbling. It was like Brock's fateful back-pass had broken the spell.

Early in the second half, Heath continued his goalscoring form after breaking Oxford's offside trap, rounding Steve Hardwick again and scoring from a tight angle. With a minute to go Paul Hinshelwood pulled one back, firing into the top-right corner from 20 yards. Seconds later Graeme Sharp broke down the right and lobbed Hardwick for 4-1.

Their quest was over, leaving Smith in a contemplative mood. The loss of Andy Thomas and Trevor Hebberd and his own over-confidence had cost them a place in the Milk Cup semi-finals and the fulfilment of one of the game's greatest fairy tales. Despite this, there was little time to dwell.

Chapter 9

Malcolm Shotton

AS SOON as Treda Shotton picked up the phone and heard the voice of Oxford United manager Ian Greaves, she knew there was a problem. Malcolm Shotton's combative style often left scars but this was different, this was bad.

After three minutes of their away game at Walsall in February 1982, a week after Oxford's dominant giant-killing against Brighton, Shotton had collided with Gary Briggs in an aerial challenge with Walsall's Don Penn and Richard O'Kelly. Briggs shattered Shotton's nose, causing blood to pour from his face. Ken Fish, used to patching up his granite-strong centre-backs, called for a stretcher as Greaves readied substitute Ollie Kearns.

Shotton went straight to hospital so Greaves suggested Treda drive up from their home in Bicester to see him. With little prospect of being discharged, she asked Jim Hunt and Ken Fish if he could be moved nearer to home. That evening, Robert Maxwell called, addressing her as 'Mrs Malcolm'. He'd arranged an ambulance to transfer Shotton to the Acland private hospital in north Oxford. It was Maxwell at his most gregarious and generous.

Shotton was used to battling. Signed by Leicester City, he was released before making an appearance. 'It was a terrible shock,' he said. 'I hadn't even played a league game. So there I was planning to get married and out of a job.' He was tempted to return to his native north-east and follow a path out of the game. Instead he stayed in the Midlands, drifting into non-league football with Atherstone Town. To make ends meet, he worked at Poole, Lorimer and Taberer as a knitter, making hosiery for Marks & Spencer. With training and playing he'd sometimes have a couple of hours of sleep before his 6am shift started.

In 1979, Roy Barry signed him for Nuneaton Borough. When Barry moved to Oxford a year later to assist Bill Asprey, he recommended that Shotton come with him. Greaves valued Shotton's steel, which represented the culture he wanted at the club. 'Whether you succeed or fail in soccer,' Greaves reasoned, 'is much more than a matter of being skilful enough.' When Billy Jeffrey left for Blackpool, Shotton was the obvious candidate to take over as captain.

'Nobody's going to take a life in soccer away from me,' Shotton said. 'It beats the days when I'd be up before dawn to ride my old Suzuki to work.' Oxford's Milk Cup dream may have imploded in the snow at Goodison Park, but Shotton wasn't going to let that be the end of it.

It was only January, yet Oxford had already played 39 games in the 1983/84 season. With the loss of Trevor Hebberd and Andy Thomas, Jim Smith feared a cruel revenge for their glorious run – the sacrificing of promotion.

Oxford's new-found national profile allowed Smith to be more ambitious in the transfer market. He narrowly missed out on Nottingham Forest midfielder Danny Wilson before turning to 22-year-old Chelsea winger Peter Rhoades-Brown, snapping him up for £85,000.

Most seasons, progressing to the fourth round of the FA Cup was a reason for celebration, but the visit of Blackpool became a sideshow in comparison to what had just passed.

An excellent debut from Rhoades-Brown and two penalties from Bobby McDonald saw Oxford ease to a 2-1 win with the prize a visit in the next round by Sheffield Wednesday.

In the league, a familiar problem returned during the 2-0 win over Preston. Celebrating goals by Mick Vinter and Hebberd – returning from his injury against Everton – fans pulled away the mesh fencing on the London Road terrace and there were reports that the Preston goalkeeper was spat on. It was a sobering reminder that Oxford's ambition had outgrown their surroundings, leading to fears the FA might intervene.

With so many cup ties, Oxford slipped to third, four points behind leaders Walsall with three games in hand. Promotion beckoned and Oxford were a rare bright light during football's bleakest time, one of the few clubs that escaped the blight of falling crowds and negative headlines.

Even the biggest clubs were suffering; having been humiliated by Oxford, Manchester United's season was falling apart. They'd won two of their eight league games since and had been dumped out of the FA Cup by Bournemouth. As the dark clouds gathered, chairman Martin Edwards issued a statement saying he'd secured their future by finding a new owner willing to invest.

His name was Robert Maxwell.

Every setback seemed to fuel Maxwell's rampant ambition even more. It was the rumour that scuppered the Asa Hartford deal. Maxwell was still agitated by Oxford's failed merger with Reading and the lack of progress on a new stadium, so he'd briefly considered bidding for Birmingham City because he was, by his own modest assessment, 'a First Division chairman'.

Edwards and Maxwell issued a joint statement to ease investor concerns, promising that negotiations would continue at pace. The media speculated that £10m would secure a deal, although Maxwell wasn't alone in making a bid with shareholder James Gulliver also interested in gaining control.

As with the merger, Maxwell's plan appeared fully formed; he would resign as a director of Oxford, passing his shareholding to one of his sons. Ron Atkinson would remain manager at Old Trafford – ending speculation that Jim Smith might be in line for the job.

Perhaps distracted by the pantomime, Oxford fell to a 2-1 defeat at Millwall. The following day, Manchester United routed Luton Town 5-0 at Kenilworth Road live on TV. The jubilant Atkinson joked that each goal would cost Maxwell another £1m. When Edwards and Maxwell met again to secure a deal, the price had indeed risen to £15m. Maxwell walked away in disgust, saying, 'Manchester United is unfortunately a closed book but who knows what the future will bring?'

Edwards seemed relieved despite missing out on a rumoured payout of £6m. 'I'm happy the talks have broken down,' he said. 'It's been a disruptive time and on occasions it got a little out of control. It's something I now regret having gone into as chairman, not a thing I want to give up lightly.'

After the defeat to Millwall, there was an immediate opportunity to respond against Wimbledon, the team that had outmuscled Smith's men a few months earlier.

A thick fog descended on the Manor, threatening a postponement, but this time Oxford were ready to battle, outclassing their aggressive opponents. In the seventh minute Steve Hatter sent Kevin Brock crashing to the floor for a penalty which was dispatched by Bobby McDonald.

Visibility worsened as Vinter looked right to put George Lawrence away; his cross was volleyed into his own net by defender Mark Morris. A minute later it was nearly three, but John Trewick, playing his last game before returning to Newcastle, failed to convert Lawrence's cross.

Oxford had overcome their Achilles heel of direct, physical teams; a running battle between McDonald and Wally Downes ended with Downes being sent off for a forearm smash on the full-back, a prize for McDonald's deliberate provocation. In the stand, Sheffield Wednesday manager Howard Wilkinson could only have been impressed by whatever he saw of the performance.

The tie against the Owls was Oxford's 18th cup game of the season. Only West Ham and Southampton remained from the top ten in the First Division, giving them another chance of a run to Wembley.

Visiting fans filled the Cuckoo Lane End; the open, cold, sun-drenched Manor Ground didn't seem as cramped and foreboding as it was at night. Wednesday, a team Smith labelled 'grafters', found Oxford in a passive mood as the intensity of the Wimbledon game had taken its toll. Wilkinson's uncompromising philosophy – 'we get fit, then we practise' – quickly paid dividends.

With five Wednesday defenders stretched across the pitch, Lawrence and Brock couldn't dominate on the wing. Inevitably, the visitors' breakthrough came from a set piece just before the half-hour mark as shambolic defending allowed Imre Varadi to fire through a crowd of bodies for 1-0.

Shortly before half-time, Gary Bannister doubled Wednesday's lead from close range. A third after the break put the game beyond doubt as Oxford exited the cup with an uncharacteristic whimper. The defeat ended a run of 21 unbeaten cup games at the Manor. Smith admitted that his team were emotionally drained, although he was secretly grateful for their exit.

With their cup adventures over, Smith knew the season would only mean anything if he delivered the promotion his chairman demanded. Having played more domestic games than any team in the country, cool heads and stamina would be critical. For all its talent, the team needed something to manage tighter games. Smith needed a player like Ray Train, an emotional anchor.

The answer came from an unlikely source as he took a call from Jennifer Todd, the wife of former England international Colin. Todd had once commanded a British record transfer fee when joining Derby County in 1971, where he won two league titles and a PFA Players' Player of the Year award before Smith took him to Birmingham in 1979. He moved to Nottingham Forest three years later, but Jennifer confided that her husband had fallen out with Brian Clough and was looking to leave. At 34 he was reaching the twilight of his career; he fitted the bill perfectly.

Oxford's 19th cup game of the season, their Associate Members' Cup debut against Swindon, promised little and delivered less. In front of fewer than 5,000 fans, the damage came in a five-minute period in the second half when Jimmy Quinn and Alan Mayes scored. Quinn added a third in the 67th minute before Colin Bailie put into his own net for a consolation ten minutes from time.

Following a narrow 3-2 win over Bournemouth at the Manor, the squad headed for a mid-season break in Scarborough after missing out on a golfing trip to Spain due to their cup commitments. Todd made his debut against Hull City at Boothferry Park, replacing Gary Briggs. It was the first of their three games in hand; a Mick Vinter goal after two minutes put them back on top of the table.

With promotion looking likely, Oxford continued to push for a new home, but instead the council challenged architects to draw up plans to increase the Manor's capacity to 19,750 with new stands replacing the Beech Road and Osler Road sections. Maxwell's mood darkened; his patience wore thin.

Oxford's stadium troubles were insignificant compared to the existential problems many clubs faced. Derby County were one example, owing £129,000 in PAYE arrears. With just ten days to find the money, director Stuart Webb desperately contacted Maxwell. Rebuffed by Manchester United, Maxwell seemed keen to help, saying his interest was to protect the Rams' 'illustrious tradition'.

His report for Oxford's AGM revealed more, 'If after 30 years the Oxford City Council continues to block and prevaricate, the club will close down either at the end of this season or at the latest by the end of the next.' If he was looking for a way out, Derby County offered an off-ramp.

The squad remained in Yorkshire after a 1-1 draw at Bradford at the beginning of March, allowing Jim Smith to enjoy the award-winning cocktail bar in their team's hotel while the players slept. The point retained Oxford's position at the top of the table as teams faltered under the relentless pressure. The final game of the Scarborough trip was an away win at Sheffield United. Goals from Steve Biggins either side of half-time – taking his season's total to 16 – extended their lead at the top of the table further.

The following day, Smith and a few of the players took part in the Blenheim Fun Run and a week later a 2-0 win at home to Port Vale saw them take a commanding five-point lead at the summit with two games in hand. Promotion and the title were there for the taking.

Smith started planning for the Second Division. On deadline day, Neil Whatmore was loaned to Bolton and he raided his old club to sign Les Phillips from Birmingham City. His biggest coup was striker John Aldridge, who'd scored 70 goals in five years for Newport County. Aldridge had expected to sign for Sunderland, managed by his former Newport boss Len Ashurst – an old golfing buddy of Smith's. Newport wanted to avoid Aldridge leaving for a discounted fee via a tribunal but when Sunderland couldn't raise the funds, Maxwell met the asking price with a full cash payment.

Oxford went into their next home game with Gillingham without Paul Hinshelwood, Mick Vinter or George Lawrence. The disruption had an immediate effect when they conceded after 42 seconds from Phil Cavener. Despite Oxford dominating with 23 corners and Peter Rhoades-Brown hitting the underside of the bar, Gillingham claimed maximum points and Smith's team fell to their first home league defeat of the season. They put it right three days later with a 2-1 win at Brentford with 3,000 travelling fans roaring them on.

In London, a High Court judge refused to sanction Robert Maxwell's bail-out, plunging Derby County's future into further doubt. Maxwell took his frustrations out in a protest against Oxford City Council. Two years after fans had marched against Maxwell, they marched with him in their thousands.

As they protested, Aldridge's family gathered at the Manor hoping to see him make his debut against Plymouth. Instead, Smith opted for stability and was rewarded with a Steve Biggins hat-trick and Bobby McDonald brace securing a dominant 5-0 win.

Not content with strengthening on the pitch, Smith knew he needed support off it. After Roger Smee's takeover, Reading's fortunes were turning around, but with the club sitting fourth he'd unexpectedly sacked Maurice Evans and replaced him with Ian Branfoot – a man Evans had appointed as his assistant.

Evans was devastated, feeling that Smee had used his 30-year association with Reading to gain control of the club. He'd expected to be offered a general manager's role but was now redundant with a derisory compensation package. There was such a backlash, Reading's players bought him a gold watch and the supporters' club made him an honorary life member.

Managerial opportunities came up at Torquay and Brentford but Evans wanted to stay in his home in Tilehurst. Smith knew Evans's technical knowledge was second to none, asking him to go on a scouting mission to watch Wimbledon against Exeter.

As Reading fans sang Evans's name during games, Smith offered him the role of chief scout and youth development officer at the Manor, the role previously filled by Fred Ford.

'I'm very pleased indeed,' Evans said. 'I'll be watching teams for Jim Smith and helping to bring on the youngsters. Oxford chairman Robert Maxwell obviously thinks I've got something to offer. He told me that football can't afford to lose a man of my talents.'

Three days later, a 1-1 draw at Burnley saw Oxford move eight points clear. In the stands was the club's new director, 23-year-old Ghislaine Maxwell. Maxwell's youngest child, and by all accounts his favourite, was studying modern history with languages at Balliol College on a scholarship funded by her father having attended Headington Girls' School, a short walk from the Manor.

Outwardly, Ghislaine's appointment, the first female director in professional football, was to attract the next generation of Oxford fan and enrich the club's social activities. But, lacking in experience, she seemed skittish and fearful of saying anything out of turn. Most likely, her role was to consolidate Maxwell's power over the board as his attention turned towards Derby County.

An uncharacteristically dour 1-0 win over Scunthorpe ensured Oxford stayed at the top of the table but Smith started to worry that fans were becoming complacent. They weren't just expected to win games, they were expected to win them with panache.

As promotion edged closer, Maxwell rowed back on his desire to become Derby chairman. The High Court accepted a plan from Stuart Webb, funded by Maxwell but without any operational involvement.

Maxwell insisted his commitment to Oxford remained, but there was little doubt the two clubs would vie for his attention. Derby's long-term potential seemed better than Oxford's even though they were set to swap places in the second tier at the end of the season.

For Oxford, the rewards kept coming. Trevor Hebberd became the *Sunday People* Third Division Player of the Year and him, Kevin Brock, Bobby McDonald and Malcolm Shotton made the PFA Third Division Team of the Year, reflecting Oxford's dominance of the division.

Aldridge finally made the bench as Oxford travelled to Walsall. As usual, the visitors were impatient to make an impression, Shotton's header crashing off the crossbar after a short-corner exchange between Hebberd and Brock.

Walsall responded with several half-chances, pinning Oxford back. Towards the end of the first half, Dave Bamber outpaced McDonald down the right flank, drawing a clumsy challenge at the byline which brought the Walsall striker crashing to the floor. The referee had no option but to award a penalty. Ally Brown stepped up and struck a thunderous drive to the right of Steve Hardwick, who instinctively palmed it to safety.

Almost immediately, Peter Rhoades-Brown responded, driving an awkward bouncing shot across the Walsall keeper, forcing a save before crossing for Brock to drive fiercely over the bar.

Walsall continued to threaten on the break as the pace of the game stayed high long into the second half. With 26 minutes to go, Paul Hinshelwood launched a 40-yard crossfield pass which was half-cleared by defender Brian Caswell. Rhoades-Brown picked up the loose ball inside the Walsall box on the left with his back to goal. In a single movement, he twisted his body and volleyed the ball over and beyond the Walsall keeper into the top-right corner.

Late on, Aldridge finally made his debut to replace Vinter, but Rhoades-Brown took the glory, his stunning winner giving Oxford a club record tenth away win and their 23rd in total, putting them 11 points clear with a game in hand.

Brock, having recovered from his devastating mistake against Everton, was creating waves beyond the Third Division title race. England's under-21s were preparing to face Italy in the semi-final of the European Championship but with key club games coming up, several First Division players pulled out of the squad. Having been recommended to Bobby Robson at the start of the season by Jim Smith, Robson's under-21 manager Dave Sexton invited Brock to join the squad.

During extraordinary times, being ordinary was a challenge. In the offices at the Manor, Jim Hunt had pinned a sign on the wall which read 'Promotion is not to be mentioned in this office until further notice'. Even the sedate Oxford United social scene caught the winning bug with the ladies' section of the supporters' club securing their darts league title and Gary Barnett, Steve Biggins, George Lawrence, Paul Hinshelwood, John Aldridge, Mark Jones and David Fogg beating the social club in a darts, pool and bar billiards games night.

Biggins' brace secured a 2-1 win over Southend as Brock headed off on international duty. Dave Sexton's promising squad included striker Mark Hateley, who'd scored against Oxford in the FA Cup for Coventry in 1982, and Manchester United goalkeeper Gary Bailey, who Brock had tormented four months earlier. The Italians featured Roberto Mancini and Giuseppe Bergomi, a member of their World Cup-winning team that had beaten West Germany in Madrid two years earlier.

Fewer than 5,000 fans rattled around Maine Road, the smallest crowd Brock had played in front of all season, but destabilising illustrious opponents was what he'd been doing all year. His impact was immediate; after six minutes, his corner was flicked on by Tommy Caton to Mark Chamberlain make it 1-0.

Four minutes before half-time, Brock, wide on the left, jinked and accelerated, leaving his marker floundering, opening up space to cross to Ipswich striker Mich d'Avray for the second.

After the break, full of confidence, Brock picked the ball up again, cut inside Mancini, and drove a fierce 25-yard shot off the bar. Mel Sterland put the tie beyond Italy's reach with 20 minutes to go from the spot after Stewart Robson was fouled.

A late Caton own goal gave the Italians a flicker of hope but for Brock, it was the perfect debut.

He returned to league action, with Gary Briggs – for the first time in five games – against Bolton Wanderers on Good Friday at the Manor. On arrival, fans in the London Road terrace faced the consequences of their unruliness, having to watch the game through the ever-expanding mesh behind the goal.

The team's focus wasn't diminished as Biggins laid on the first goal for Hebberd after ten minutes before Briggs celebrated his return 12 minutes later with number two. Gerry McElhinney turned the ball into his own net after 40 minutes before Biggins equalled the club's goalscoring record for a season before half-time. Not bad for a striker who Jim Smith didn't think could score.

Oxford sat back in the second half and had to wait until the last five minutes for Aldridge to complete the rout. There was no point in being shy about it; Smith said he would put £1m on Oxford going up.

Aldridge made it two goals in as many days, coming on for Mick Vinter to snatch a point at Bristol Rovers and leave Oxford one win from promotion.

Their first opportunity came a week later with a trip to Aldridge's old club Newport County. Immediately before the game, Colin Todd announced that he was leaving to play in the North American Soccer League with Vancouver Whitecaps. His contribution had lasted 12 games, but he'd been critical in steering Oxford steadily to the edge of promotion.

At Somerton Park, County put up a stubborn resistance, and although Aldridge scored again, Oxford came away with a point leaving them needing a draw for promotion and a win for the title.

The following Wednesday they faced Wigan Athletic at the Manor. There was one word on everyone's lips: promotion. Brock missed out as he flew to Italy with England under-21s as just under 9,000 fans packed the ground expectantly. The Manor had been the scene of so many great giant-killings and nights of attacking flair; the team were in the unfamiliar position of being overwhelming favourites.

The warm evening set the scene; an expectant buzz surrounded the ground, but Oxford's performance was stilted. Wigan, lacking any incentive to attack, were happy to contain their opponents. Their keeper denied Lawrence after eight minutes before Biggins had a goal ruled offside. When Aldridge hit the post after half an hour it was clear that although it wasn't going to be Oxford's night, it would be their season.

The game petered out to a goalless draw, which was enough for promotion – in a season which had everything, perhaps it was asking too much to top it off with another barnstorming win. 'It turned out just as we'd feared,' Jim Smith lamented. 'We hoped to pull a special night out, but it didn't happen.'

As the referee blew his whistle and sprinted for the tunnel, Oxford fans ignored pleas from the PA to stay off the pitch, swamping the players as they scrambled for safety. For once, it was an invasion full of joy. Under the Beech Road stand, the players and management celebrated, although Robert Maxwell, forever unpredictable, left early.

After an eternal wait and chaotic scenes, the players appeared at the front of the stand, stumbling across the antiquated bench seats. The title was for another day – the U's were going up.

As the celebrations died down over the next few days, attention turned to the win that would secure the title. Three days later Exeter City arrived at the Manor already relegated and rooted to the bottom of the table. The stands were full and weighed down with expectation.

This time Oxford seemed unburdened. After three minutes Hebberd fired wide as they carved Exeter open, and not long after, Briggs's thundering header from Brock's corner gave them the lead.

But a second didn't come and Oxford sat back, content they could see the game out. Exeter grew in confidence. In the final moments with the title within sight, fans climbed over the perimeter wall and lined the pitch anticipating another jubilant invasion. The moment was coming.

The distractions grew: the noise from the pitch, the throng on the touchline. Knowing the melee to come, the players looked to the referee awaiting his signal. In a momentary lapse, Exeter's Martin Ling seized an opportunity to drive past the Oxford players and pass the ball to former Manor loanee John Sims. With little to lose, Sims unleashed a speculative shot. Rather than smother the ball and secure the title, Hardwick let it squirm under his body for the equaliser. The championship was still a point away.

The quest continued on May bank holiday Monday. Oxford travelled to east London for an evening game against Leyton Orient but all eyes were on Wimbledon's home game against Gillingham 15 miles away, which kicked off at three o'clock. If Wimbledon dropped points, the title would be Oxford's.

Needing a point for promotion, Wimbledon led after just ten seconds through Kevin Gage. The Gills looked stunned but recovered, stifling more Wimbledon attacks.

Five minutes after the break they equalised through Steve Bruce and a minute later, Tony Cascarino headed a second. A third, direct from John Sitton's free kick, handed Oxford the championship in the most understated way. In a season which had everything, it seemed an inglorious end.

Oxford celebrated with a 2-1 win over Leyton Orient with Vinter and Aldridge scoring – his fourth goal in six games, a promising return in his brief cameo.

For Jim Hunt, the man who made the call to Robert Maxwell 18 months earlier, it had been an exhausting season, but after eight years of dragging the club through one crisis after another he was finally tasting success – and celebrated by buying the office a new Canon photocopier.

Malcolm Shotton was presented with the new Canon League trophy from Bob Daniel of the Football League before the final home game against Rotherham. Jim Smith left out Aldridge and Les Phillips, allowing the players who'd made the biggest contribution to take centre stage.

Biggins opened the scoring, breaking Colin Booth's 20-year goalscoring record for a season. Despite Oxford dominating, Rotherham equalised, before George Lawrence restored the lead. Another Rotherham equaliser threatened to dampen the celebrations again, but in the last minute substitute Aldridge slipped the ball to Vinter for the winner.

A timely end to a blockbuster season and the greatest day of Jim Smith's career.

Oxford had played 65 games, losing ten, scoring 118 goals – 24 more than their nearest rivals. They'd beaten Newcastle, Leeds and Manchester United and reached the fifth round of both cup competitions. They were Third Division champions with a record 95 points. The only player not happy was Neil Whatmore, whose difficult season ended with him being involved in a car accident as Shotton paraded the trophy.

Kevin Brock was voted Player of the Year and Malcolm Shotton the Clubman of the Year. Four days later, the team returned to the Manor to play the Second Division champions Chelsea in a friendly billed as 'Battle of the Champions'. Free of pressure and fear, Oxford ran out 2-1 winners with goals from Aldridge and Lawrence.

With the squad finally released for a well-earned rest, Brock joined the England under-21s for their two-legged European Championship Final against Spain.

In front of 30,000 fans in Seville, England twice went close when Hateley headed Brock's cross off the post, before returning the favour for Brock to shoot at Andoni Zubizarreta. After 20 minutes, Hateley was elbowed by Sanchís and had to go off with breathing problems. On 51 minutes England capped a mature performance when Mel Sterland exchanged passes with Paul Bracewell for the only goal.

The return leg was held the following Thursday at Bramall Lane. Needing a draw, manager Dave Sexton focussed on experience, selecting Gary Bailey in goal, Everton's Derek Mountfield and Watford's pacy winger Nigel Callaghan, who'd just returned from the FA Cup Final. Brock retained his place having been transformed over the season.

In the face of physical intimidation, Brock showed the steel that Smith had instilled in him. Hateley volleyed home after half-time before Howard Gayle squeezed a weak shot under the goalkeeper to double England's lead. A third goal secured the championship, ensuring Brock would end the season with promotion and an international title. Was this the peak? Somehow, it didn't feel like it.

Chapter 10

Dave Langan

FINALLY, DAVE Langan broke down in tears; for 18 miserable months his knee had been gorged and his back twisted. After all the pain and setbacks, he could take no more.

Growing up, all Langan wanted to do was play football and represent his country. As an attacking full-back he'd achieved both; signed by Brian Clough for Derby County in 1977, Jim Smith took him to Birmingham City for a record fee three years later. He made his debut for the Republic of Ireland against Turkey in 1978 and neutralised teenage Argentine sensation Diego Maradona in a friendly in Dublin in 1980. Popular with his team-mates, playing made him happy and he was content to be tossed around by life's ebb and flow.

A year after his triumphant game against Argentina, Langan lined up for his 14th cap in the feverish atmosphere of Lansdowne Road. Ireland were edging toward possible World Cup qualification. Victory in their final game against France would leave their opponents needing to win their last two matches to qualify on goal difference.

The Irish started at a savage pace, overwhelming the stylish French threat, including Europe's most elegant player,

Michel Platini. Bundled up in the occasion, Langan raided the right flank, pressing the French threat back into their own half.

After just five minutes, Ireland scored with an own goal from Philippe Mahut before Platini equalised four minutes later. After half an hour, Ireland maintained a breathless tempo, disrupting the French passing game. Irish goalkeeper Seamus McDonagh bowled the ball out to Langan, who played it forward under pressure from Monaco striker Alain Couriol.

Langan's hasty clearance was easily intercepted but it returned to him at pace. The ball ran free and the defender threw himself into a crunching challenge with Platini. As they came together, Platini's studs raked down the side of Langan's knee.

He felt a sharp pain but played on, jumping up to defend the French threat. When the referee blew for a free kick, he slumped to the floor. The atmosphere lulled and pain seeped into Langan's consciousness. He tried to massage the injury away and absorb the discomfort as best he could. As he lay on the turf, Langan's life was taking a new and darker path.

After a few minutes of rudimentary treatment he was back on his feet, his desire to help his team overriding any concerns for himself. It was a cruel mistake fuelled by adrenaline and a sense of purpose; each stretch contorted the ligaments in his knee as the Irish held on to register a glorious 3-2 win.

Despite the triumph, Langan returned to Birmingham in agony and missed the next month of games. Cortisone injections controlled the swelling, allowing him to return for a humiliating 3-0 defeat to local rivals Wolves at St Andrew's. Birmingham's dismal run of one win in 13 saw them plunge from mid-table to just above the relegation zone, costing Jim Smith his job.

Ian Greaves' first game in charge against Charlton in December 1981 – a 1-0 win over the league leaders.
Steve Daniels

Ian Greaves, the former Busby Babe who kick-started the club's remarkable turnaround.
Steve Daniels

Robert Maxwell (pictured in 1985), enigmatic and charismatic, ruthless and cruel all at the same time.

Celebrating a famous 3-0 FA Cup giant-killing against First Division Brighton in 1982. Steve Daniels

Jim Smith (pictured in 1985)

Trevor Hebberd, Jim Smith's best signing.

Steve Biggins. Despite a hatful of goals and the winner against Manchester United, Biggins was never one of Smith's favourites.
Steve Daniels

Billy Hamilton celebrates scoring Oxford's second against Arsenal in 1984.
Steve Daniels

Dave Langan unleashes a 35-yard piledriver to make it 3-2 against Arsenal.
Steve Daniels

Kevin Brock, the local boy who became a European U21 Championship winner whilst still a Third Division player.

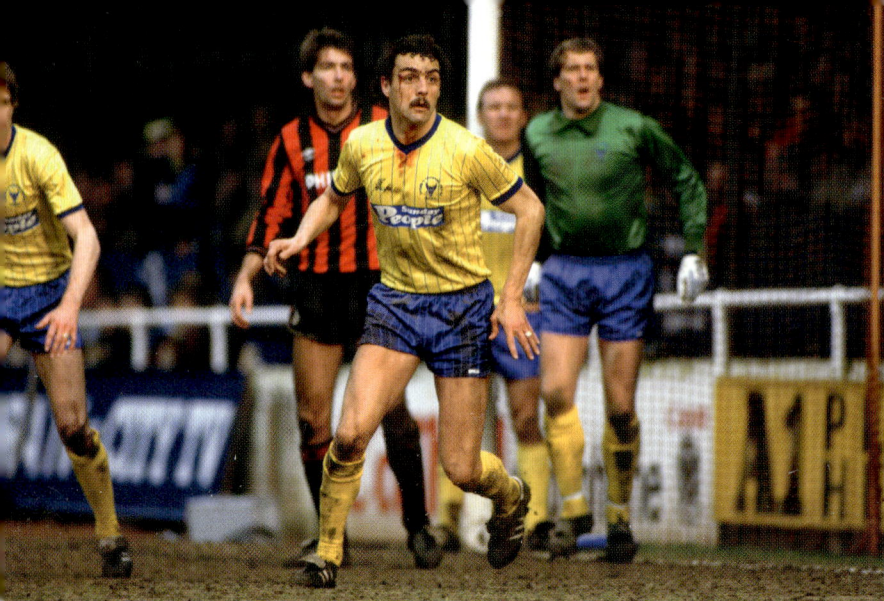

Gary Briggs, fearsome centre-back – pictured against Manchester City in 1985.

John Aldridge scores against Barnsley to secure the Division Two title in 1985.
Steve Daniels

Every time Langan put pressure on his knee he felt a shooting pain. During matches, adrenaline disguised the discomfort, but training was impossible and he settled into a routine of physiotherapy and gym work to maintain his strength like future Republic international Paul McGrath, whose ability to play while not training was celebrated as an act of superhuman power. It gave Langan a false belief that everything would be fine.

In February, he broke down again, and was finally referred to renowned Greek orthopaedic surgeon Dr Apostolos John Polyzoides. Polyzoides' expertise was reassuring, but he was paid by the club to get their players fit; longer-term consequences were secondary.

Polyzoides admitted Langan for keyhole surgery and found a large ulcer inside his knee joint. He drilled the ulcer out and rebuilt the cartilage. Langan was told he'd be out for six months.

For the first three, Langan did nothing, and drink was a constant companion. During his rehabilitation, it was clear something wasn't right. He was given more cortisone injections and was sent home to rest. A few weeks later it happened again so Polyzoides cleaned the knee out and sent Langan home. His isolation grew, and when he broke down for the third time, he was sent for more surgery.

This time Langan committed to his rehabilitation, building his upper-body strength, but one day in the gym he twisted and felt a shooting pain through his back. He'd cracked a vertebra which put him in a cast for eight weeks, and when it didn't heal he was put in a rigid corset for another month. When Langan next kicked a ball, it was clear he'd need another operation and another six months out of the game.

Langan's drinking became excessive, impacting his mental health. Birmingham's club doctor worried that he might be a suicide risk. By his ninth operation, to remove bolts in his back, Langan thought there might be some light at the end of the tunnel. He returned to rehab; his knee started swelling again. Finally, Langan broke down in tears.

At the end of the 1983/84 season Birmingham manager Ron Saunders told Langan his contract wouldn't be renewed. He hadn't played for 18 months. Unfit and unreliable, his prospects were bleak.

In July the phone rang; the voice at the other end was the familiar drawl of Jim Smith. Smith believed in Langan, trusted him, had invested in him. The call couldn't have come at a better time.

Smith's success had brought a renewed interest. The attacking flair that gripped so many had penetrated the bleak crumbling wastelands of English football. Newcastle United, who'd lost their manager Arthur Cox to Robert Maxwell's new project at Derby County, enquired about his availability. Maxwell responded by securing Smith on a new two-year contract, which he hoped would see him at the helm in the First Division. This was more than one of Maxwell's inexhaustible fantasies – Oxford were now competing with the biggest clubs, reinforcing Smith's desire to bring more success to the Manor.

To win another promotion, Smith needed to strengthen his squad again and provide cover for Paul Hinshelwood. Smith knew that Langan was capable, available, and someone who'd sacrifice himself for his team.

Langan was desperate, he was invisible and in a deep hole of despair; in haste he reassured Smith that his injuries were behind him. He was barely able to jog without feeling pain. Smith invited him to join the squad for pre-season training, offering him a three-month contract.

As Oxford thrived, Maxwell finally realised his own lofty ambition: to own a national newspaper. In his quest to control the narrative that surrounded him, he'd acquired the Mirror Group, putting him in direct competition with his nemesis, Rupert Murdoch, owner of *The Sun*. It signalled the start of a circulation war which Oxford would quickly become wrapped up in when Maxwell changed the club's shirt sponsor from BPPC to his weekend tabloid, the *Sunday People*.

Back at the club, Smith prepared for his assault on the Second Division by signing former loanee John Trewick on a permanent deal from Newcastle. Trewick, once Newcastle's record buy, had been blighted by injuries, allowing Smith to secure him on a free transfer.

Pre-season opened with shooting practice: a 10-0 destruction of a North Bucks League XI preceded a 5-0 win over Wantage in early August. Smith was impressed by Langan's fearlessness and energy, despite the risks he was taking with his injuries.

Smith turned his attention to the first meaningful friendly, against Southampton the next day, where he planned to play his strongest side with Hinshelwood reinstalled at right-back.

On the morning of the game, Hinshelwood called in sick, so Smith needed Langan to make his second start in as many days. It would normally have been like playing with his friends at home, but he hadn't played for 17 months and now he was being asked to play twice in 48 hours. There would be grave consequences if the lies he told Smith were revealed – it would set his recovery back further and maybe end his career.

Langan couldn't back out, but even to his own amazement, despite a 3-0 defeat, he was as industrious and creative as he'd ever been. The form which had attracted Brian Clough to sign him for Derby, made him Birmingham's record signing under Jim Smith and had given him his cherished international honours sprung back to life.

Two days after a 2-1 win against Cambridge United the following week, Smith unveiled his next pre-season signing: Billy Hamilton from Burnley for £95,000 with Neil Whatmore heading to Turf Moor. Hamilton had always impressed when playing Oxford and wanted to get out of the Third Division. When Smith heard that manager John Bond thought Hamilton's only quality was goalscoring, he made his move.

Hamilton went straight into the side for Oxford's final friendly against Reading. More significantly, Smith chose Langan over Hinshelwood at right-back. After ten minutes Langan crossed for Brock to open the scoring, before driving into the box two minutes later to win a penalty which Bobby McDonald converted. Brock and Vinter secured a 4-2 win, but Smith's attention was already turning to the league campaign and he substituted Langan with 14 minutes to go. Smith had unearthed another diamond – Langan's three-month trial would soon be extended to a two-year contract.

As the new season approached an old story raised its ugly head.

According to Reading chairman Roger Smee, Maxwell was using his 19 per cent stake in the Royals to make mischief by opposing key decisions at the club's upcoming AGM. Smee complained to the Football League that Maxwell's interests in Reading, Oxford and Derby contravened their ownership rules. Maxwell assured the league that he would sell his shareholding to retired bank executive Cyril Townsend, but couldn't promise the deal would be completed before the AGM.

Maxwell's reshuffling priorities continued in mid-August. His son, Ian, resigned as an Oxford director to become Derby County chairman, lending them £550,000 to buy back the Baseball Ground. Maxwell's grip over Oxford was as tight as ever, but his interest was waning.

Smith was also making changes; as the season approached, he allowed Mick Vinter to move to Mansfield Town, now managed by Ian Greaves after a disastrous six-month spell at Wolves.

Although most were happy to consolidate Oxford's position in the Second Division, Maxwell wanted another promotion. Smith wasn't sure; the bookies had Oxford at 10/1 for promotion, and despite everything that had happened the previous season, the prospect of reaching the First Division still felt further away than their days in the Southern League.

The opening game at the end of August was a trip to Huddersfield. Oxford started cautiously with Steve Hardwick making some good saves. After 35 minutes they found their attacking rhythm and Trevor Hebberd pounced on Sam Allardyce's mistake to round the keeper for 1-0, before John Aldridge scored a minute later. In the second half David Burke deflected Langan's shot into his own net. They'd swung their first punch and found the division had a glass jaw; Billy Hamilton gushed, 'It's a joy to play in such a good footballing side.'

Three days later, they travelled to Hereford in the first round of the Milk Cup, the competition which had provided so much joy the previous season. Hebberd scored again after four minutes but the lead only lasted until the eighth minute when Jim Harvey equalised from a penalty. Ten minutes before half-time, he grabbed a shock second from a free kick. Oxford struggled to break down the stubborn Fourth Division side and were thankful for Hamilton's equaliser just after the hour.

Their home campaign started against Portsmouth. The echoes of the riot in the London Road terrace two years earlier were clear to see. The sun shone, attracting Portsmouth fans in large, expectant and threatening numbers. The mood around the terrace was tense and it was clear that Pompey supporters were again intent on gaining entrance to the home end. They swarmed into the stand, inciting Oxford fans to react. Fighting spilled on to the pitch as trouble swelled again. Eventually, the police regained control and despite a sense of unease, the game kicked off on time. Oxford took the lead when Hamilton caused panic in the box, forcing Gary Stanley to prod the ball into his own net, but despite constant pressure they were pegged back three minutes from time for a 1-1 draw.

For Jim Hunt, the trouble against Portsmouth highlighted the precarious balance between the club's limitations and his chairman's unquenchable ambition. He ruminated about what more he could do. Lots of visiting teams would bring large numbers in the Second Division. How would they control everyone? Fence them in?

There would be no such pressure four days later when fewer than 5,000 fans turned up for the second leg against Hereford. Oxford eased to a 4-1 lead with two goals apiece from Hamilton and Aldridge, but unbeaten Hereford hit two goals in three minutes to bring the tie back to 4-3. Oxford were reliant on Dave Langan's goal-line clearance to prevent an equaliser before Hamilton crashed home his third to flatter the scoreline.

Wimbledon were next in the league. After a goalless, listless first half, Jim Smith unleashed his rage on Peter Rhoades-Brown. When Rhoades-Brown arrived at the club, George Lawrence warned him to expect the brunt of Smith's fury by virtue of playing in front of the dugout.

Smith produced ten pence and told Rhoades-Brown to phone his wife and tell her to put their house up for sale. Fearing the worst, the winger asked Smith for a ten-minute reprieve to turn his performance around.

It was a characteristic Smith outburst. The players were used to ducking the teacups; his explosive anger could reduce them to tears. Only Maxwell's presence tempered him and the players would invite their chairman into the dressing room to help ease the tension. On one occasion Maxwell walked in during a team talk to ask Malcolm Shotton how his family was, leaving Smith dumbfounded.

On the pitch, Rhoades-Brown's efforts to impress backfired and his over-enthusiasm resulted in a booking. Smith hauled him off and brought on Steve Biggins. Despite the winger's tribulations, Oxford raced to a convincing 3-1 win, including a spectacular 35-yard Bobby McDonald free kick that opened the scoring on the hour. Where the team had been humbled the previous season by Wimbledon's muscular style, the result extended their record-breaking unbeaten run to 16 games.

Knowing the fate of Mick Vinter and Neil Whatmore before him, Rhoades-Brown thought his time at Oxford was over, but Smith took him aside to congratulate him on his renewed efforts.

Despite success on the pitch, Jim Hunt was suffering an *annus horribilis*; ticketing, crowd trouble and fixture congestion filled his in-tray. The government were readying to make clubs accountable for hooliganism, suggesting membership cards should control access to grounds. Hunt was alarmed by the prospect of more delays at the turnstiles and, regardless, he felt the problem reflected broader social ills.

Settling into life in the Second Division, Smith felt that upcoming games at home to Fulham and Wolves, and a trip to Grimsby Town, would provide a clearer indication as to how realistic the club's ambitions were.

Fulham proved stubborn opponents, with the midfield being controlled by the tenacious Glaswegian Ray Houghton starving Oxford's supply to the wings. Thankfully, Fulham's leaky defence proved their undoing when Jeff Hopkins' under-hit back-pass allowed Aldridge to open the scoring. Clifford

Carr equalised from a Houghton cross before Aldridge restored the lead with a brilliant finish from Rhoades-Brown's cross. The winger laid on the third for Hamilton before Peter Scott pulled one back to make for a tense final 20 minutes.

Hamilton's five goals in six games saw him selected for Northern Ireland against Romania in their World Cup qualifier, the first Oxford player to be called up for an international in nearly a decade.

But it was Aldridge creating the headlines; a brace against listless Wolves made it eight in seven games. Steve Biggins sealed a comprehensive 3-1 win with only a late Dave Langan own goal marring the performance.

Smith's critical trilogy concluded with maximum points at Grimsby. If he wanted assurance that his team were ready for the division, the table told him all he needed to know. Oxford were second by two points with a game in hand. The only catch was that Ron Saunders' Birmingham, Smith's former club and managerial nemesis, topped the table.

As Oxford's season progressed, Maxwell continued to frustrate Reading, threatening to sell his shareholding to Aclind Ltd – a company, it was revealed, that was owned by Gladys and Michael Waller, the family of former United chairman Frank, who'd colluded with Maxwell over the merger.

Oxford took a break from their league programme to draw 1-1 at Blackburn Rovers in the Milk Cup with Peter Rhoades-Brown scoring. Their style suited the higher division; they had more space to play in and more attacking threat. Langan offered a fruitful supply line for Hamilton, whose style complemented Aldridge's poaching instincts.

Defending their 22-game unbeaten run Oxford faced Carlisle United, opening the scoring when Langan crossed for Rhoades-Brown to claim his third goal in as many games.

Hamilton added a second after good work from Hebberd and then turned provider to let Kevin Brock score the third before half-time. A fourth from Aldridge, after Hebberd had broken clear, sealed an emphatic victory. The *Oxford Mail* boldly declared that the team would be promoted.

Smith too was content to set promotion as his primary objective, but only if Oxford could navigate their daunting October programme against Brighton, leaders Birmingham, and first, Manchester City.

With both clubs starting the season well, the TV cameras were present at Maine Road for Oxford's visit. But rather than a spectacle, the game descended into a gritty midfield tussle as the fear of defeat blunted both teams' attacking instincts. Oxford defended stoutly and could have had two penalties, firstly when Steve Biggins was tripped by Mick McCarthy inches outside the box before John Trewick went down after a clumsy challenge from Nicky Reid.

With five minutes to go Oxford created their first clear chance, but Alex Williams saved Brock's shot. With the game heading towards a stalemate, City substitute Jim Tolmie launched a high ball into the Oxford area from a Paul Power throw-in. Striker Tony Cunningham beat Briggs for the first time all afternoon and the ball dropped to Steve Kinsey, who lashed home from ten yards out.

Facing defeat for the first time in nearly six months, Oxford responded instantly and thought they'd equalised within a minute when Graham Barker, under pressure from McDonald, put the ball into his own net. The players wheeled away only to see the linesman flagging for offside. Smith freely shared his frustrations about the referee with the press, resulting in a warning from the FA about his conduct, but City had been more adventurous and deserved their win.

The following Monday, the team drowned their sorrows at a civic reception to celebrate their Third Division title at

Oxford Town Hall. The event was enthusiastically hosted by Olive Gibbs, former lord mayor of Oxford, avid Oxford fan and wife of former club secretary Edmund Gibbs.

Determined to bounce back, Oxford welcomed Blackburn to the Manor for their Milk Cup second leg, settling their nerves after 16 minutes with a Billy Hamilton goal.

Blackburn's hustling disrupted Oxford's attacking flow and Simon Garner equalised, forcing the game into extra time. Hamilton then assumed control, scoring his second early in the first period and completing his second hat-trick of the campaign a minute before half-time. Afterwards, Hamilton emerged from the changing room not with the match ball, but a bag of wild mushrooms a fan had given him after he was spotted picking fungi at the team's training ground by a reporter. The legend of 'Mushroom Billy' was born.

The draw couldn't have been more enticing and once again, the Manor would host one of England's greatest clubs: First Division league leaders Arsenal. A year on from the triumphs against Leeds, Newcastle and Manchester United, Oxford were ready to slay more giants.

Fuelled by that glorious run and a stronger squad, expectations were high as Jim Smith described it as a taster for the following season, when he expected to face Arsenal as equals in the First Division.

Oxford returned to the Manor the following Saturday to face Brighton. One visiting fan, C.A. Dickerson, travelled from his home in Herefordshire to find he'd forgotten his entrance money. Fearing a wasted journey, a stranger, Mr Clay of Abingdon, lent him the cash as a gesture of goodwill.

Despite a patchy display, the 2-1 victory returned the team to winning ways. The *Sunday People*, emblazoned across the victors' shirts for the first time, were quick to declare themselves a lucky omen and celebrated, featuring glamour model Sam Fox wearing the new kit and 'trying on a different strip to the one she's used to'.

With success came more strain on the Oxford squad, as in addition to long-term absentee Andy Thomas, the influential combination of Bobby McDonald and Kevin Brock were also missing through injury. Despite the depleted squad, to the evident frustration of the fans, Maxwell's links with Derby drew closer when Oxford's leading goalscorer, Steve Biggins, signed for the Rams for £20,000.

Oxford followed their win over Brighton by welcoming Sheffield United to the Manor. With Arsenal tickets on sale, the large crowd were treated to four rapid-fire first-half goals and a 5-1 win including a majestic brace from George Lawrence. Despite carrying an injury, Lawrence was denied his hat-trick by a narrow offside decision as Oxford returned to the top of the table.

Although Arsenal were on the horizon, for more personal reasons, the trip to St Andrew's to face fourth-placed Birmingham City loomed larger in Jim Smith's mind. For the first time, he'd return to the club who'd sacked him unceremoniously two years earlier. Dave Langan was also returning to the scene of his injury nightmare. The press were keen to play up the grudge match between Smith and Ron Saunders, the Saturday morning football show *On the Ball* with Ian St John and Jimmy Greaves stoking the flames with a feature.

Smith was careful not to rise to the bait. He was happy at his new club and took little satisfaction at Birmingham's demise under Saunders. Langan was less diplomatic, and despite lodging with avid City fans Gordon and Margaret Powers – celebrating their ruby wedding anniversary at the game – he joked, 'I still want United to win even if it means I haven't got a bed.'

Saunders had little time for the realpolitik of the game; he was under pressure having delivered nothing more than relegation after some fierce cost-cutting. Smith's over-spending was to blame, he argued, but that did little to alleviate the sense of underachievement.

As the players emerged, Smith briefly headed for the home dugout. 'Force of habit,' he'd explain. If the managers were keen to play the grudge down, the players were happy to live up to its billing. The crowd swelled to over 20,000 with 4,000 fans travelling from Oxford, some fresh from wrecking a pub in Hatton near Warwick.

Both sets of players were at each other's throats from the first whistle. Despite the unrelenting physicality of the game, only George Lawrence was booked for not returning the ball for a throw-in. 'The longest period of possession in the whole game,' mocked one reporter.

Smith wanted three points but struggled against Saunders' resolute back five. Despite the defensiveness, the home side went closest when Billy Wright's free kick was saved by Steve Hardwick. Des Bremner then hit a post before Robert Hopkins headed narrowly wide.

Amid the fury, there was one moment of light when Hopkins fouled Langan, forcing the referee to reach for his pocket. Langan jumped to his feet and persuaded the referee not to book his former team-mate. For a moment, peace broke out and Langan's name reverberated around St Andrew's.

The point ensured Oxford retained top spot and proved they were no pushovers. Trevor Hebberd, often considered lightweight, was happy to mix physical aggression with the robust Birmingham midfield. Smith believed his side were ready for the First Division. Their next test, Arsenal, would prove if he was right.

With both sides topping their respective divisions, Arsenal, without England striker Paul Mariner or defender Tommy Caton, welcomed back Tony Woodcock after a period out and drafted England youth international Tony

Adams on to the bench. Smith made one change, replacing Peter Rhoades-Brown with Kevin Brock.

It was Halloween, the stands bristled, and unlike the year before when it seemed enough just to be welcoming Manchester United to the Manor, this time Oxford's public wanted more. Even Robert Maxwell was caught up in the mania, delaying a planned mercy dash to famine-ridden Ethiopia and a plane carrying 30 tonnes of food and medicine.

Early Arsenal pressure stretched Oxford in the opening minutes, but the combination of Langan and Lawrence down the right proved a constant menace. This was the old Langan, the one before his life had been derailed by Platini's challenge all those years ago.

After 17 minutes, Arsenal nearly opened the scoring when Charlie Nicholas broke through the Oxford back four to shoot narrowly wide. The resulting corner was worked short to Graham Rix whose weak, daisy-cutting drive somehow squirmed through Steve Hardwick's hands and into the net for the opening goal.

Arsenal had the momentum; Oxford absorbed more pressure with Bobby McDonald clearing twice in quick succession from Stewart Robson. Having survived the storm, the home side slowly re-established their composure. In the 37th minute Billy Hamilton won a header which dropped to Lawrence, who clipped a looping cross into the box for the onrushing John Aldridge.

Aldridge instinctively focussed on the trajectory of the ball, squeezing between Viv Anderson and Pat Jennings to head the equaliser into the empty net.

The Manor erupted, the London Road terrace throbbed, and the noise from the crowd was amplified by the terrace's low roof. It all distracted from Aldridge, who was motionless in the penalty box. Jennings' momentum had poleaxed the striker, knocking him unconscious. As the euphoria died down, attention focussed on Aldridge, who was quickly surrounded by St John Ambulance men and trainer Ken Fish; their grave expressions suggested something wasn't right.

After a lengthy delay, Aldridge was carefully lifted on to a stretcher and carried around the pitch towards the tunnel, motionless. In the dugout, Jim Smith prepared Peter Rhoades-Brown and bellowed instructions to his shocked players as the winger nervously adjusted his socks.

With half-time approaching, Smith resisted sending on the replacement, and instead he waited for news from the dressing room. Mr Fish set to work while the game continued. Despite being down to ten men, Oxford were buoyed by the equaliser and pressed forward relentlessly. Within five minutes Kevin Brock released Langan down the wing. His cross dropped to Hamilton whose bullet header landed beyond Jennings for 2-1, his eighth Milk Cup goal of the campaign.

Oxford were beating the First Division leaders – and with ten men. The Manor unleashed a triumphant roar; it was happening again. The noise was still echoing around the terraces as the Beech Road stand bristled. Fans strained to see what was happening. Down by the dugout wasn't Peter Rhoades-Brown, but John Aldridge, fully recovered and ready to rejoin the fray. It had been a breathless opening half.

The second half didn't relent; kicking up the slope towards the Arsenal fans in the Cuckoo Lane End, Lawrence and Langan raided the flanks, leaving the visitors desperately trying to plug holes.

Then, against the run of play, a poor goal kick from Hardwick fell to Nicholas, who fed Ian Allison to slide the ball past the keeper. Stranded, Hardwick turned to see the ball crash off the base of the post. The rebound fell to Brian Talbot, whose full-blooded drive from ten yards seemed destined for the net. From nowhere, Bobby McDonald scrambled to head the ball off the line for a third time.

An injury to Stewart Robson saw the introduction of teenager Tony Adams on the hour, the change disrupting Oxford's flow. Arsenal counter-attacked; Woodcock and Nicholas combined to leave Allison one-on-one with Briggs. With Oxford in retreat, Allison calmly side-footed the equaliser beyond Hardwick.

Undeterred, Oxford persisted, making a mockery of the gulf between the sides. Never leaving a moment for Arsenal to settle, intricate interplay on the edge of the box saw Hamilton clip the ball to Lawrence, who fired high into the Cuckoo Lane End when he should have scored. Graham Rix retaliated, driving across Hardwick's goal, but this time the keeper collected safely.

With 20 minutes remaining, a long ball was half-cleared by Tommy Caton. As it dropped, John Trewick harried Viv Anderson into a rushed clearance. Retaining possession, Oxford worked the ball back to Trewick on the left, who played it inside to Brock.

Composed, Brock slid a pass with the outside of his boot to Langan in space 30 yards out. Langan set himself and a thought flashed through his head, a morsel of information fed to the players by Jim Smith before kick-off.

Anticipating a cross, Aldridge and Hamilton headed into the box, causing the Arsenal defence to retreat. Langan's first touch opened a space in front of him. He had his moment and let fly, his feet lifting off the ground with the force of his strike. The ball looped towards Jennings, who Smith had heard was suffering with a hand injury. The manager had told his players to shoot from distance to exploit the weakness, and Langan was happy to oblige. The big Irish goalkeeper reached to pluck the ball from the sky but, weakened by the injury, he couldn't contain its force and it dropped apologetically into the net. Oxford were beating the First Division leaders.

Arsenal were now chasing the game and Kenny Sansom's snap shot from a similar distance bounced in front of Hardwick, deceiving him and hitting the post. The league leaders flailed desperately as whistles filled the air; a final crossfield ball drifted over the touchline, giving the referee a moment to blow for full time. Fans cascaded on to the pitch, celebrating another famous night at the Manor. Through all the pain and setbacks, in a team which channelled his natural enthusiasm, Dave Langan had found a home.

Chapter 11

John Aldridge

JOHN ALDRIDGE was frustrated; Newport County had drawn 2-2 at Orient, leaving them drifting in 13th place in the Third Division. Despite scoring 27 goals, he'd gone nearly a month without finding the net. Perhaps it was the growing speculation about his future. His goals were attracting interest from several clubs. Newport were feeling financial pressures and Aldridge was their most bankable asset.

Signed from non-league by then manager Len Ashurst, he'd scored over 70 goals during a period of giant-killings, promotion, a Welsh Cup win and an appearance in the European Cup Winners' Cup.

Ashurst left to manage First Division Sunderland but remained in contact with Newport's chairman Richard Ford. Fearing Aldridge's transfer would be decided by a tribunal, Ford invited Ashurst to bid for Aldridge.

Aldridge needed to move. He was 26, two years older than Ian Rush, the Liverpool striker who looked and played like him, but who'd already scored 50 top-flight goals. If Aldridge was going to make a breakthrough, he'd need to find his path soon.

Finally, after the Orient game on 17 March 1984, a bid arrived, but it wasn't from Sunderland. On the other side of

London, Oxford had beaten Brentford 2-1, giving them a dominant seven-point lead at the top of the Third Division. Jim Smith had been impressed by Aldridge's performance for Newport earlier that season, likening him to Jimmy Greaves. Smith had assumed that Sunderland would be his next destination. When the Wearsiders couldn't match County's asking price of £75,000, Robert Maxwell moved.

Aldridge picked up the phone to find Maxwell in a characteristically direct mood. 'Do you want to join me?' he boomed, offering to double Aldridge's salary.

Aldridge wanted to talk to his wife Joan, so Maxwell gave him 24 hours to make his decision. Oxford had all but secured the Third Division title, but they weren't the club Aldridge imagined joining. On the other hand, there were no other bids, and the money Maxwell was offering couldn't be ignored. Despite his reservations, Aldridge phoned Smith the next day to confirm, just as Sunderland submitted their bid of £50,000.

Injury meant Aldridge's debut was delayed for three weeks before he came on as a second-half substitute for Mick Vinter against Walsall. Two weeks after that, on Good Friday, he scored his first goal in a 5-0 rout of Bolton Wanderers. By the end of the season, he'd score four times and quickly set about ousting Steve Biggins as the club's leading striker.

The addition of Billy Hamilton gave Aldridge the cover he needed as Oxford began their assault on the Second Division. By the end of October they'd scored 21 goals with Aldridge contributing 12. Aldridge may have hoped to join a bigger club before signing for Oxford but beating one came a close second.

The win against Arsenal inspired a spontaneous outpouring of creative energy. Graham Butler of Bicester wrote a poem celebrating the victory, while 12-year-old

William Cowan won an *Observer* competition for his report of the game. Ten-year-old Arsenal fan Stephen Gray wrote to the BBC to ask if they would help overturn the result.

Unlike the previous year, when each giant-killing unlocked even bigger prey, Oxford drew Ipswich Town at Portman Road. For Jim Hunt, it offered respite from the ticketing headaches of recent months.

Four days later, Oxford returned to the Manor to face Blackburn for the third time that season. Both teams were keen to maintain their form; Oxford having lost just twice in their last 33 games. A brace from Billy Hamilton, including a last-minute winner, secured a 2-1 win to consolidate their position at the top of the table and make Hamilton joint top scorer with Aldridge.

But there was cruel luck days later when Hamilton suffered a knee ligament injury in training before their trip to Shrewsbury. Ken Fish predicted he'd be unavailable for several weeks, forcing him out of Northern Ireland's must-win World Cup qualifier with Finland in Belfast.

There was better news for Dave Langan, whose form and goal against Arsenal helped force his way back into the Republic of Ireland squad for the first time in three years for their qualifier against Denmark in Copenhagen.

Despite Hamilton's absence, Oxford raced to a 2-0 lead against Shrewsbury with a brace from Aldridge. But a missed penalty for his hat-trick proved costly as Shrewsbury fought back after the break, equalising in the last minute through Gary Stevens. The result was costly for Langan too, who had to withdraw from the Republic of Ireland squad with a hamstring injury.

The following day Jim Smith took some of his frustrations out as teams led by Ron Atkinson and Ray Graydon competed at the Manor for the Fred Ford/Maurice Kyle Memorial

Trophy, featuring George Best, Brendon Batson, Lou Macari and Maurice Evans.

But his frustrations continued at Oldham the following weekend with a goalless draw leaving four teams at the top of the table separated by just three points. Afterwards, Hunt phoned Les Bateman to turn on the Manor's floodlights so Robert Maxwell could land his helicopter and join a protest, organised by Ghislaine, against the new £2m Oxford ice rink in Oxpens, which Maxwell described as funding a minority sport.

The following morning, Maxwell's *Sunday Mirror* broke an exclusive: Jim Smith had leaked that his chairman had given permission to open negotiations with his old Birmingham striker, England international Trevor Francis, who had been playing in Italy for Sampdoria. Another sign of Maxwell's seemingly limitless ambition.

The Ipswich Milk Cup tie may have been an underwhelming prospect, but Oxford were keeping heady company. Liverpool, Manchester United and Arsenal were all out but five of the top eight teams from the First Division remained in the last 16.

Oxford's reputation meant they were the most feared team in the draw, despite being the lowest-ranked. Hamilton's injury had impacted their league form, so his return to the squad ahead of schedule gave Smith confidence his team could progress.

Ipswich's glory days in the early 1980s were far behind them – they were sitting 16th in the First Division and had suffered a comprehensive 3-0 defeat to Tottenham Hotspur the previous Saturday. In response, manager Bobby Ferguson promised to attack Oxford, hoping that some of the good fortune that had revitalised Everton after their fortunate draw at the Manor might rub off on his team.

With many of their best players gone, two youngsters, Trevor Putney and Mark Brennan, seized their opportunity to control the midfield in the opening minutes. Oxford were given an early warning in the first half when Eric Gates volleyed against the crossbar but they responded well with Peter Rhoades-Brown's header rebounding off the post.

After 28 minutes, Mich d'Avray's glancing header gave Ipswich the lead. Oxford struck back three minutes later when Kevin Brock's 25-yard drive was misjudged by Paul Cooper and snuck in off the post.

Ipswich continued to attack after the break as Oxford tried to hold out for a replay, but midway through the second half, George Burley's clever pass found Romeo Zondervan in space to shoot past Steve Hardwick for the winner. It was an anticlimactic end to the campaign compared to the previous season.

Smith saw a clear advantage to bowing out of the competition: an opportunity to focus on the league and get back on track after two frustrating draws. There was no better place to do it than at the Manor against sixth-placed Leeds United, a year to the day since Oxford had humiliated them in the Milk Cup.

Despite a fall from their 1970s heyday, Leeds retained the experience of 38-year-old midfielder Peter Lorimer and goalkeeper David Harvey alongside youngsters Denis Irwin and Andy Linighan, a mix they hoped would take them back to the First Division.

Before the game, Smith picked up another Bell's Manager of the Month award in front of Oxford's largest league crowd of the season, which included FA secretary Ted Croker and the TV cameras from *Match of the Day*.

Persistent rain during the week made the pitch heavy, but Trevor Hebberd made light work of it when crashing a long-distance drive off the post in the opening moments. Leeds responded when Scott Sellars put Tommy Wright through on goal. Steve Hardwick reacted slowly, allowing

Wright to clip the ball round him but his cross slowed in the mud and Langan scrambled to clear off the line from Andy Ritchie's shot.

Maxwell, delayed by a meeting in London, pulled his Rolls-Royce into Beech Road as a loud roar erupted from the ground. As he weaved his way through the narrow space behind the main stand, he assumed an Oxford goal and gave a wry smile to a camera crew from the BBC who were filming him for a feature on *Sportsnight*.

But Oxford hadn't heeded the early warnings. Langan, trying to inject some energy into the attack, had bustled infield, but his heavy pass back to Hebberd cannoned into the path of Wright, who had the simple task of sliding the ball beyond Hardwick for 1-0.

Oxford pressed for a response and a half-chance for Hamilton was wasted before Leeds struck again. The lively Wright crossed to Lorimer, who slid the ball past Hardwick for number two. Maxwell took his seat next to a concerned-looking Jim Smith. Oxford were facing their fourth game without a win, overrun by Leeds' mix of youthful pace and experienced guile.

Peter Rhoades-Brown, mindful of Smith's previous half-time roastings, led the response, battling down the wing to force a corner. Brock's inch-perfect kick was met emphatically by Gary Briggs to head home for 2-1. At the break, Maxwell headed under the Beech Road stand for a cup of tea as Smith got to work, imploring his team to not overplay in the difficult conditions.

The second half started with the pitch looking like a potato patch, its stickiness frustrating Leeds' passing, allowing Oxford to take command in midfield. Within two minutes, Hebberd controlled the ball in the centre circle with the help of the mud and combined with Brock and Langan to loop a cross to the back post for Hamilton to chest the ball down and poke it inside the post for the equaliser. Momentum shifting, six minutes later, Brock floated a perfect back-post cross to Aldridge, whose header made it three. Leeds buckled as their fans, a mass of bodies in the Cuckoo Lane End, grew increasingly frustrated.

As Leeds' discipline collapsed, Oxford seemed to be floating across the pitch. Just beyond the hour, Hamilton sent Aldridge clear to slide past Harvey for 4-2. Moments later an innocuous tussle involving Aldridge left Lorimer clutching his face on the floor. Lorimer jumped to his feet as the two players were booked but he refused to give referee John Moules his name. Moules raised his finger and sent Lorimer to the dressing room.

The dismissal sparked fury in the packed Cuckoo Lane End. Leeds fans dismantled the TV gantry at the back of the terrace, throwing planks of wood and scaffolding on to the pitch. A coin hit Steve Hardwick. 'I've never faced anything so frightening,' he said later. The trouble highlighted Oxford's paradox; the more they won the greater their problems became. When the referee finally restarted the game, Brock crossed to Aldridge for 5-2. 'Five, not bad,' Maxwell purred in the Beech Road stand, oblivious to the riot to his left.

Oxford's fightback and Leeds' brutality reverberated around the country. With recriminations to come, they were relieved to visit bottom side Notts County the following week. Despite the chasm in class, Oxford contrived to concede an unfortunate opener from David Hunt before a shocking miss from Rhoades-Brown moments later confirmed their worst fears. With 13 minutes to go, a sweeping second, with a suspicion of offside from Alan Young, made the game safe. The shock defeat allowed Blackburn to take top spot on alphabetical order. Maxwell, frustrated, returned to the Manor in his helicopter, again using the floodlights to guide its landing.

Oxford hadn't won away since the middle of September but their home form was sensational, and next to face their onslaught were the financially stricken Charlton Athletic. Smith was growing concerned that his team were too reliant on Hamilton and Aldridge for goals. George Lawrence responded, scoring on his return, before Aldridge got his 18th goal of the season. Hebberd made it three from a deflected shot before he was brought down in the box to allow McDonald to score the fourth from the spot. The rout was completed when Briggs headed in Brock's cross for five.

Two days later, Ghislaine Maxwell travelled to London to accept more silverware: an unusual silver tray with matching milk and coffee pots, an award for Club of the Year from the Football League Executive Staffs' Association.

A surreal week continued as the BBC made good on their promise to overturn Oxford's Milk Cup win over Arsenal, broadcasting Stephen Gray refereeing a rerun of the game in front of 4,000 fans at the Manor. Gray sent off most of the Oxford team, allowing Arsenal to ease to victory.

As Christmas approached, Jim Smith and former England rugby captain Bill Beaumont faced off at the Minchery Farm Club in Littlemore for Radio Oxford's *Question of Sport Christmas Special*.

Maxwell's benevolence overflowed: discovering that only 12 players had medals for winning the Third Division, he ordered one for every member of the staff including Bill Palmer, who swept the terraces, and Doreen Baker, who cleaned the kit. Then, he and Chelsea owner Ken Bates loaned Southend United £70,000 after they faced bankruptcy due to their debts to the supporters' Christmas savings club. When Maxwell was happy, so was everyone else.

Three days before Christmas, Oxford took their stuttering away form to Fratton Park to face second-placed Portsmouth in front of the TV cameras. On a heavy pitch,

Hebberd struggled to make an impact in midfield and Brock got bogged down, isolating Hamilton and Aldridge up front.

With 20 minutes to go, Langan broke free on the left, digging out a cross into the box for Brock, who slid in at the far post for 1-0. Portsmouth responded, using their physical advantage to push forward. With the home fans growing restless, the game paused when an inebriated fan dressed as Santa Claus wandered on to the pitch, causing a delay for several minutes.

The obstruction removed, in the final minute, Alan Biley – who'd been given an award by lookalike cartoon character Roy of the Rovers before the match – headed an equaliser. Then, in the time added on due to the festive invasion, he channelled his doppelgänger by snatching the winner. Although Hamilton hit the crossbar, it was all for nothing as Oxford dropped to fourth after eight away games without a win.

The following week they travelled to Barnsley, but the poor weather took its toll and just under two hours before kick-off the referee postponed the game.

Oxford fans en route with the London Road Club heard the news on the radio and decided to divert to Mansfield Town to watch Mick Vinter, Neil Whatmore and Ian Greaves. Arriving at Field Mill, they found that this match had been called off as well. It was the only other game postponed that day.

Smith continued to refine his squad to rediscover their form. He sent Gary Barnett on loan to Fulham and welcomed Peter Foley back on a non-contract basis. He also dipped into the transfer market to sign Reading goalkeeper Alan Judge as cover for Steve Hardwick.

On Boxing Day, Oxford welcomed relegation-threatened Cardiff City to the Manor. The team had scored three or more goals in nine of their 12 games at home and the

Christmas holiday ballooned the crowd to over 12,000. For the second Boxing Day running, the club were forced to close the gates early, leaving fans trapped outside. Those who got in were rewarded with a characteristically vibrant attacking display as the team waltzed to a 4-0 win with Hamilton and Aldridge both scoring twice, taking their combined total for the season to 36.

Three days later, Crystal Palace arrived defending an eight-game unbeaten run. To celebrate Oxford's 1,000th league fixture, Jim Hunt signed four programmes offering a £25 voucher towards the cost of season tickets for the following year. Realising a flaw in his plan, he was quick to clarify that if more than four people claimed the prize, he would be the sole arbiter of who had forged his signature. Oxford crushed Palace 5-0 with two goals apiece from McDonald and Hamilton and another from Aldridge.

After the game, Smith announced the £30,000 signing of 23-year-old midfielder Brian McDermott from Arsenal. With 60 top-flight appearances, Smith hoped McDermott's experience would bring solidity to the midfield, an area where the team were sometimes exposed, particularly on the road.

At the turn of the year Oxford sat comfortably in second, a point behind Manchester City with two games in hand. To Jim Hunt's frustration, the players were forced to spend New Year's Eve in Darlington before their 1-0 win over Middlesbrough. McDermott's signing paid immediate dividends as he supplied the goal for Trevor Hebberd and a first win on the road since September. With McDermott on board, two days later one of the heroes of the previous season's Milk Cup run, George Lawrence, returned to Southampton after drifting from the starting line-up due to the form of Peter Rhoades-Brown.

Hopes of building on the Middlesbrough win were dashed immediately when the weather wiped out practically the whole of January. Only a 2-0 victory over Shrewsbury in the FA Cup survived the conditions. To retain their sharpness, Smith flew the team to Portugal for a 5-1 win in a friendly over local side Farense, giving Andy Thomas the opportunity to play, for the first time for a year. The lack of league action allowed Blackburn to build a lead at the top of the table but there was plenty of activity off the field. Jim Smith missed out to Newcastle for Manchester United's Welsh midfielder Alan Davies, and he also accepted a transfer request from Paul Hinshelwood, whose opportunities were limited by Dave Langan's form. Hinshelwood was due to join Swansea City before opting instead for Millwall.

There was relief as the FA found the club not to blame for crowd trouble against Leeds, only criticising their decision to erect the TV gantry in the Cuckoo Lane End that provided ammunition for the visiting fans.

As January came to an end, the weather improved and there was a familiar foe in the FA Cup as Oxford faced Blackburn for the fourth time that season. The tie, postponed from the Saturday to the Wednesday evening, meant as they prepared to play the draw for the next round was made, setting up a potential rerun of the previous season's epic Milk Cup ties with the winners due to face Manchester United at home. The TV companies quickly targeted it as their live game of the round.

After 13 consecutive home wins, the Manor bubbled with confidence. But, as fans planned for the arrival of Ron Atkinson's side, under the Beech Road stand, there was drama. Before each game, Ken Fish would put the players through a rigorous warm-up in a cramped room under the stand. As the team built up a sweat, Billy Hamilton, who'd already scored five goals against Blackburn, jumped and landed awkwardly, injuring his knee.

Oxford started with ten men as Mr Fish tried in vain to massage Hamilton's knee back to health. He appeared just after kick-off, but within minutes, clearly unfit, Smith replaced him with Mark Jones.

Despite the disruption, Oxford started well; Jones missed a chance after ten minutes before Brock went close. But a minute before half-time, against the run of play, Blackburn's Jimmy Quinn headed the opening goal.

After the break, Oxford poured forward in search of an equaliser. Just after the hour they were rewarded when Glenn Keeley handled Trewick's cross and the referee pointed to the spot. Bobby McDonald stepped up, but Blackburn goalkeeper Terry Gennoe guessed right, saving brilliantly, bringing Oxford's hopes of a dream rematch with Manchester United to an end.

Jim Smith was frustrated by the stop-start nature of the season and the patchy form that came with it. The cup game had been too tough after a three-week break. To add to Hamilton's injury, McDonald picked up an abdominal strain that would keep him out for weeks.

As Smith considered a move for another striker, Oxford's first game without Hamilton saw Kevin Brock give them their third away win in a row, at Carlisle, leaving four teams at the top divided by goal difference.

With no margin for error, three days later Oxford headed to Selhurst Park to face struggling Crystal Palace. The omens weren't good when the team bus broke down on the way to the London hotel they were using for their pre-match meal. With the vehicle blocking the road, two police vans transported the players to the hotel.

After nine minutes, Langan's long ball sent Brock through, but his shot was beaten away by keeper George Wood. Oxford continued to press but Palace were threatening on the break; first Jerry Murphy hit the bar. Then Andy Gray set up Alan Irvine only for him to clip the post.

After the break, Palace's physical strength started to tell. Gray and his strike partner Trevor Aylott pressurised Gary Briggs and Malcolm Shotton, drawing a save from Hardwick five minutes into the half. Phil Barber then set up Aylott but he directed his header over the bar.

Eight minutes from time, Aylott made amends, turning in Irvine's cross for the winner. It had been Oxford's worst performance of the season with only Steve Hardwick coming away with any credit. They'd been undone by another physical side, leaving Smith to question whether his team had the moral and physical courage to win promotion. 'We were lightweight without Billy and Bob,' he said.

There was mixed news in the following days: McDonald was advised he could manage his injury through painkillers rather than an operation but Hamilton was set to be out for months. He'd missed five games in five years at Burnley but the intensity of Oxford's programme was complicating his rehabilitation, making him increasingly injury-prone at the Manor.

Smith moved quickly to bring in versatile Welsh international Jeremy Charles from Queens Park Rangers for £100,000. The 25-year-old was equally at home up front or in defence, offering the cover Smith needed.

Postponements meant Jim Hunt was forced to sell tickets for the pivotal games against Birmingham and Manchester City weeks in advance. The challenge was shaping his thinking for a season in the First Division, pondering whether Oxford would need to be the first club in the country to force every game to be all-ticket.

It wasn't their only problem as the contract for the Football League's TV deal was due for renewal. Clubs were benefitting from £8.7m a year but a four-year renewal, worth

£17m, including 16 live league games a season, was causing concern; most clubs feared the expansion of live games would impact crowds and revenue.

The Football League were torn. Most believed their future was with the BBC and ITV, but Robert Maxwell wanted to focus on the opportunities offered by subscription television, an area he was investing in with his British Cable Services company.

The Football League added Maxwell and heavyweight chairmen Irving Scholar and Ken Bates to their negotiating team. Their first move was to increase the price to £19m. But with the TV companies unmoved, the prospect of going into the following year without a deal was growing. Clubs like Oxford relied on the money and exposure; without it they risked heading back to the brink of extinction.

Following the defeat to Crystal Palace, after another two-week break, Oxford had the opportunity to regain top spot with a rearranged trip to Fulham. With only a friendly against Tottenham at Bisham Abbey between the games, they may have been forgiven for being rusty, but they started brightly with McDermott and Brock probing to make chances for Aldridge and Charles on his debut.

The influential Fulham midfielder Ray Houghton nearly opened the scoring but he fired over, before McDermott retaliated with a low drive. As the game progressed, the home side gradually gained control. Clifford Carr and Kenny Achampong – on his debut – tested Hardwick before teenager Achampong fired in just after the hour to give Fulham the points.

It consigned Oxford to their first back-to-back defeats in major competitions for two years and they seemed to be, again, locked in a sequence of frustrating narrow losses on the road. The last thing they needed was another trip north, particularly against a promotion contender, and an over-familiar face.

For the fifth time in the campaign, Oxford faced top-of-the-table Blackburn. It was their fifth consecutive away game. Jim Smith brought in Tony Spearing, on loan from Norwich, to replace McDonald with Charles deputising for Hamilton.

Oxford fans occupied the Darwen End of the ground with a Union Jack featuring a swastika displayed prominently on the terrace, a reminder that even during the club's resurgence, dark forces lurked.

There was an early scare when Shotton escaped a handball appeal while trying to clear a stray knock-on from Briggs. After five minutes, Charles nodded a long ball wide to McDermott, whose cross landed for Brock to connect with the diving header for the opening goal.

With the home side battling a flu bug and Langan outstanding at both ends of the pitch, Oxford looked comfortable attacking on the break. Brock's constant threat pegged Blackburn back, their wayward passing failing to utilise the pace of Noel Brotherston and Ian Miller.

Blackburn looked more positive after the break, although Oxford limited them to half-chances until the 68th minute when Simon Garner forced Spearing to concede a corner. The ball was floated towards Derek Fazackerley to flick on to Jimmy Quinn, who fired the equaliser in off Brock. In frustration, Smith replaced McDermott with Rhoades-Brown, but neither side could fashion a winner as their over-familiarity seemed to neutralise the game.

Oxford's first home league game of 1985 was on 2 March against Smith's old club, Birmingham City, still promotion rivals. With just one league win since the turn of the year, it was a welcome return home where they'd dropped just two points all season.

Jim Hunt expected the game to sell out and Birmingham quickly sold their allocation, but with only a reserve match against Swindon for fans to visit the Manor, sales in the home areas were slow. Things were complicated further when Hunt refused to sell tickets to anyone with a Birmingham accent.

Ron Saunders' side were Oxford's worst nightmare: physical and direct, they'd plundered ten away wins in the season. Dave Geddis targeted Briggs with a series of robust challenges. His strike partner, Wayne Clarke, focussed on Shotton, forcing him off with damaged ligaments to be replaced with Peter Rhoades-Brown.

Without McDonald, Hamilton or Shotton, and with Briggs under pressure, Birmingham broke through after seven minutes when Clarke pounced on a poor punch from Steve Hardwick. Twenty minutes later they doubled their lead when Martin Kuhl's free kick deflected to Geddis to fire home.

The ticketing problems had left the home terraces with 3,000 spaces, with the Cuckoo Lane End sold out, and despite Hunt's best efforts Birmingham fans had found a way into the Beech Road stand. When their celebrations spilled over, Oxford fans reacted, invading the pitch for a confrontation. An FA reprimand was surely due.

The biggest police presence the club had ever seen cleared the pitch before Clarke sealed the win, heading Birmingham's third and condemning Oxford to their first home defeat of the season. The whole day had been a grim spectacle, illustrating the brutal effectiveness of a physical style against Oxford. What had been written off as poor form was threatening to become a crisis.

Smith accused Geddis of committing 20 fouls without being booked and lambasted Clarke for injuring Shotton. Saunders responded by describing Smith as a 'squealer'; their feud showed no sign of abating.

The club's season-long problems with hooligans at the Manor hardened Jim Hunt's resolve. The government needed to act and introduce identity cards, while for persistent offenders, he suggested the birch.

The following Saturday, Oxford, needing to address the slump, were given a boost as Billy Hamilton returned for the first time in five weeks. Despite a much-improved performance, they could only muster a point at Sheffield United with Jeremy Charles's diving header grabbing his side's only goal before he was carried off. Moments later, Hamilton pulled up lame, but struggled on. It was a well-earned point, but at what cost?

Chapter 12

Jeremy Charles

IN THE unremarkable residential district of Cwmbwrla in the Welsh town of Swansea lies a row of modest multi-generational terraced houses known as Alice Street.

The area was the product of an exploding urban population that grew during the 18th and 19th centuries. Industrialisation and specifically copper smelting drew large numbers of people to the town from the poor Welsh rural communities. Despite the comparative wealth that industrial growth brought, life was hard, the work was dirty and dangerous and the city's infrastructure struggled to cope with the influx.

Small houses without heating or electricity teemed with people, families were packed together. Crowded and noisy, generational and familial lines blurred and lives entwined. Children would spill into the parkland nearby and play chaotic games of 40-a-side football using a tennis ball.

The brutal, no-rules games of indeterminate length helped develop a fitness, steel and skill that made the more organised football at nearby Swansea Town seem tame. First to emerge from this chaotic incubator were 'Saturday gladiators' Ernie Jones and Jackie Roberts, whose careers would eventually be devastated by the Second World War.

Their path into professional football inspired the next generation – another Alice Street resident, Mel Nurse, made his debut for Swansea in 1955 and eventually followed Jones into the Welsh national side.

But it was at 9 Alice Street, the rented home of the Charles family, where two players lived who would change world football. John Charles was a phenomenon; blessed with panache, he had the build of a titan and the grace of a ballet dancer. He could play at centre-half or centre-forward. Starting his career at Leeds, in 1957 he moved to Juventus where he'd eventually secure three *scudetti* and two Italian Cups. To many, he was the greatest foreign player in Italian football and perhaps the best player in the world.

A year after moving to Italy, John led Wales to the 1958 World Cup in Sweden but was injured in the final group play-off against Hungary. In the quarter-final, Wales slipped to a narrow defeat against Brazil with 18-year-old wunderkind Pelé grabbing the goal.

For once, John was outshone by his younger brother Mel, who was regarded as the best player of the tournament. Pelé called him the best centre-half he'd ever played against. Mel was four years John's junior, and could also play in defence or attack. A year after the World Cup he moved to Arsenal from Swansea. After three years at Highbury, he moved to Cardiff City where he was eventually joined by John. Just as they had been on Alice Street as they became footballers, the Charles boys lived on the same street as their careers came to an end.

Into this extraordinary environment, in 1959 Mel's only son Jeremy was born. Jeremy also lived on Alice Street and enjoyed the same versatility his father and uncle had, allowing him to play up front and in defence. Like Mel, he joined his hometown club, by now known as Swansea City, making his debut two years before John Toshack took over as manager.

Toshack guided the Swans on a remarkable journey through the divisions with Jeremy a key member of the squad. He scored Swansea's first goal in the top flight before his season became dogged by injury. The surge was short-lived and relegation in 1983 saw Charles transferred to QPR before Jim Smith swooped to sign him for Oxford. Despite the step down, he hoped the move might bring more glory to the family name.

Without a win in five, Oxford had dropped to fourth, seven points behind leaders Manchester City. They needed some rhythm and a route through their injuries, but promotion would depend on their formidable form at the Manor where ten of their remaining 15 games would be held.

Despite Charles's first goal for the club, against Sheffield United, he and Billy Hamilton missed the visit of Wimbledon so Mark Jones was drafted in to partner John Aldridge up front.

Any fears that Oxford would shirk the challenge of Wimbledon's uncompromising and muscular style were set to rest after five minutes when Aldridge scored his first league goal of the calendar year. Jones nearly doubled the lead before Malcolm Shotton showed uncharacteristic agility to turn and shoot into the corner of the net for number two.

A third came ten minutes after the restart when Aldridge latched on to Jones's pass, sidestepped the keeper and slotted home his 24th goal of the season, equalling Steve Biggins' record. Three minutes from time Brian McDermott raced down the right wing before cutting inside and scoring his first goal for the club. Oxford had absolutely dominated a team they once feared and fans purred contentedly on their way back down London Road.

The buoyant mood was in stark contrast to events 40 miles away, where Luton Town were hosting Millwall in the quarter-final of the FA Cup live on BBC television.

Unfashionable and unpopular, Millwall had struggled for years, but manager George Graham had revitalised them and they were now fighting for promotion from the Third Division.

Luton were at the foot of the First Division, their FA Cup run a welcome distraction from their league problems. Despite the reputation of both clubs, and against Millwall's advice, the hosts resisted making the game all-ticket.

Word spread across London's hooligan firms that something was brewing, an opportunity to put on a show live in front of the nation. Fans gathered in the town throughout the afternoon as windows were smashed and the police were attacked. As kick-off approached, the stadium was overwhelmed with 10,000 people gaining entrance to the cramped Millwall end alone. Fans spilled on to the pitch, throwing bottles, nails and coins, and heading towards the Luton section.

Amazingly, the pitch was cleared in time for kick-off, but the tense atmosphere ruptured after 14 minutes when another invasion caused a 25-minute delay. When the players eventually returned, Brian Stein fired Luton ahead.

Trouble continued throughout the game with Luton keeper Les Sealey hit on the head with a missile. In another pitch invasion, Luton coach Trevor Hartley was attacked and a policeman, isolated in the centre circle, stopped breathing after being struck with a concrete block. His colleague was attacked while trying to resuscitate him. Rioting continued outside the ground and 81 people were injured but only 31 were arrested, many claiming in court to be fans of other clubs.

Live on television, the riot shook the country; hooliganism couldn't be dismissed as the mis-channelled exuberance of youth. Violence was nationwide and organised, and there was impetus to act at the highest levels of government.

The introspection and soul-searching began. Oxford were one of football's rare redemption stories, their likeable manager leading a quirky band of no-hopers and never-weres. But even they couldn't escape the malaise, and at in-form Brighton hundreds of fans were contained by mounted police following a riot after a goalless draw three days later, a game which sparked into life on the hour when Dave Langan was sent off after Brighton defender Hans Kraay collapsed off the ball. Smith accused the Dutchman of diving.

Despite one win in seven and sitting fourth, Smith felt his team were finding their form. With league leaders Manchester City their next visitors, they needed to turn performances into points.

City, unbeaten in five, had lost twice in 21, but Smith was able to welcome back Billy Hamilton and Bobby McDonald. Peter Rhoades-Brown softened the City defence with a series of surging runs down the wing before Langan fed Aldridge to open the scoring on 29 minutes. Two minutes later Brock swung in a cross from Paul Power's weak clearance for Trevor Hebberd to head number two. Power capped a wretched display just after the hour, handling Rhoades-Brown's cross in the area, allowing Aldridge to score from the spot past Alex Williams.

With none of their promotion rivals winning, Oxford were catapulted to second. Optimism flooded through the Manor, talk of promotion returned, and with it, the need for a new stadium. 'Trouble is,' Smith joked, referring to the benefits of the Manor's famous slope, 'we'll need a site with a hill on it.'

The celebrations continued the following night at the PFA awards at the Hilton Hotel in London with Bobby McDonald, John Aldridge and Billy Hamilton all selected for the Second Division team of the season. His team receiving national plaudits, Jim Smith prepared for life in the top flight with a £70,000 bid for Irish international Gerry Armstrong, Billy Hamilton's strike partner during the 1982 World Cup. Armstrong, playing for Real Mallorca, was keen to return home.

Next, though, were Grimsby Town at the Manor, and with Hamilton injured on international duty, the fluidity they enjoyed against Manchester City was missing. Despite constant pressure, by half-time the game was still goalless. The players returned to the changing rooms anticipating a rocket from their manager. But Smith seemed downbeat; John Aldridge thought he looked hungover, and quietly the Bald Eagle asked the players to go and enjoy themselves.

Bemused by their manager's demeanour, the struggle continued after the break and they were delivered another blow after an hour when Jeremy Charles went off injured. Substitute Brian McDermott seemed to reflect Smith's malaise with his crossing becoming more wayward as the desperation grew.

As injury time approached the crowd grew anxious; Oxford's momentum was seeping away. But McDermott hadn't dropped down a division for the club's ambition to disintegrate in front of him. He made one last drive towards the Cuckoo Lane End and launched another desperate cross, hoping to find its target. It looped to the back post, the Grimsby defence froze for a split second and Rhoades-Brown ducked, the ball glancing off the crown of his head, beyond the keeper and into the net for the winner. Smith, who'd been so detached, was revitalised. 'If we don't get up into the First Division now,' he said, 'we never will.'

If Smith thought the team was ready for the First Division, the Manor certainly wasn't. A stadium swap with Reading was considered and Fulham chairman Ernie Clay offered Craven Cottage as a temporary home. In response,

Oxford City Council identified four green-belt sites beyond the city boundary. Maxwell was not impressed.

An opportunity to retake top spot came three days later as Oxford travelled north for their rearranged game against Barnsley. Hamilton returned, but with full-back Joe Joyce and winger Gordon Owen putting pressure on Malcolm Shotton and Gary Briggs, Oxford were thwarted by another aggressively organised opponent. The breakthrough came after 11 minutes when Nicky Law's free kick was flicked on by Rodger Wylde to Owen, who crashed the ball in off the bar. It was the first goal Oxford had conceded in seven and a half hours of football.

Settling to their task, Hebberd and Brock battled to regain control of midfield but as they were edging their way back into the game, McDonald conceded a corner. The delivery fell to Billy Ronson, who scrambled to get his shot away. As Rhoades-Brown tried to clear, Ronson stole in, robbed the winger and crossed to Owen to head the second.

Oxford peppered the Barnsley goal looking for a route back into the game with McDonald's set pieces offering chances for Aldridge and Hamilton. Just after an hour, another set play saw Futcher and Hamilton go up for the ball. As they landed, there was a blast of the referee's whistle for a push on Hamilton but Aldridge's low spot kick was saved by Clive Baker. Eleven minutes later, Shotton stumbled under pressure, freeing Ronson to cross to the unmarked Owen to complete his hat-trick.

Despite the setback, Oxford returned to the top of the table three days later with a comfortable 2-0 win over Cardiff. Aldridge scored with an overhead kick after four minutes, before feeding Charles for the second. In the closing minutes, Aldridge was fouled in the box by keeper Gary Plumley, but McDonald fired his penalty wide.

It wasn't unusual for Robert Maxwell's interventions to come at inconvenient times. As Jim Smith prepared his team talk for the visit of relegation-threatened Middlesbrough, he was summoned to the phone. Calling from Spain, Maxwell asked how Smith was planning to address the problem of missed penalties. Smith assured his chairman he'd given the responsibility to Dave Langan.

After three minutes, Hardwick launched a ball into the Boro penalty box. As Aldridge shielded possession, Tony Mowbray clumsily bundled him over for yet another spot kick. As planned, Langan stepped up, and his strike was true and hard, but keeper Daniel O'Hanlan got a hand to it. Another miss.

Middlesbrough had chances to score, but in the 23rd minute Rhoades-Brown's corner found Briggs, who sent Charles into the box to play a one-two with Shotton and fire under O'Hanlon for the only goal of the game. It was another step towards promotion, although Smith kept the details of another penalty miss from Maxwell.

Oxford travelled to struggling Wolves. Molineux, once the envy of Europe, had become a stricken wreck. Oxford fans filled the corner terrace, while the other run-down stands remained sparsely populated, a reminder of how times were changing.

Oxford struggled to find their rhythm during a drab first half, but after the break McDonald cannoned a free kick off the bar and Briggs threw himself at the rebound to direct the ball into the net for 1-0.

The lead lasted a minute as Molineux erupted when Humphrey crossed to Chapman to rifle past Hardwick; their first home goal in five months. Oxford looked set to drop more points before Charles beat his defender to centre for Brock, who stabbed home the winner eight minutes from time, but the result was tainted by yet another injury to Charles.

The following Tuesday Birmingham City moved within a point of Oxford, beating Crystal Palace 3-0. Following a stumbling February, Smith felt his side were now playing their way into form, with seven games remaining and five at home. Despite injuries to Hamilton and Charles he had confidence in the ever-reliable Mark Jones and Andy Thomas, who'd scored for the reserves against Crystal Palace.

Oxford continued their formidable form against Huddersfield four days later, going ahead after six minutes through McDonald. They were out of sight after half an hour when Brock's corner was flicked on by Briggs for McDermott to drive into the far corner. Nine minutes later, Aldridge netted his 28th goal of the season from Langan's free kick, confirming a convincing victory.

Oxford were now nine points clear of Blackburn in fourth with six games left. Jim Hunt, making plans for the First Division, promoted Mick Brown to ticket manager and appointed Mick Moore, groundsman at Morris Motors, to replace Les Bateman, who was leaving the club after 36 years.

The *Match of the Day* cameras were at the Manor for the visit of Oldham Athletic the following week. Among the guests was the newly crowned Miss Oxford, Heather Cameron, fresh from a photoshoot wearing an Oxford shirt and little else that would feature in the *Sunday People* the following morning.

Mindful of their sluggish start in front of the cameras against Leeds, Mark Jones, replacing Hamilton, supplied Kevin Brock for the opening goal after 18 minutes. Jones was on hand three minutes later to set up Aldridge for the second.

McDonald's mistake allowed Quinn to score before half-time but five minutes after the restart he made amends, latching on to Brock's header for 3-1.

Man of the match Jones limped off midway through the second half after crashing into a perimeter fence, allowing the spotlight to fall on Aldridge. He scored his 30th goal of the season 12 minutes from time, and six minutes later he connected with Langan's cross for his hat-trick. A last-minute consolation from McGuire did nothing to dampen the celebrations. Twelve points clear with a vastly superior goal difference, Oxford were effectively three points from promotion.

Their remaining game in hand was at home to Shrewsbury the following Wednesday. Sensing destiny, the stands filled once more with fans ready to witness history.

Mindful of their sluggish display against Wigan the previous season, Oxford started brightly. After just a quarter of an hour Langan collected the ball on the right, exchanged a one-two with Hebberd, controlled the pass on his chest and volleyed in off the post, sparking mayhem in the London Road terrace. The doorway to the First Division was open.

Oxford couldn't capitalise further, but it didn't matter. At the final whistle, for the second year in a row, chaotic scenes descended on the Manor as fans flooded the pitch, and a chorus struck up to the tune of 'Yellow Submarine', celebrating Jim Smith's triumph. Smith looked on at the choir, his shirt soaked with champagne. He was back. The players had been transformed by this ramshackle little club and catapulted into the top division. They emerged at the front of the Beech Road stand with fans clamouring on any vantage point to see.

Match-winner Dave Langan, fresh from a call-up by the Republic of Ireland and ten months on from his injury nightmare at Birmingham, trained his sights on his former manager. 'I regard what I have done as a kick in the teeth for Ron Saunders,' he said with glee. 'I've proved him wrong to write me off.'

Amid the celebrations, one man, by his own admission, was furious. Robert Maxwell had delivered his side of the deal when taking over Oxford United in 1982. Silencing the celebrations, he announced that the club would boycott a civic reception in their honour, saying, 'We will refuse to go until the city council give us a definite financial commitment on a new ground. Now they must deliver. We don't know whether we will be able to play First Division football here next season.'

The misjudged intervention deflated Smith; for everything he'd done, it would never be enough. His footballing parable about guile, ingenuity and spirit had been shrouded by petty local politics and the great looming shadow of Robert Maxwell.

Despite the shifting mood and chaotic scenes, afterwards, Maxwell was delighted to see a group of players gathered outside the dressing rooms looking composed in their matchday suits. 'Well done lads,' he said. 'We'll do even better in the First Division.' It was a surprise message for the Shrewsbury players who were waiting to get on their coach home.

Promotion celebrations went on through the night with Radio Oxford holding a champagne breakfast for the bleary-eyed manager and players. Ron Saunders snapped back at Langan, saying, 'The wages Dave Langan was on, he would have to be the equivalent of Beckenbauer to stay and he's a million miles away from that.' With Birmingham sitting second in the table, the title race was now personal.

A seven-point cushion meant Oxford were one win from the championship. Forty-eight hours after beating Shrewsbury, they headed to Leeds United suffering from a literal and metaphorical hangover. In the days that had followed their promotion the headlines had focussed on Maxwell's outburst, and it was no surprise that Jim Smith was in demand for Saturday morning TV.

As Smith prepared for a live interview with *On the Ball* hosts Ian St John and Jimmy Greaves, he was unaware that Maxwell had already phoned the show. 'There can be no football at the Manor Ground or anywhere else in Oxford next season,' Maxwell announced with typical bombast. Moments later Jim Smith was live as St John asked him about Maxwell's comments. The manager said he was probably joking.

An hour before the game, Maxwell summoned Smith to the phone to chastise his manager for undermining him. The cloud hanging over Smith darkened. On the pitch, his weary team held out for 68 minutes before Ian Baird fired the home side ahead. Oxford couldn't respond, but Smith was circumspect: 'I knew it would be difficult for the lads to find any fire today. I think they're still celebrating.'

With 15 minutes to go, the mood brightened when Smith introduced Andy Thomas from the bench after 15 months out of the game. On the way home on the coach, Smith confided with BBC Radio Oxford commentator Nick Harris that relations with Maxwell were approaching breaking point.

Birmingham's win at Barnsley narrowed the gap to four points. Before Oxford's visit of relegation-threatened Notts County, Smith put on a united front, echoing Maxwell's call for a new stadium for financial and safety reasons.

On the pitch, the lethargy suffered at Leeds continued as County fought to stay in the division. Aldridge, without Hamilton, had a goal disallowed after five minutes for offside. Moments later County hit the bar, before Steve Hardwick made a series of fine saves. They broke the deadlock with ten minutes to go, Justin Fashanu firing in from Mark Robinson's pass.

With the crowd anticipating celebrations to match those after Shrewsbury, Oxford sprung to life. Hebberd headed over the County defence for Andy Thomas to fire the ball into the roof of the net for the equaliser but with Birmingham confirming their promotion against Cardiff, Oxford's lead narrowed to two points.

Birmingham had an opportunity to take top spot against Middlesbrough the evening before Oxford's penultimate game, at Charlton. But their own hangovers blunted them and they could only come away with a goalless draw. There was just a point between the teams.

More than 3,000 supporters travelled to Charlton anticipating the title. But, once again Oxford's form deserted them. A minute before half-time Mike Flanagan fired in from 30 yards, before crashing the ball off the bar after the break.

Briggs equalised three minutes later. The title drew closer when Charles nodded down another Brock corner to Aldridge to fire home for 2-1.

Charlton were not ready to give in and Flanagan equalised before Robert Lee's diving header made it 3-2. With three minutes remaining Oxford won a corner on the right. The visiting fans bellowed encouragement. 'Come on you yellows,' echoed around the half-empty Valley. The delivery was low and flat, but an Oxford flick-on landed two yards out and Charlton midfielder Alan Curbishley panicked, hooking the ball into his own net for 3-3.

While the title chase continued, Jim Hunt announced ticket prices for the 1985/86 season: £65 for terrace tickets and £120 for seating, making the Manor one of the most expensive places to watch football in the country. A week later, the club added another 20 per cent due to the demand. For fans, success came at a price.

One game and one point would now give Oxford the title; Jim Smith felt one final effort in front of a full house at the Manor would see them over the line. Birmingham were hosting Leeds at St Andrew's ready for any slip-up while Oxford entertained Barnsley.

The Manor was full and anxious, an atmosphere that had become so familiar, as success rolled through the club like a series of tidal waves. This time there would be no slip-ups, just fluid, attacking, dominant football. Within five minutes, all doubts were swept away when John Aldridge fired home John Trewick's pass. Jeremy Charles doubled the lead minutes later, heading in Kevin Brock's cross, before Aldridge got his 34th goal of the campaign. Aldridge had another ruled out for a foul before McDonald steered his header into the net for 4-0 after just 26 minutes.

The rest was a procession; Oxford were champions, Jim Smith had the title his team deserved. The only losers were the bookmakers, one of whom had to pay out £8,000 on a 16/1 bet placed on Oxford for the title. The lucky punter? Robert Maxwell.

As the players navigated their way wearily around the Manor Ground, soaking in their achievements, elsewhere, the troubles that had faced football for more than a decade finally swelled up to engulf it.

Some 180 miles away in West Yorkshire, Bradford City had been celebrating their promotion to the Second Division when a discarded match was dropped on to a pile of rubbish left under their antiquated wooden stand, turning it into a horrifying inferno. Fans spilled on to the pitch and watched as trapped supporters raced to find a route to safety. With the turnstiles locked, fans couldn't escape the raging fire, and the silhouettes of the victims could be seen against the flames. Fifty-six fans died and hundreds more were injured.

Elsewhere, as Birmingham chased Oxford for the Second Division title, fighting broke out between over 1,000 fans at St Andrew's. Riot police closed in on the trouble and a wall collapsed, killing a 15-year-old boy. The day of Oxford's greatest success was the day of one of English football's most catastrophic disasters.

Fans digested the news from Bradford and Birmingham, the saturated coverage highlighting woeful inadequacies and complacency across the game.

The following day, the Oxford squad climbed on board two South Midland Bus Company tour buses to weave their way through the city to the civic reception Maxwell had threatened to boycott. The parade toured the city for an hour and a half before arriving at the Town Hall.

The following day, Jim Hunt arrived in the office to find a letter of congratulations from Accrington Stanley, who Oxford had replaced in the Football League 20 years earlier.

On the Tuesday, they played Manchester United in Peter Foley's testimonial. Two days later they boarded a plane to Sofia for a hastily arranged trip to Bulgaria courtesy of Maxwell's friendship with the country's president, Todor Zhivkov. Maxwell, who maintained high-level connections within the Soviet bloc, seemed the only person who wanted the game to be played.

The squad flew from Heathrow before playing against the Bulgarian national team the following day. In front of 30,000 fans, after a goalless first half, Jim Smith made two changes that allowed the Bulgarians to overwhelm their exhausted opponents with five second-half goals.

The local football federation hosted a dinner that evening and the following day, the players toured Sofia before attending a cocktail party hosted by the president of the International Youth Foundation, beneficiaries of the money raised from the match.

On 17 May the squad travelled to Mihaylovgrad in the north-west of the country to play second-tier side Septemvriiska Slava, winning 2-1. Some of the players headed home while others travelled to the Black Sea resort of Varna for a well-earned holiday.

Back home, there was an end-of-season dinner to attend – the Championship Ball – at Pressed Steel in Cowley, with director Kevin Maxwell hosting, Peter Brackley as guest speaker and Bernie Winters closing the evening's entertainment.

Before the club could take a well-earned break and prepare for the First Division there was one last formality: a new contract for Jim Smith. On 29 May, Maxwell hosted a party in London to watch the European Cup Final between Liverpool and Juventus to sketch out the deal in a convivial atmosphere. Maxwell ushered Smith into a private room, a familiar routine where he would shuttle from one meeting to another. When he finally had his chairman's attention, Smith asked for £50,000 a year; Maxwell counter-offered with £47,000. As the discussions got under way, Maxwell's secretary Jean Baddeley, who Smith had met at his interview, came into the room and suggested the two men needed to see what was unfolding on television.

The BBC's build-up to the game had taken a dark turn. Reporting on English fan violence was not unusual, but as host Jimmy Hill introduced the coverage, it was clear that football was taking a back seat. Hill, Terry Venables and Graeme Souness traded rumours about the trouble that had flared before the game. Inside the inadequate stadium there was a sense of chaos as police milled around the perimeter running track. A wall had collapsed after rioting Liverpool fans had penned their Juventus counterparts into a corner of one of the stands. There were reports of injuries, rumours of fatalities, then confirmation. Thirty-nine people would be declared dead in the stadium, mostly Italians. Maxwell and Smith's negotiations were put on hold as the disaster unfolded.

The following day, prime minister Margaret Thatcher asked the FA to withdraw English clubs from European competition and a week later UEFA announced an English ban for the foreseeable future.

On 3 June, Maxwell phoned Jim Hunt to call a board meeting for 3pm. Hunt said it wouldn't be possible to get all the directors to attend at such short notice. Maxwell assured him that it wasn't necessary for everyone to be there if Smith could make it.

Smith and Hunt walked in to find Maxwell with former Fulham financial director Brian Dalton and introduced him as the club's new managing director. The chairman explained that Dalton would take control of everything apart from team affairs. Three days later, Dalton was unveiled to the press, much to Smith's growing discomfort.

Dalton's appointment was the breaking point and Smith was now actively considering his options. Lawrie McMenemy had just left Southampton and Smith thought the role suited him perfectly. Then he was contacted by Dennis Signy, a football journalist, and the former chief executive at Queens Park Rangers. Signy had links with QPR chairman Jim Gregory, who'd dispensed with their manager Frank Sibley the previous week.

Smith was making his move; in London he met with Gregory, who had a reputation for being tricky to work with. Smith reasoned that nobody could be more difficult than Maxwell.

After four hours of negotiation, Smith and Gregory struck a deal. On Maxwell's 63rd birthday, Smith handed in his resignation. He'd got his £50,000 salary and phoned the players in Portugal to announce he was leaving. There was a disbelieving silence; Jim Smith had walked out on Oxford United.

Chapter 13

Maurice Evans

THE BOOMING voice, the statements framed as questions; the only thing unfamiliar about Robert Maxwell's offer to Maurice Evans to replace Jim Smith as Oxford manager was that Evans said no.

The club Maxwell had transformed had just two months to prepare for the biggest season in its history without its chief architect. Norwich City striker Mick Channon was quick to apply for the vacant job, but Maxwell's first choice was Evans, Smith's right-hand man. The problem was that Evans didn't want the job.

Maxwell's bungled merger had been at the heart of his resistance: he'd been broken by the saga. A quintessential football man, he'd been brutally exposed to the greed in the game, forced to defend his club's integrity while his employers sold it for the highest price. His association with Reading lasted for nearly 30 years but his sacking by Roger Smee was a betrayal that left him never wanting to work in football again, let alone manage a club.

Jim Smith lured him out of exile as chief scout and youth development officer. The role played to his strengths but on his first day he unpacked his files and sat in his office, it was unfamiliar territory, away from the training ground and players. He was desk-bound, an office worker, he had to teach himself to type. He hated it. He didn't think he'd last a week. But the two men complemented each other perfectly, Smith outgoing and exuberant with Evans studious and detailed, mining the divisions for talent to fit Smith's vision.

He didn't want to return to the front line and didn't fear the consequences of his resistance. Nothing could be as bad as his experience at Reading, which stripped him of everything but his integrity, something Maxwell couldn't buy.

Smith tried to take him to QPR, but instead he agreed to stay and take temporary charge so preparations for the new season could continue; the team deserved that, at least. Evans refused to sign a contract, saying they weren't needed when people trusted each other. It tied Maxwell into an agreement more powerful than anything written on paper. Any misstep, Evans would walk and Maxwell would flounder; a constant tension to put his chairman at arm's length.

In the aftermath of Heysel, Bradford, Birmingham and Luton, the authorities had a mandate to act. There'd long been a frothing debate about how to cure the 'English disease' with commentators and media suggesting everything from longer prison sentences to national service. Maxwell wanted the FA and Football League to merge and walked out of the league's AGM when they wouldn't discuss Heysel.

Chelsea chairman Ken Bates installed an 11ft-high electrified barbed wire fence around three-quarters of Stamford Bridge, identical to one he erected at his dairy farm, treating the fans like cattle.

The government appointed Lord Justice Popplewell to lead an inquiry. His interim report, in July 1985, was damning. It recommended improvements to stadiums, stewarding, fire safety, and controversially, identity cards for football fans and the exclusion of away supporters. The FA had little option but to accept the recommendations, only resisting identity cards while the practicalities were worked out. Oxford were enthusiastic signatories to the plan.

The European ban had an early bizarre consequence; Oxford's pre-season friendly against Newport County was cancelled when the team was prevented from crossing the Welsh border to play.

Maxwell was sanguine; the problems were the result of a long decline and incompetent administration. He likened it to the newspaper industry and his battle with the print unions. He'd won that, allowing for modernisation, and he was ready for more confrontation.

The first clash came as negotiations between the Football League and the BBC and ITV over TV rights stalled. After another deal was rejected, the Football League changed strategy, trying to split the two channels by auctioning the rights to the highest bidder.

To sharpen the league's commercial resolve, Maxwell tabled a motion to remove Norwich City's Sir Arthur South as chairman of the negotiating team. Maxwell's preferred candidate, Everton's Philip Carter, had no idea he was about to be nominated and had no intention of standing. When the proposal was rejected, Maxwell resigned from the committee, taking it as a sign of the League's inadequacies. To add to his humiliation, the committee chose not to replace him.

Back at the Manor, secretary Jim Hunt received the confirmation he'd long feared: new stadium regulations would hit his club more than any other. The Manor was small and antiquated, and as Oxford's rise had been so rapid, even without the new rules their infrastructure was at breaking point. With a capacity over the threshold of 10,000, a new safety licence was required. Home secretary Leon Brittan issued a declaration to the club at the beginning of July confirming the need for changes.

With the support of £250,000 from the council, a programme of work started with construction firm Bovis as lead contractor. The total cost would be more than £1.25m, a bill out of the reach of most clubs. The Osler Road terrace was rebuilt, creating two seated stands, and the pitch was surrounded by a high, obstructive fence. The London Road terrace was partitioned with a steel divide. The only aesthetic upgrade was an angular arch over the London Road entrance.

Stewards and fire marshals were recruited and gates preventing fans from moving between stands were constructed, meaning some turnstiles were no longer operational. Those in charge worried about how they would get fans in for kick-off and, mindful of the challenges of getting them into the ground for big Milk Cup ties, they declared every game all-ticket.

The preparations affected every aspect of the club; alongside the construction, ticket office manager Mick Brown worked overtime to process 7,000 season ticket applications. The hive of activity and Evans's reluctance to take the manager's role permanently meant there was just one pre-season signing: Welsh international full-back Neil Slatter from Bristol Rovers.

By August, the Manor had gone through a miraculous transformation, sacrificing some of its soul in the process. *The Times* described it as being like 'the home of a builder who specialises in extensions and has taken advantage of lavish planning permission'; it was a Frankenstein's monster of the archaic and modern.

The top flight offered other opportunities. The club opened Top Gear, a new club shop on the corner of London Road and Osler Road, and filled it with merchandise including their new Umbro kit.

Before his departure, Jim Smith knew the club's commercial value was growing and called his contacts at

Adidas to negotiate a new kit and equipment deal. He knew they couldn't feature the *Sunday People* on their shirt if they wanted coverage in rival newspapers, so Smith asked Maxwell who he wanted in its place.

Maxwell was incensed at Smith's deal, saying it was tiny compared to Manchester United and Liverpool. He cancelled the arrangement and approached Adidas's rivals Umbro, returning with a new kit agreement. When Smith asked who were supplying their training equipment, Maxwell had no idea. Smith had to sheepishly returned to Adidas to do another deal, meaning the team would play in Umbro while using Adidas equipment.

The new shirt departed from the bright yellow and royal blue of the Spall Sports kit in favour of a paler yellow with navy blue shorts and socks. On the front, the club's new sponsor, American computing corporation Wang Computers, a £300,000 deal struck by Maxwell.

The season opened on 17 August with a trip to West Bromwich Albion. John Aldridge, fresh from signing a new four-year contract, couldn't sleep in anticipation of his and the club's biggest day. Maxwell, unable to attend, sent an idiosyncratic message of encouragement, 'If you win the toss, go for an early goal.'

Albion had finished mid-table the previous season and invested heavily in a new frontline of Imre Varadi from Sheffield Wednesday and former Tottenham and England under-21 forward Garth Crooks.

Backed by 3,000 Oxford fans, after six minutes, Gary Briggs marked his arrival in the top tier with a crunching challenge in the box which swept Crooks's legs from under him. The referee waved away appeals for a penalty. Encouraged, 12 minutes later, he landed another juddering challenge in the centre circle, leaving Crooks limping badly. With less than 20 minutes of the season gone, Crooks was replaced due to ligament damage. Briggs had claimed his first victim.

The two sides went in at the break level. As the second half progressed Oxford grew more confident, and with half an hour remaining West Brom were reduced to ten men when Tony Grealish was stretchered off after colliding with Trevor Hebberd.

Having overcome initial stage fright, Oxford found themselves in control but the Baggies' enforced reshuffle disrupted their rhythm. Minutes after Grealish's departure, Carl Valentine fed Jimmy Nicholl, who miscued his cross into the box. Steve Hardwick misjudged its flight, allowing Varadi to bundle him and the ball into the net for the opening goal.

With Oxford chasing the game, Billy Hamilton tired up front so Maurice Evans introduced Jeremy Charles to regain some composure. With 15 minutes to go, as Oxford pressed, Malcolm Shotton's shot was deflected for a corner. Kevin Brock's first cross was cleared straight back to him. He re-set, delivering a composed cross to Bobby McDonald to head home the club's first goal in the top flight. Despite a late scare when Steve Mackenzie hit the bar, Oxford saw the game out to take their first point in the First Division.

Four days later, they welcomed Tottenham Hotspur to the Manor for their first home game in the top flight. Illustrating the new world Oxford now occupied, Spurs had spent over £1m on Chris Waddle and Paul Allen to add to a host of internationals including World Cup winner Osvaldo Ardiles and generational talent Glenn Hoddle. It was the kind of league fixture a club like Oxford could only have dreamed of a few years earlier.

Before the game, scenes at the turnstiles were chaotic. The club had offered combined tickets for Tottenham and the upcoming fixture against Leicester City to prevent touts from benefitting from the anticipated demand. The Manor had sacrificed 1,500 from its capacity due to its questionable improvements, but only 10,600 tickets were sold, 3,000 fewer than the last game of the previous season.

Those unaware of the new ticketing policies arrived trying to pay with cash, while others baulked at the price increases. Inside the ground, many were confronted for the first time with the new-look Manor. Each stand was caged in, even the homely, shallow Osler Road terrace, where many young fans first experienced Oxford United before graduating to London Road. The Manor was a prison with the innocent trapped alongside the guilty. In the home end, fans mockingly sang their allegiance to the right or left side of the terrace, a slave song.

Starting without Aldridge, suspended after a sending-off in a pre-season friendly against Brighton, the warm, sticky evening threatened to stifle the game as Shotton and Briggs settled into their role of First Division enforcers, containing Spurs' attack.

After half an hour, Ardiles wriggled through the Oxford defence and gave himself the opportunity to cross, from which the ball fell to Mitchell Thomas with time to pick his spot and make it 1-0.

Kevin Brock nearly equalised immediately after half-time as rain cleared the muggy atmosphere. Hamilton battled valiantly without his strike partner, having a goal disallowed for a foul on England keeper Ray Clemence. For the second game running Jeremy Charles made a telling contribution, coming on for the injured Mark Jones and looping a header over Clemence for the equaliser with two minutes remaining.

A breathless week continued with the announcement that Robert Maxwell was publishing a book about the club's rise through the divisions. *The Rise and Rise of Oxford United* would be released in November and given free to all Pergamon employees. 'It wasn't until manager Jim Smith and chairman Robert Maxwell took over that the club enjoyed its meteoric rise,' gushed the press release, ignoring their recent acrimonious split.

On the field, Oxford returned to the Manor to face Leicester, who'd beaten the league champions Everton on the opening day. Again, the crowd failed to break the 10,000 mark, but any sense of inadequacy was cast aside when Hebberd finished a fine move after 25 minutes for 1-0. Fifteen minutes later it was two as Hamilton fired past keeper Ian Andrews. The third came after an hour from Charles. Ten minutes later Trewick scored a penalty before Hamilton completed the thrashing.

Gordon Milne, Leicester's manager, was magnanimous; his team had been outclassed in every department. Although Maurice Evans had publicly declared his resistance to taking on the manager's role permanently, the win – and a Fiat Performance of the Week award – encouraged him to accept the job until the end of the season.

Oxford United had arrived in the First Division, winning in the style that had taken them to two championships.

Sadly, nobody outside the stadium could see or hear any of it. The stalemate over broadcasting rights meant not only that there were no live games or highlights on television, BBC Radio Oxford were reduced to half- and full-time news reports.

The contention was the number of live games channels were permitted to broadcast, but there was a deeper issue. Football was synonymous with violence and disaster; England had qualified for one World Cup in 15 years and its clubs were banned from Europe. The league's star player was Manchester United's Bryan Robson, a tough-tackling midfielder, not a box-office celebrity like George Best, Stanley Matthews or Jimmy Greaves. The TV market was limited to two channels at a time when other sports were thriving, family friendly and easy to cover. The epic World Snooker Championship Final in April 1985 between Steve Davis and winner Dennis Taylor had attracted an audience of 18.5 million viewers despite finishing after midnight. Football was squeezed to the margins.

The mantra was that TV and football needed each other, but Robert Maxwell felt the Football League should determine the terms of a deal; more money and less coverage to protect attendances. He envisaged a model like American football, whose pay-per-view *Monday Night Football* broadcast was a lucrative national institution. Traditionalists were less sure; the league's lumbering committees meant gaining a consensus was difficult.

Oxford had more immediate problems: crowds had exceeded 10,000 just once and fans who attended complained about the new obstructions. Jim Hunt immediately set about seeking permission to alter the fencing, but the response from the council was slow, leaving the club to endure complaints when they could do little more than wait.

Worse still, the team were soon struggling. John Aldridge returned for a bad-tempered visit to Birmingham, scoring his first top-flight goal with a 25-yard drive after 14 minutes. But it would prove to be his first defeat when scoring for Oxford after a deflected own goal from Briggs brought Birmingham their equaliser before the team were out-muscled 3-1.

Afterwards the managers traded insults, continuing the war of words from the previous season. Evans said, 'I couldn't believe what I was watching. If this is First Division football, I wouldn't pay to watch it.' Ron Saunders responded, '[Bobby McDonald] elbowed Hopkins in the face and the referee didn't even book him. Oxford started the trouble and couldn't finish it off.'

A 1-0 defeat to workaday Sheffield Wednesday in front of just over 9,300 followed. For two years Jim Smith's side had entertained with fluid attacking football, but now Oxford needed to find a way to grind out results.

Usually a purist, Evans's tone changed, praising the merits of Wednesday's style and admitting, '[Owls boss] Howard Wilkinson has got ordinary First Division players, organised them, made them work and here they are in second place.' Perhaps he needed to do the same, though it was hardly in Smith's original vision.

September opened with a 5-2 defeat to Coventry, despite twice taking the lead through McDonald, the first after just two minutes. Oxford had shown their attacking threat and their defensive weakness. For the second time in three games Briggs put the ball in his own net and they lost Hamilton to another injury, forcing him out of the Northern Ireland squad.

By contrast, Ron Atkinson at Manchester United had made a dream start to his season, registering six consecutive wins and winning the Bell's Manager of the Month award, although a post-Heysel ban on alcohol meant the traditional prize of a bottle of whisky couldn't be presented on the pitch.

While the rest of the league floundered with falling attendances, over 50,000 people were at Old Trafford for Oxford's visit, a marked departure from the dour half-empty stadium of their Milk Cup replay in 1983. The visitors were quickly overwhelmed, happy to reach the break only two down after goals from Bryan Robson and Norman Whiteside. In the second half, Gordon Strachan fed Peter Barnes to drive past Hardwick for three. It was the middle of September; Oxford were 19th and their top scorer was full-back Bobby McDonald.

As glamorous as facing Manchester United and Arsenal in the Milk Cup was, United were searching for their first title for 20 years, while Arsenal's 1971 championship had been their only such success in 30. They felt like ageing bar-room crooners occasionally hitting the right notes.

Their failure was because of one club: Liverpool, the dominant winning machine of the era. The previous season, though, had been a humiliation, ending without a trophy for the first time in a decade and losing the title to rivals Everton by 13 points. Then Heysel stained their period of dominance. The ban on English clubs in Europe meant they were tethered to the domestic game and blamed for a blight that was far bigger than them.

Elsewhere, the continental competitions that had lifted Liverpool to another level were about to resume without them. Visiting the Manor, with its now curious mix of ramshackle and modern, seemed both incongruous and appropriate. For the foreseeable future, Liverpool's dominance would be faintly parochial by comparison to their recent past.

Nonetheless, their starting 11 contained nine European Cup winners – only Jan Mølby and Steve Nicol hadn't won it, and both were full internationals. Oxford, at least, could field their new signing, midfielder Ray Houghton from Fulham.

The big games at the Manor over recent years had been shrouded in a claustrophobic darkness. The low glow of the ground's floodlights created an isolating and uncomfortable environment for teams used to playing in vast, open theatres. When Oxford attacked out of the gloom, it had been disorientating, discomforting and devastating.

By contrast for the visit of Liverpool, the early autumn sunlight presented the Manor as a rustic idyll. Liverpool fans used to occupying the terraces of Munich, Milan and Madrid were packed into the Cuckoo Lane End lined with lush green beech trees.

The hosts needed to generate an intensity to dislodge the visitors from their rhythm. Liverpool may have been an all-dominating force across Europe, but they were also uncompromising, particularly with the addition of Steve McMahon, making his debut in midfield.

Oxford opened tenaciously, forcing their opponents to rush passes and snatch at shots from range. When the opportunity came to attack, they did so with numbers. When a combination of Houghton, Charles and Briggs bundled Bruce Grobbelaar and Mark Lawrenson into the back of their net following a corner, Liverpool knew they were in a game. It was a sobering introduction; their imperious captain Alan Hansen would later admit that Oxford – with the fearsome Shotton and Briggs – were the first fixtures he'd look for at the start of the season.

Another corner nearly dropped to John Aldridge but he couldn't react quickly enough; Liverpool were rattled. After 15 frantic minutes, Steve Hardwick collected a feeble Craig Johnston chip and cleared to Aldridge, who won a throw from Alan Kennedy. Dave Langan took it quickly to Trewick, who combined with Houghton. Houghton released Langan, who reached the byline and chipped to Aldridge unmarked on the six-yard line to head home into the far corner beyond Grobbelaar for 1-0. Oxford had cut the Merseyside giants to ribbons.

They weren't going to give up their advantage easily. Five minutes later, during an untidy passage of play, Trevor Hebberd forlornly headed a loose ball high into the air. Ronnie Whelan leapt, but as he made contact, he felt the full force of John Trewick's boot in his face, enraging McMahon. Whelan, blood pouring from his head, left the field to be replaced by Paul Walsh.

The challenge took the sting out of the game, giving Liverpool time to regain their composure. Oxford defended stoutly with McDonald clearing off the line from Steve Nicol before another robust challenge, from Briggs on Walsh, saw him go into the book.

In the second half, Oxford briefly threatened before Liverpool's class started to tell. A beautifully worked move shifted from left to right before finding Mølby in space in the middle. His clever lofted ball released Rush, whose first touch appeared to hit his shoulder. A second touch beat the on-rushing Hardwick. The Welsh striker continued beyond the keeper, forcing the ball home for the equaliser.

Liverpool smelt blood, and with quarter of an hour to go, Rush's crossfield ball found Johnston, who emphatically fired in the second. The Cuckoo Lane End descended into chaos as Johnston paraded in front of them like a triumphant bullfighter, his prey bloodied on the floor.

Five minutes later, with Liverpool camped in Oxford's half, Kevin Brock was sacrificed for Peter Rhoades-Brown. Trevor Hebberd and Dave Langan, their socks rolled down to their ankles, chased shadows. Liverpool looked fresh, the gulf in class seemingly unbridgeable.

Three minutes remained and Liverpool relaxed, satisfied they'd secured the three points. Then Alan Kennedy's lazy free kick was easily cleared by Bobby McDonald to Rhoades-Brown just inside the Oxford half. Still fresh, Rhoades-Brown broke clear, running 40 yards and weaving through the Liverpool midfield. But as he threatened, he under-hit his through ball to Jeremy Charles, and Kennedy moved across to intercept. Sensing Grobbelaar was on his line, the full-back played the ball back to the safety of his goalkeeper. For someone with Kennedy's experience, it was a foolish blind pass. Unknown to Kennedy, Grobbelaar had advanced to the penalty spot, anticipating a cross. Stranded, the pass wrong-footed the Zimbabwean keeper and, unable to adjust his feet, he watched the ball bounce into the goal for the equaliser. The Manor exploded into chaos; another giant had been humbled.

With a draw that felt like a win, Oxford were ready to fight for what they had. To survive, they needed fortitude and fortune, ingenuity, grit and teamwork. The First Division was going to be a wild ride.

Chapter 14

Ray Houghton

RAY HOUGHTON may have been forgiven for thinking his football career was cursed. Born in Castlemilk in Glasgow, a couple of miles from Hampden Park, he grew up a Celtic fan, idolising Kenny Dalglish whose busy, industrious style he emulated.

But, before he had the opportunity to follow his neighbour Arthur Graham into the professional game, his family moved to London. He left school and took an office job while playing for Willesden.

Aged 17, Houghton went to watch a friend playing in a trial for West Ham and was invited to play, showing enough promise to be offered a deal. Finally able to realise his dream, he signed professional terms at Upton Park and set his sights on international recognition. Manager John Lyall sent him to Scotland for under-18 trials. But national team boss Andy Roxburgh ignored the English-based players; Houghton described it as the worst week of his life. He never heard from them again and his national career seemed over before it started.

Back in London, West Ham were recovering from relegation in 1978, winning the FA Cup in 1980 and promotion the following season. They were built around a stable midfield of Trevor Brooking, Alan Devonshire and Geoff Pike, limiting Houghton to one substitute appearance. In 1982, Lyall offered Houghton a free transfer.

Dejected, Houghton went to Majorca on holiday, returning to find a letter from Malcolm Macdonald offering him an opportunity at Fulham. Houghton grabbed his chance, putting in a man-of-the-match debut at home to Rotherham before scoring his first league goal against Bolton at the beginning of September. He was ever-present that season and became a key player; he even became a local hero when he saved two elderly sisters from a mugging in King's Cross that made the national papers.

Despite topping the table in October, on the final day of the season Fulham were outside the promotion places behind Leicester on goal difference. Fulham travelled to the Baseball Ground to face relegation-threatened Derby needing to better the Foxes' result to go up. Leicester ground out a 0-0 draw with Burnley, raising the Londoners' hopes of snatching promotion.

But Fulham conceded with 20 minutes to go. Sensing survival, Derby fans gathered around the perimeter of the pitch as the final whistle approached. Steve Cherry tipped over Houghton's fierce drive, causing one fan to come on and pat the keeper on the back. With seconds remaining, referee Ray Chadwick blew for offside. Thinking it was the final whistle, Derby fans streamed on to the pitch. Fulham defender Jeff Hopkins was punched and had his shirt torn. With little prospect of order being restored, the referee abandoned the game and Fulham's chances of promotion withered away.

Following Houghton's breakthrough season, Reading manager Maurice Evans enquired about his availability, but Fulham weren't keen to give up their prize asset. A ligament injury contributed to a poor run of form before, in April and with the team sitting in 16th, Macdonald resigned.

Fearing his opportunity to play top-flight football was being affected by Macdonald's departure and their mid-table finish, Houghton asked new manager Ray Harford for a transfer. Despite interest, there were no bids and by November rumours circulated that Houghton might be ready to commit to a new long-term deal.

With his contract running down, vultures began to circle. Derby enquired, but the transfer deadline passed and Houghton along with three team-mates presented their manager with a cake as a token of their commitment until the end of the season.

After another mid-table finish, Houghton waited for offers. Steve Coppell at Crystal Palace kept a close eye and Jim Smith, initially keen to bring him to Oxford, wanted him to move to Queens Park Rangers.

Houghton wanted First Division football and to stay in London where he'd settled with his wife, but Sheffield United were first to open negotiations. He asked for more time to think over the offer, knowing Smith was waiting for Jim Gregory to return from holiday before making a bid. Houghton continued his pre-season preparations with Fulham, including a private game against Oxford.

Negotiations between Fulham and QPR were slow, and eventually Smith pulled the plug on the deal. 'It's dragged on so long that I decided it couldn't be right for us,' he said. Houghton was stunned; his career seemed to be stalling again.

Newcastle showed interest but Houghton started the new season at Craven Cottage. West Brom made an enquiry when their midfielder Steve Hunt put in a transfer request. Injuries at The Hawthorns offered opportunities and by the end of August, Houghton looked certain to sign.

But, with their season starting poorly and with Houghton stuck in a transfer chain waiting for other deals to be completed, progress was sluggish. He agreed terms, but the Baggies were reluctant to pay the £150,000 fee. Then another club stepped in.

The press speculated that the mystery club was Newcastle, but in fact Maurice Evans had swooped in with £125,000 in cash, plus Gary Barnett and reserve Jim Hicks. Houghton was an Oxford man, ready for his debut against Liverpool.

Oxford were so used to outclassing their opponents in the Second Division that adjusting to the harsher realities of the top flight took time. They hoped to build on the draw against Liverpool at Newcastle but fell apart in the last 25 minutes when Peter Beardsley drove home the opening goal before combining with prodigious teenager Paul Gascoigne to set up Neil McDonald for the second five minutes later.

In the last minute, Gascoigne waltzed through the Oxford defence to score his first senior goal. Evans's day got worse when he had to race home ahead of the team coach after hearing his teenage son had lost two teeth in a car accident.

Home form was more encouraging – John Trewick's penalty gave Evans his first official win as manager in a 1-0 victory over Manchester City, but on the road was different.

Evans knew his team would score goals, but he also knew they'd concede. There was no greater illustration than at Filbert Street against Leicester the following Wednesday. Andy Thomas opened the scoring after three minutes only for Alan Smith to equalise after 24. Ian Wilson grabbed a second three minutes later. Just before half-time, John O'Neill was harshly punished for a challenge on Houghton, allowing Trewick to score from the spot for 2-2.

There was no let-up after the break as John Aldridge latched on to Trevor Hebberd's through ball for 3-2 only for Gary McAllister to level again with 18 minutes to go. Seeking their first away win of the season, Aldridge was pulled down inside the box by O'Neill. Expecting a penalty, the Oxford players were perplexed by the referee's decision to award a free kick. Minutes later Aldridge hit back, making it 4-3 from 12 yards but with a minute to go Gary Briggs barged Mark Bright over in the box and Steve Lynex equalised from the spot for 4-4.

Evans seethed at the wasted opportunity as Oxford travelled to Goodison Park to play Everton. A Graeme Sharp goal two minutes before half-time gave the home side the lead, but the game descended into controversy when teenage defender Ian Marshall appeared to catch the ball inside his own penalty area.

Oxford appealed but referee George Tyson judged that Marshall had been pushed. Rather than award a free kick, he played advantage, and Everton broke at speed, allowing Paul Bracewell to fire in a deflected shot for the winner. Evans stormed from his bench and had to be restrained by players and the police.

Evans's brush with officials peaked a week later at the Manor. Trailing to a 24th-minute goal by Brian Stein against Luton, John Aldridge was sent off for fighting with Mitchell Thomas. Deep into the second half, with Oxford chasing the game, referee Ray Lewis stopped play. He refused to restart until Aldridge and Thomas, dressed in suits and sitting in the dugout, returned to the changing rooms. Another confrontation was averted when Hebberd equalised two minutes from time.

With one league win in ten, Oxford were 18th, needing an edge to survive at the top level. Third-placed Chelsea were the next visitors, on a run of five successive wins. Maurice Evans wasn't impressed. 'I've seen them twice before,' he said dismissively. 'I didn't think they were quite as good as their position.'

Fighting fire with fire, after half an hour Briggs disposed of left-back Doug Rougvie with an injured shoulder. The change allowed Houghton and Hebberd to seize control of midfield. A Dave Langan cross found Aldridge for 1-0 before Hebberd fed Peter Rhoades-Brown, whose thunderous drive made it two ten minutes later. Oxford sat back, allowing Evans's protege at Reading, Kerry Dixon, to pull a goal back, before they survived a late David Speedie miss to secure three valuable points.

Evans was warming to his task; although a man of principles, no reputation or form guide could be respected. Each point had to be fought for.

Oxford travelled to Watford, who were on a run of seven consecutive home wins, without the suspended John Aldridge. After four minutes, Watford led from a Wilf Rostron header and looked set to secure another win when Nigel Callaghan curled in a free kick for the second.

Despite the desperate situation, Hebberd and Houghton's influence in midfield began to tell again. With 19 minutes to go, Rhoades-Brown cut in from the left and chipped to the back post over the head of goalkeeper Tony Coton. The ball dropped, clipped the post and crept over the line for 2-1.

With something to chase, seven minutes later Langan broke down the right and crossed for makeshift striker Thomas. Coton parried Thomas's shot into the path of Houghton, who poked in the equaliser.

The emergence of Houghton and Hebberd couldn't disguise the fact Oxford were missing Billy Hamilton's commanding presence up front. This exposed Aldridge, who'd scored just four league goals. The lack of firepower put pressure on Oxford's shaky defence so Evans made Brian McDermott available for transfer and tabled a £150,000 bid for Hull City's combative striker Billy Whitehurst.

Nonetheless, unbeaten for most of October, Oxford were a point above the relegation zone. The season was taking shape; Oxford and their fellow promoted clubs – Manchester

City and Birmingham – were battling for survival with fading stars Ipswich Town and West Brom.

With a relegation battle in prospect, Oxford's favourite competition offered some relief. Their Milk Cup campaign opened inauspiciously against Northampton Town in front of just 5,600 fans. The Fourth Division side led after 21 minutes from Ian Benjamin before Rhoades-Brown equalised and Houghton scored with 17 minutes to go. In the last minute, Steve Hardwick brought down Trevor Morley for a penalty, but Oxford avoided an embarrassing draw when Phil Cavener put the ball wide. They finished the job in the second leg after a 2-0 win with goals from John Aldridge.

In the third round, they drew Newcastle United at the Manor in a rerun of their breakthrough win in 1983. With Aldridge suspended and Hamilton injured, Evans partnered Jeremy Charles with Andy Thomas, who converted Houghton's corner after 19 minutes. Tony Cunningham equalised before half-time, but five minutes into the second period Thomas got another and nearly had a hat-trick, shooting wide with the keeper to beat before capping a man-of-the-match performance by crossing to Hebberd for 3-1 with 15 minutes to go.

The win set up a third-round tie against holders Norwich City. It was a less glamorous campaign than in recent years but offered a more navigable path through the competition.

In the league, November started badly with a 2-0 defeat at Aston Villa and 2-1 reverse at home to title-chasing West Ham, despite leading through John Aldridge. They then travelled to Highbury to face Arsenal. Thirteen months on from their giant-killing, they were now peers as Jim Smith had predicted.

Goals from Paul Davis and Tony Woodcock in the first half put the Gunners in command before Jeremy Charles's goal pulled it back to 2-1. Oxford had the ball in the net a second time, but it was ruled out for offside. The three defeats saw them drop to 19th, with only goal difference keeping them out of the relegation zone.

This wasn't ideal form to face the Milk Cup holders for a place in the quarter-finals. Confidence was dented further when Kevin Drinkell opened the scoring after 14 minutes. The lead lasted ten minutes before Thomas beat Steve Bruce to cross to set up Aldridge for the equaliser. Thomas beat Bruce again before lobbing the keeper for the lead for 2-1. On 63 minutes, he completed another man-of-the-match performance by slaloming past two defenders before passing to Les Phillips for the third, setting up a quarter-final against Portsmouth.

Three days later Oxford returned to the Manor to face Norwich's East Anglian rivals Ipswich, who'd thrown a two-goal lead away against Everton to lose 4-3 the previous week. Keen to put that result behind them, Ipswich started brightly. After 24 minutes Kevin Wilson got on the end of a move between Trevor Putney and Jason Dozzell for 1-0 before Ian Cranson hit the bar minutes later.

Aldridge had a goal ruled out because Thomas was offside, but Ipswich were dominating. A minute before the break, Hebberd brought down Wilson in the box and Mark Brennan converted for 2-0. Aldridge went close early in the second half before Putney crossed to Mich d'Avray to knock down to Dozzell, who volleyed in number three after 53 minutes.

The Manor was dejected; Oxford's defence crumbled with every attack. Kicking towards the London Road terrace, they had one option. A minute after the restart, Trewick crossed for Aldridge to volley a goal back. Spurred on by the breakthrough, Langan raided the wing, crossing to Aldridge for another; in three minutes, the score had gone from 3-0 to 3-2.

With Aldridge hunting his first top-flight hat-trick, and the ghosts of the previous week haunting the visitors, Oxford swarmed forward. Just after the hour, young keeper Jon Hallworth buckled, dropping a cross at the feet of Aldridge, who prodded the equaliser. It had taken eight minutes to turn the game around.

With half an hour to play, Oxford surged down the slope, a primal roar thundered from the terraces, and the breakthrough finally came with ten minutes remaining when Houghton's corner dropped to Neil Slatter to prod home the winner. The frenetic London Road terrace surged with unbridled elation.

'We were rubbish in the first half,' Evans said with characteristic honesty. 'The only way we were going to get back in the game was to attack and fortunately we're good at it.'

Aldridge's lightning-quick hat-trick announced his arrival in the First Division, highlighting the fact that the more he scored, the better Oxford did, but also the more others took notice.

At the end of November, inspired by the novelty of a trip to Wembley Arena, Oxford fans turned out in vast numbers for the annual *Daily Express* five-a-side tournament. The noisy following, by far the biggest of any club, inspired a strong Oxford squad to dispatch the holders Watford in the first round and beat West Ham to set up a semi-final against Nottingham Forest. Goals from Hebberd, Aldridge, and star of the tournament Houghton set up a final against Arsenal.

Oxford fielded a strong side, featuring goalkeeper Paul Whittington, emergency cover from Oxford City. The tight game went to a penalty shoot-out where Whittington saved from Ian Allison, allowing Aldridge to score the trophy-winning spot kick.

December opened with a visit to Nottingham Forest. After 19 minutes, Neil Slatter, selected in place of the suspended Gary Briggs, fired a 30-yard pass to release Andy Thomas, who stylishly lobbed Forest keeper Steve Sutton for the opening goal.

The home side were booed off at half-time having failed to create a single chance, but they weren't allowed sanctuary for long when just five minutes later, the players reappeared on the pitch to wait for their opponents, an idiosyncratic punishment from the charismatic Brian Clough.

The public humiliation worked; Forest became more purposeful after the break and the pressure told almost immediately. Phillips was booked for a foul on Gary Mills before Bobby McDonald almost gave away a penalty for nudging over Nigel Clough.

As the game opened up, Oxford persevered with their directness. On the hour McDonald's clearance released Thomas again, but he shot wide. Forest responded and as Peter Davenport prepared to shoot, Slatter scythed him down for a penalty. Davenport converted, limiting Oxford to their fourth away point of the season.

Any confidence from the Forest result evaporated six days later as Oxford travelled to White Hart Lane to face Tottenham. Playing with Trevor Hebberd as a sweeper, after 12 minutes Andy Thomas, a highlight of the early season, clashed with Graham Roberts. The sharp pain was ominously familiar and Ken Fish quickly confirmed a broken foot.

By this point Oxford were already a goal down, and they trailed by three at half-time. Despite Aldridge's consolation, they collapsed to a 5-1 defeat. As they licked their wounds in the White Hart Lane dressing room, the draw for the third round of the FA Cup took place. Oxford were pleased to be at home, but their hearts sank when out of the hat next came the name Tottenham Hotspur.

After months of deadlock, there was finally some good news from the Football League. The league and TV companies struck an interim deal that would allow six live games for £2.5m. After nearly four months of blackout, Oxford's breakthrough season would finally be seen and heard by those at home.

Maurice Evans worried about Oxford's defence, who'd conceded 46 goals including 12 in their last four games. Even with the visit of bottom side West Brom to the Manor, he focussed training on the team's defensive shape.

There were few concerns up front; Aldridge's 16th goal of the season gave Oxford the lead from the spot before a rasping 25-yard drive from Steve Hunt brought Albion level. Imre Varadi made it 2-1 two minutes later, latching on to a 50-yard pass. On the hour, Jeremy Charles turned in Ray Houghton's cross to make it 2-2.

Despite the point, Evans was uncompromising in his verdict. 'Bloody awful,' he said. 'I thought it was rubbish out there. The way we defend is sheer recklessness.' With half the season complete, as Oxford's relegation fears lingered, Evans was forced to deny the club were in crisis, but there was little doubt that to survive, something had to change.

Evans was becoming more defensive in his tactics and towards his own performance. He pointed to the fact Andy Thomas was out for two months, Billy Hamilton was a long-term casualty, and Steve Hardwick, Jeremy Charles and Peter Rhoades-Brown were all on the treatment table, while Dave Langan, Les Phillips and Ray Houghton were carrying knocks.

The echoes of his predecessor returned as Robert Maxwell closed the Jim Smith era with the publication of *Rags to Riches*, the book celebrating Oxford's double championship win. It was distributed to Pergamon's 25,000 employees and inscribed with a note celebrating the company's expansion, scant compensation for the 1,600 Mirror Group workers he'd just made redundant.

Evans's Christmas present was 23-year-old striker David Leworthy from Tottenham for £175,000, a deal rushed through with minutes to spare before the FA closed for the holiday. Leworthy had suffered disciplinary problems at Portsmouth and was released after one appearance. He dropped into part-time football with Fareham, where Tottenham were alerted to his performances. Coming from non-league hung over him as he failed to make the breakthrough at White Hart Lane. Rumour was that Robert Maxwell signed him on the advice of the *Mirror*'s sports editor without consulting Evans, whose prime target had been Fulham's Dean Coney.

After one training session, Leworthy went straight into the side for the Boxing Day game against Southampton at the Manor and was even deprived of an introduction to the fans when the stadium's public address system failed. He lined up alongside Aldridge, with whom he hoped to build a strike partnership as potent as Kerry Dixon and David Speedie at Chelsea, Mark Hughes and Frank Stapleton at Manchester United and Gary Lineker and Graeme Sharp at Everton.

Steve Hardwick's injury meant Alan Judge also made his league debut. Southampton, without Peter Shilton or Mark Wright, were immediately exposed. Within two minutes Leworthy opened his account, finishing a decisive move. After 21 minutes, John Aldridge fired a penalty wide, hitting a cheerleader standing to the side of the goal. Nine minutes later Leworthy got his second after Phil Kite in the Southampton goal dropped the ball at his feet. Aldridge completed the scoring with a chipped effort from the edge of the box, but it was Leworthy's day.

After a mild December, temperatures plummeted and Oxford's visit to Coventry was postponed, meaning Evans was able to focus on their New Year's Day game and a trip to Jim Smith's Queens Park Rangers.

Smith had undergone a patchy start at Rangers: they'd progressed in the Milk Cup, but were mid-table and on a run of five defeats. Loftus Road's artificial surface offered some protection and only Arsenal had taken three points there all season.

Their luck was in after just three minutes when Houghton's goal was ruled offside and 20 minutes later Martin Allen miscued a shot that wrong-footed Alan Judge for the opening goal. The star of the show, John Byrne, then set up Wayne Fereday for the second with a majestic through ball.

In the second half, Oxford dragged themselves back into things with Leworthy getting his third in two games, but just as they thought they might salvage a point, Byrne capped a fine display with the third from close range, registering Smith's first win over his old friend.

Three days later Oxford returned to the Manor for their FA Cup third round tie against Tottenham. Attacking the London Road terrace, Oxford piled forward, over-running the midfield and isolating Spurs' attacking threat. The breakthrough came when Kevin Brock picked out the unmarked Neil Slatter to head home.

The game was held up for a short while after the referee was struck on the head with an object from the London Road terrace; the fences and other precautions hadn't quelled the perpetual unrest in the crowd.

With Briggs dominating, Clive Allen was replaced by the pacy John Chiedozie who, with 14 minutes remaining, connected with Glenn Hoddle's free kick to send the tie back to White Hart Lane.

With temperatures near freezing, the replay four days later was under threat. Heavy snow in London tested Spurs' new £11,000 plastic covering, but the referee declared the game on after an 11am pitch inspection. For Oxford, it was a distraction from their relegation worries but for Spurs, it was an opportunity to salvage a disappointing season.

Early on, Chris Waddle had the ball in the back of the net, firing past Judge, but Chiedozie was ruled offside. Oxford chipped away at Spurs' fragile confidence with Aldridge, Hebberd and Jones, in to replace Brock who was missing due to a stomach upset, going close.

On the half-hour mark, the pressure told as Phillips's cross created confusion in the box and Aldridge arrived at the far post to score past Clemence.

Spurs responded as Hoddle's back-heel set up a chance for Chiedozie before another chip nearly found Paul Allen. Under increasing pressure, Hebberd brought down Allen for a free kick, and as Oxford complained Hoddle slid the ball to Waddle to fire in the equaliser.

Rhoades-Brown nearly regained the lead and with four minutes to go Aldridge had a gilt-edged chance from Houghton's lob but couldn't force the winner.

The first half of extra time was goalless, but with eight minutes remaining, Hoddle's superb crossfield pass found Waddle whose low drive was turned smartly into the net by Clive Allen.

The brutal exit added to Oxford's injury problems; Evans had eight players on the sidelines with Phillips, Brock and Briggs all ruled out for the visit of league leaders Manchester United.

Depleted, Oxford battled to contain United, nearly conceding an early Hughes effort, returning to where he'd made his scoring debut two years earlier. They finally conceded when Norman Whiteside poked home after 11 minutes when Judge failed to hold Strachan's far-post free kick. Leworthy equalised just before the hour, a reward for Oxford's persistence, stealing in to get on the end of Trewick's free kick.

Oxford's injury problems began to tell as the game entered its final third. Seventeen minutes from time a spectacular volley by Hughes from Terry Gibson's cross made it 2-1, and within eight minutes Gibson directed Stapleton's wayward shot into the net for three.

The First Division could be a humbling environment; where once Oxford terrorised Manchester United over three titanic games, their systemic frailties were exposed. Each point was a precious gem and even when full and noisy the Manor could feel like a whimper. A 2-1 defeat at Sheffield Wednesday, including an own goal from Malcolm Shotton, underlined the challenge.

As always, the Milk Cup offered hope. For years Portsmouth had been a club that Oxford had aspired to be, and now the roles were reversed. The quarter-final brought no certainties; Portsmouth had beaten Tottenham in the previous round and were pushing for promotion from the Second Division.

After crowd trouble in 1982 and 1984, the club increased prices to £5 for a terrace ticket, inviting criticism from fans who saw the rise as opportunistic.

For all the great Milk Cup nights at the Manor, this one offered the best chance yet to progress to the semi-final.

Oxford took no chances, and after two minutes Phillips's shot deflected off Briggs past keeper Andy Gosney for the opening goal. Portsmouth's response played to Oxford's attacking strengths. Moving the ball with the verve of previous big nights, both Trewick and Charles went close, before Houghton robbed Lee Sandford at the corner flag, neatly passing it into the path of Phillips, who found the bottom corner for 2-0.

After the break Oxford played with poise and intelligence, their difficult First Division education paying dividends. With 20 minutes to go Charles was replaced by Mark Jones due to concussion before Slatter slammed home the third from a free kick. A last-minute consolation by Gary Stanley from 35 yards didn't dampen the mood and Oxford would play either Aston Villa or Arsenal in the semi-final.

Despite the progress, January concluded with a frustrating 1-0 defeat to Coventry which Maurice Evans called 'absolutely pathetic', and the team's league troubles continued as they faced Birmingham City, who were in an even deeper slump having not won for 17 games, costing Ron Saunders his job.

New manager John Bond had promised flair and imagination, but the game lived down to its expectations and a largely uninspiring relegation tussle was decided with 12 minutes to go when Wayne Clarke burst through to score, sending Oxford to their third home defeat in a row.

The defeat dumped Oxford into the relegation zone, and their season was being compared to Norwich City's who had won the Milk Cup while being relegated the previous year. Maurice Evans made a defiant but ominous prediction: 'We're too good to go down.'

Chapter 15

Jim Hunt

JIM HUNT was a committeeman who believed in collective will and strong administration, a tradition born of Victorian values and hewn through the war years. For Hunt, sound governance and stoic pragmatism was the cornerstone of success. When Robert Maxwell joined Oxford United he demanded 'loyalty, workmanship and honesty'. Hunt had all three.

Agelessly well presented, he seemed to be in perpetual middle age. Part of the wartime generation, he looked like he'd absorbed the great worries of the age. A sweep of grey hair was carefully lacquered into the style of an always man; his skin was sallow and his deep-set eyes framed by large, bushy eyebrows.

Despite 30 years with engineering firm Lucy's, he was mostly known across Oxfordshire sport through a close association with Kidlington Cricket Club. He joined Oxford United's supporters' club in 1969 as secretary before Tony Rosser invited him to become club secretary five years later.

During the 1970s, the stars who'd catapulted Oxford into the Football League faded and the club settled into a life of lower-league struggle. Hunt became the voice of the fans as hooliganism built a sinister momentum. He was resolute; the violence was youthful malevolence, a common view among those whose youth had been shredded by global conflict. The ill discipline of the postwar generation, indulged by a decade of liberalism, overshadowed the real supporters. For those who didn't live the values he felt so strongly, he advocated police dogs, national service and corporal punishment.

But beneath the stoic facade was a man of deep compassion and a fierce loyalty to his club and those within it. He showed an unquestioning allegiance to his chairmen, indulging Robert Maxwell's eccentricities, supporting anything beneficial to the club. He was almost paternal when negotiating transfers, ensuring that players got the best possible deal for themselves as well as the club.

Despite this, little could prepare him for 20 March 1977. Oxford had just lost 1-0 to Crystal Palace at the Manor after the visitors' Paul Hinshelwood had capitalised on an uncharacteristic mistake from reliable midfielder Peter Houseman.

Houseman had been a marquee signing by manager Gerry Summers in 1975, joining from Chelsea where he'd become a hero after scoring in the 1970 FA Cup Final. His time at Oxford had been less successful, but he and his wife Sally had settled into a comfortable life at their new home in Witney with their three young children.

The Housemans commiserated with friends Allan and Evelyn Bennett at a charity fundraiser for the club at Cowley Workers' Social Club that evening.

On the way home, the foursome were driving along the A40 near the Godstow Flyover in their Hillman Avenger. As they overtook another car, a Maserati came over the brow of the hill travelling at nearly 100mph. The force of the collision broke the Maserati in two and killed the Housemans and Bennetts instantly, orphaning six children.

Bartholomew Smith, the 22-year-old son of Conservative MP John Smith, was returning from a dinner party. He had a history of reckless driving and was later banned for ten years, only escaping jail because the John Radcliffe Infirmary didn't have time to test whether he'd been drinking on the night of the crash.

Hunt was thrust into the spotlight, the solemn, reassuring voice of Oxford United on a national stage. He absorbed the overwhelming tragedy, the club's darkest day. Hunt's resilience protected those he felt most deeply about – the club and the people within it. He was the rock around which others flowed.

During the early 1980s, Hunt took the burden of responsibility as the club was steered towards its financial abyss. Where others may have fled, he remained determined to find a solution. It was he who picked up the phone to Robert Maxwell.

Success brought a landslide of new challenges. For years Hunt had battled to get fans into the Manor, and now with the stands overflowing, ticketing was a constant problem as well as crowd trouble and FA investigations. Now in the First Division, he faced a formidable new force: the biggest clubs in the land. But Hunt wasn't someone who backed away from a challenge.

In February 1986, a blanket of snow covered the UK as temperatures dropped to the coldest on record, decimating the football calendar including Oxford's Milk Cup semi-final against Aston Villa, after they'd beaten Arsenal.

Firmly in the First Division's relegation zone, Oxford travelled to third-placed Chelsea, who were two points behind leaders Everton with two games in hand. Everton's visit to Watford was a victim of the weather and Manchester United's game against Liverpool had been moved to Sunday to feature live on television, giving Chelsea the opportunity to top the table for the first time in 20 years.

It wasn't Oxford's first trip to Stamford Bridge that season; since reaching the Second Division in 1984 they'd become full members of the Football League. With only a year to get used to their new status and navigate the politics of the game they were still naive to the power structures that existed although, with Maxwell, they feared no one.

Stadium safety, hooliganism, financial collapse, a potential Super League and the role of TV all competed for attention. But first, the Football League had to fill the gaps in the fixture calendar left by the European ban. It led to the creation of the English Super Cup for those who would have qualified for Europe. To ensure the idea was voted through, a Full Members' Cup was introduced for the remaining teams in the top two divisions.

The media were hostile, questioning the value of a competition without the country's biggest teams. For Oxford, the absence of the bigger clubs offered a realistic chance of progressing. Jim Hunt, a vocal supporter, found an ally in Chelsea's Ken Bates, who argued that, given the state of the game, any innovation was worth a try.

Others disagreed and the competition quickly ran into trouble: adding 200 fixtures to the calendar 'only makes sense in the land of greed', argued *The Times*.

Arsenal, West Ham, QPR, Blackburn Rovers and Wimbledon all withdrew, creating a more navigable path to the final for Oxford. The disagreements and a failure to find sponsorship meant the tournament was delayed until the middle of September, when Oxford drew Fulham and Shrewsbury Town in Group Six. Three days after the draw, more clubs pulled out.

At home to Shrewsbury, who Oxford had beaten to confirm promotion five months earlier, a strong side blew their Second Division opponents away 3-0, but the dismal crowd of 1,898 demonstrated the antipathy towards the competition. Managing director Brian Dalton remained unfazed. 'We went into the competition to fly the flag and not with the sole purpose of making money. Events will prove us right,' he said, incorrectly.

A 2-0 win over Fulham at Craven Cottage confirmed their passage to the quarter-finals where a single goal from John Aldridge overcame Stoke City, lining up a two-legged semi-final with Chelsea.

The first leg at the Manor was bad-tempered. After a quarter of an hour, Malcolm Shotton and Jerry Murphy exchanged blows, resulting in a melee. Fifteen minutes later, Keith Jones received a red card after a crunching challenge on his old team-mate, Peter Rhoades-Brown. With Chelsea down to ten men, Oxford's Wembley prospects seemed to be growing.

Then, seven minutes after the sending-off, Neil Slatter needlessly put the ball into his own net and the whole performance turned sour. Kerry Dixon doubled the lead shortly after half-time. Oxford responded with an Aldridge penalty, but as they chased the game, Dixon added two more in the last ten minutes for an emphatic 4-1 win. Maurice Evans fumed at the missed opportunity.

The second leg was turgid and processional. Steve Hardwick was injured, breaking a sequence of 150 games, giving Alan Judge his first team debut. Bobby McDonald and Dave Langan were also missing. Chelsea contained Oxford's limp threat until moments before half-time when Les Phillips threaded a pass to Trevor Hebberd to drive past Eddie Niedzwiecki for the winner.

Just after the break, Briggs broke two of David Speedie's teeth in an aerial challenge, leaving him concussed. At the final whistle both teams were booed off the pitch. It was an acrid tie in a wretched competition.

The chairmen of the finalists – Chelsea's Ken Bates and Manchester City's Peter Swales – argued that the final should be played at Wembley on a Saturday to maximise the crowd but even by the semi-finals, the format hadn't been agreed nor Wembley booked.

Before the second leg, and with Oxford still technically in the competition, City and Chelsea approached the Football League for permission to postpone their fixtures on 1 March to play the final, the same day as Oxford were scheduled to play at City in the league. The authorities agreed when Bates and Swales promised to underwrite the cost of hiring Wembley. With Oxford's fixture against Everton the following week also likely to be postponed due to the FA Cup sixth round, Jim Hunt complained to the Football League Management Committee, claiming they'd broken their own rules.

The appeal was upheld, and the final was moved to Sunday, 23 March, the day after a full set of league fixtures, including the Manchester derby. Fittingly, it ended in a bizarre 5-4 win for Chelsea with David Speedie scoring the fastest hat-trick in Wembley history and Manchester City responding with three goals in the last five minutes. It had not been a normal competition.

When the news of Oxford's protest broke in January, the media were quick to pounce on the story branding Oxford 'spoilsports' for blocking the game. When Hunt arrived at the Manor the following morning, he found the club's answer machine full of abusive calls from Chelsea and Manchester City fans threatening an attack on Robert Maxwell. A note attached to a brick was delivered, threatening to burn the Manor to the ground. The club called the police.

By February, the outrage seemed to have passed and despite the weather, Oxford headed to Stamford Bridge, an archetype of 1980s football, with great swathes of uncovered, unloved terracing, a huge and incongruous cantilever main stand and The Shed, a lawless badlands and breeding ground for far-right hooligans. The pitch was surrounded by a running track with cars parked behind one goal. Ken Bates's anti-hooligan barbed wire fencing – its electricity thankfully turned off – topped off a cathedral of the unlovely.

It was a far cry from the sophisticated glamour of the 1970s but, unbeaten in the league since October, Chelsea sought to reclaim some of that lustre, attracting Scandinavian television to broadcast the game live.

Chelsea's form was underpinned by the goals of Dixon and Speedie, but with Dixon injured and Speedie suspended they were replaced by Duncan Shearer and Pat Nevin.

The snow and heavy conditions left the pitch saturated. Shearer toiled under the pressure of deputising for Dixon, and Nevin, a light, elfin winger, was bogged down in the heavy turf. By contrast, Briggs and Shotton resurrected their days in the lower tiers as Hebberd and Houghton controlled the midfield.

After 11 minutes, Colin Pates fouled Hebberd on the edge of the box. Houghton and Rhoades-Brown stood over the ball with Slatter favourite to take it. Houghton knocked the ball to Rhoades-Brown, who drove it beyond the wall and into the net for 1-0.

But for an air shot, Aldridge would have doubled the lead, then five minutes before half-time his run opened a space for Houghton to shoot fiercely. Niedzwiecki parried the ball to Jeremy Charles, who gratefully tapped home for 2-0.

In the second half, the sun disappeared, the temperature dropped and snow began to fall as Chelsea tried to resurrect their dwindling chances of going top of the table. But, with every missed chance, Shearer's confidence visibly drained.

With 20 minutes to go, Chelsea won a corner. Mickey Hazard's cross wasn't cleared and the ball dropped to John

Bumstead, who'd been pushed forward to chase the game. He controlled the ball and fired in for 2-1.

Chelsea's dream flickered briefly into life, but with a blunted attack and worsening conditions, Oxford held firm. As the game drifted into a frozen stupor, Hebberd caught Hazard dithering on the edge of the Chelsea box, exchanged passes with Aldridge, took a touch and slammed the ball in the net for 3-1. Oxford's shivering fans scattered on the open concrete terrace had to pinch themselves.

Within a minute Houghton sent Aldridge through to complete the rout, breaking a run of seven games without a goal. At 4-1, Chelsea fans streamed for the exits, their opportunity to witness a little piece of history crushed by the guile and determination of a team constantly creating their own.

The win, given the Fiat Performance of the Week award, lifted Oxford out of the relegation zone but there was no opportunity to build on it as the weather claimed their next two games against Watford and Newcastle United.

As the freeze continued, Maurice Evans sought to bring stability to his side. He needed experience to guide the team to safety, a role Ray Train and Colin Todd had played under Jim Smith. Kevin Brock was transfer-listed, feeling he was stuck in a rut. Evans knew that Steve Perryman's near-20-year career at Tottenham was coming to an end. After a club record 653 league appearances, debuting in 1969, leaving was a wrench so while talks continued with Spurs manager Peter Shreeve, Evans waited.

One game not impacted by the weather was Wales's friendly with Saudi Arabia in Dhahran. It gave an opportunity to Neil Slatter to win his 12th cap for his country. He had a mixed game: after half an hour, he nearly scored a spectacular own goal when his clearance cannoned off goalkeeper Neville Southall's chest. Then, two minutes into the second half, he picked the ball up on the right and miscued his cross into the top corner for his first international goal in a 2-1 win.

It would be nearly a month before Oxford returned to action, heading north to Maine Road to play Manchester City, the game that would have been postponed had it not been for Jim Hunt's protests.

City had played five games in February to Oxford's two. With the visitors heavy-legged from their lack of action, the home side could have put the game beyond Oxford's reach in the opening moments. On three occasions they scythed through the Oxford back four but couldn't convert.

Then, against the run of play, a long clearance from Neil Slatter found John Aldridge, who broke away to slide the ball past the keeper for an unlikely opening goal.

After Slatter cleared off the line on the half-hour mark, Oxford started to look more likely to score. With half-time approaching Rhoades-Brown crossed for Charles to side-foot home, and for the second away game in a row Oxford went into the break 2-0 up.

City couldn't get a foothold in the game as Oxford threatened to extend their lead. On the hour, Rhoades-Brown tackled Nicky Reid inside his own half and evaded a lumbering challenge from Johnson, then embarked on a blistering 60-yard run to cross for Aldridge to head home number three.

Demoralised, City fans emptied the stands as Aldridge nearly completed his hat-trick, crashing a shot off the bar. Despite losing John Trewick with bruising on his knee, Oxford, without an away win in ten months, had registered two in a row. Jim Hunt couldn't ignore the irony of beating the two clubs he'd fallen out with over the Full Members' Cup debacle.

With the Milk Cup semi-final finally on the horizon, Oxford had found their form just at the right time. Maurice

Evans knew that defensively Oxford were weak, but the heart of the side was Malcolm Shotton and Gary Briggs. John Aldridge was emerging as one of the country's top strikers and Trevor Hebberd and Ray Houghton could compete with the best; his team were out of the relegation zone and fighting for every point. Now they'd fight for a place at Wembley.

Chapter 16

Peter Rhoades-Brown

ON 13 FEBRUARY 1982, as Oxford suffered their miserable
FA Cup exit at Coventry City and Jim Smith ground out his
last point as manager of Birmingham at West Ham, Peter
Rhoades-Brown was exactly where he wanted to be.

Chelsea's Stamford Bridge was teeming with raw
emotion; a crowd four times its normal size was an echo of
their lost glory. Facing European champions Liverpool in the
FA Cup, their humble mid-table Second Division status for
once could fade into the background.

Chelsea, with one defeat in 14, had climbed to ninth in
the division. But Liverpool had scored 30 goals in 11 games,
conceding just four and winning their last five. When the
draw was made, Chelsea players had one question, 'How do
we contain them?'

It was the kind of game the 20-year-old Rhoades-Brown
had dreamed of. He was full of potential; after his debut
in 1979, his frustrating inconsistency meant he struggled
to match his rapid wing play with effective delivery. His
manager, John Neal, would advise him to 'run down the
left wing … but don't forget to turn right at the corner flag'.

After eight minutes Chelsea's early probing started to
expose their opponents' mortality. Rhoades-Brown teased

Phil Neal, setting up a half-chance that Chris Hutchings sliced harmlessly wide. Moments later, catching Liverpool square, Rhoades-Brown couldn't connect with a cross from Gary Locke. There was space to exploit, and given a chance, Rhoades-Brown knew he could have an impact.

As Liverpool calmly tried to tame Chelsea's enthusiasm, moving the ball away from the menacing right-back Lock to the opposite flank, Neal played a pass to Terry McDermott and set off into midfield anticipating it back. McDermott instead turned inside but his pass slowed in the rutted turf, allowing Colin Lee to nip in and evade a lunging challenge from Mark Lawrenson. With Neal hopelessly out of position, Lee's touch set Rhoades-Brown free.

The normally composed partnership of Alan Hansen and Mark Lawrenson desperately sprinted to catch the winger, but the former schoolboy county sprint champion wouldn't be caught. At the edge of the box, he looked up to see Bruce Grobbelaar on the six-yard line, seemingly startled by the speed of the attack. Not known for his finishing, Rhoades-Brown's scuffed shot seemed to surprise the Liverpool keeper and the ball squeezed beyond him and inside the left-hand post.

Rhoades-Brown was buried by his team-mates, and when he reappeared he sucked in great gulps of air, trying to regain his composure. There were still 83 minutes to resist the European champions.

Within minutes Rhoades-Brown broke down the left and placed a dangerous cross just beyond Clive Walker before Liverpool twice hit the woodwork. Despite constant pressure, Chelsea's resolute defending and 17-year-old goalkeeper Steve Francis kept the visitors at bay.

With eight minutes to go, Mike Fillery's quick free kick found Walker, whose hopeful cross caused a mix-up between Grobbelaar and Neal, allowing Lee to poke home and confirm the shock win.

Chelsea had claimed the greatest scalp in English football, announcing Rhoades-Brown to a national audience. His hopes of fulfilling his dream to play at Wembley seemed to be coming true.

But it was as close as he'd get; a narrow 3-2 quarter-final defeat to Spurs put paid to their hopes. A year later Chelsea narrowly avoided relegation from the Second Division and were bought by Ken Bates, who set about funding John Neal's rebuilding.

Rhoades-Brown found himself drifting to the margins of the rejuvenated squad. As the team prepared for a visit to Derby in 1984, he confronted his manager to force his way back into the reckoning. Neal absorbed Rhoades-Brown's demands, raising his hopes of a recall. A few days later he arrived for training and was told that his manager wanted to see him. Rhoades-Brown assumed he was back in the team.

Neal had two pieces of news: he'd signed Mickey Thomas from Stoke, a seasoned Welsh international who played in Rhoades-Brown's left-wing position, and Jim Smith at Oxford United had made a bid for him.

Like others before him, the move to the Manor transformed Rhoades-Brown's career. After the apparent step down, he'd secured back-to-back division titles and for the first time took his place in the First Division. Just one dream remained: to play at Wembley. Improbably, with a two-legged semi-final to come, Oxford were on the verge of giving him that chance.

Aston Villa's 1985/86 season had been propped up by their Milk Cup run; in the league they hadn't won since the middle of December or scored a goal for nearly two months. Maurice Evans sensed their fragility and after two convincing away wins, he knew he needed to go into the first leg and attack.

After three postponements, the tie coincided with the suspension of Villa's striker Andy Gray for the first leg, while Nigel Spink played in goal despite a broken finger. John Trewick had recovered from the injury that forced him off at Manchester City and Jeremy Charles played despite a throat infection.

The pitch had survived the cold snap and looked in good condition but even the milder weather and prospect of Wembley couldn't rouse Villa Park, which was half-empty apart from a full and boisterous away end.

Both teams were in a hurry to establish their authority and the early exchanges were full of energy but lacked craft. Villa's pressure was matched by Oxford's counter-attacking with Rhoades-Brown and Trevor Hebberd threatening down the wings. But passes went awry in the eagerness to find an opening.

Villa had the first chance when Simon Stainrod worked the ball to Mark Walters, only for the winger to shoot narrowly wide. Oxford's response was immediate as Hebberd's industry through the middle gave Ray Houghton space to look up and place a low cross into the Villa box for John Aldridge to volley past Spink for the opening goal; a moment of quality had sliced through the home side.

Building on their experiences against Chelsea and Manchester City, Oxford pressed home their advantage; if Villa pushed forward, they were exposed to Aldridge's pace. Only a series of crunching tackles allowed them to establish any authority, but that played into the hands of Gary Briggs, who relished the physical challenge.

As Villa pushed, Les Phillips broke away and Houghton peeled left, drawing defenders with him. It left Aldridge free on the right to look up and bend the ball high over Spink's head, only for it to crash off the underside of the bar.

Houghton then charged through Villa's defence, firing directly at Spink, before Hebberd's cross was hooked away by Dean Glover with Aldridge ready to convert.

Villa responded through Paul Birch, the one player who refused to give in. First, he fired a warning shot at Alan Judge before attacking down the left to deliver a cross that Stainrod could only head harmlessly into the ground.

A long throw from Darren Bradley then caused confusion in the Oxford box. Phillips's desperate header dropped to Birch who, despite being crowded out, took a touch and lashed the ball over Judge's head and into the net.

The balance shifted and seconds later Judge dropped a long free kick at the feet of Stainrod, but the striker's weak shot was cleared off the line by Malcolm Shotton. Oxford were happy for the referee to bring the breathless half to a close.

After the break, Rhoades-Brown charged down the left and crossed for Charles, who was still labouring after a heavy challenge from Paul Elliott, his weak connection allowing Spink to collect.

As the game grew more physical, the referee struggled to distinguish between fouls and tackles. Then on 55 minutes Villa forced a corner, from which Allan Evans flicked on to Stainrod, who got his head to the ball and directed it towards goal. Judge looked like he was being blocked as it dropped over the line with Phillips lunging to clear. Oxford players surrounded the referee, but he waved the protests away; 2-1.

After such a positive start, the tie was slipping away. The Oxford fans fell silent, hoarse from urging their side on, and their energy drained as momentum shifted. Then, seconds after the restart, Oxford played it long down the left channel for Aldridge, who slid to collect the ball under a challenge from Evans. The striker got to his feet and poked the ball beyond the defender, who wrestled him to the ground. The referee pointed to the spot as Oxford fans celebrated wildly behind the goal.

Aldridge positioned the ball carefully as Stainrod tried to distract him, but his composure didn't falter and he placed his kick beyond Spink for 2-2.

Oxford were winning the psychological battle; Houghton nearly gave Aldridge the chance to grab the winner before Shotton's free kick fell to Charles. With almost too much time to think, he side-footed the ball into the grateful arms of Spink. With two minutes to go, Phillips's cross dropped to Aldridge but for once, his instincts deserted him as he prodded at the ball. A final free kick from Stainrod drifted over Judge's bar and the referee called time.

If Maurice Evans's mission was to bring football back to the people, there could have been no better advert. Villa's heads dropped, as Oxford fans filled the stadium with noise. There was no doubt who had the advantage.

In the bar, John Aldridge celebrated knowing he was one win from Wembley when the new Republic of Ireland manager Jack Charlton approached him. Aldridge was eligible to play for the Republic through his great grandmother, who was from Athlone. With England enjoying a depth of attacking talent, Aldridge's age and unfashionable club meant that Ireland offered his only realistic chance of international honours.

Charlton saw beyond reputations and wanted eligible, hard-working footballers. Billy Hamilton's absence had helped Aldridge develop an edge to his game over the season. No longer shielded by the Irishman, he'd learned to find his own space and compete with the best defenders.

Charlton was also interested in Ray Houghton, after being alerted to the fact his father was Irish by Dave Langan. The best player on the pitch, Charlton could see Houghton's battling qualities fitted his plans.

The following night Jim Smith took his QPR team and their slender 1-0 first-leg lead to an expectant Anfield to face Liverpool in the other semi-final. Rangers' chances of progressing seemed remote, although a 2-1 league win earlier in the season gave them some hope.

They hadn't banked on the benevolence of their opponents who twice led but were pegged back by own goals from Ronnie Whelan on the hour and Gary Gillespie six minutes from time, allowing Rangers to go through 3-2 on aggregate.

Despite being on the cusp of Wembley, one person was unmoved by Oxford's progress. Dave Langan hadn't started a game since New Year's Day due to injury and the form of Neil Slatter. Momentum was gathering in the Republic of Ireland squad and Langan knew that, at 29, he needed to be playing first-team football. He approached Maurice Evans with a transfer request. Evans refused.

With no game on Saturday due to the FA Cup, Oxford were unchanged for the return leg. With Steve Hardwick going on loan to Crystal Palace to cover their injured keeper George Wood, Alan Judge kept his place. The transfer-listed Jeremy Charles was preferred to David Leworthy, offering Aldridge more protection.

The mood in the Villa camp was grim after a dismal 4-1 home defeat to Arsenal had led to a protest calling for Graham Turner's head. It made Villa's £75 champagne hospitality packages seem like a folly.

Momentum was with Oxford and the Milk Cup defined an unprecedented era in their history. The scramble for tickets was so fierce that Jim Hunt forgot to reserve one for Football League secretary Graham Kelly, who was left to join the hunt for spares.

The Manor was filled with destiny, brimming with familiar expectation. In the Beech Road stand, QPR manager Jim Smith looked on, contemplating the prospect of facing his old club at Wembley. Behind the Cuckoo Lane End, one Aston Villa fan collapsed and later died in hospital.

With tension swirling around the ground, Villa started with purpose; Birch and Walters pressured the home side down the wing. Their direct football and away form offered some salvation in a poor season, playing in a style Oxford had struggled to contain.

The pressing opened opportunities for counter-attacking. After 15 minutes, Oxford had their first opening when Aldridge laid the ball off to Houghton, whose shot was parried by Spink.

Although the midfield tussle dominated, Rhoades-Brown, fired by his Wembley dream, made inroads down the wing. Ten minutes before half-time he homed in on goal only to be brought down by Paul Elliott, who was injured and stretchered off, returning a few minutes later.

Maurice Evans sensed the growing tension; his team teetered on the cusp of either their greatest achievement or their biggest missed opportunity. In the dressing room at half-time he stood quietly, waiting for a hush to descend. 'You are all far too tense,' he said quietly. 'I drove past a hospital on my way here. People are dying while you're worrying too much about tonight.' His tone quietened further, 'It is only a game of football. So go out there and relax, enjoy your game, express yourselves and you'll do better.'

Returning to the cauldron of noise and attacking the London Road terrace, the players refocussed. The new physical dimension to Aldridge's game started to tell. On the hour he rose to head a long ball from Hebberd into the path of Les Phillips, giving the midfielder acres of space to set himself and drive emphatically past Nigel Spink for 1-0.

Filled with confidence and driven by a ferocious crowd, Oxford piled forward, impatient to make the game safe. They were denied a penalty when Tony Dorigo appeared to handle in the box, but 17 minutes from time, Rhoades-Brown's driven cross found Aldridge, who headed back towards Jeremy Charles to dive in and score the decisive second.

Noise billowed around the Manor like a typhoon, willing the clock to speed up, but with three minutes to go Mark Walters volleyed spectacularly from the edge of the box, putting the game back on a knife-edge.

As the tension built, Oxford edged their way to the whistle and finally confirmed their place at Wembley. For all that had gone before, this was a new level. Fans flooded on to the pitch again and Peter Rhoades-Brown buffeted in the chaos; headed towards the London Road terrace to celebrate, he was about to fulfil his ultimate dream.

The champagne flowed in the Oxford dressing room as Robert Maxwell joined the celebrations. Assistant manager Ray Graydon, a former Villa player, took four bottles into the away dressing room, but beat a hasty retreat when he saw the ashen faces of their defeated opponents.

Jim Smith would now face the team he'd created, a perfect narrative. For Maurice Evans, it was a nightmare; eight months into the job, he still felt like an imposter. 'What's happened hasn't changed my feeling that I never wanted to go back into management,' he said. He even joked that Smith should lead both teams out.

Evans didn't want the publicity that the final would bring, and even claimed he wasn't concerned about the result. 'I don't care what the score is,' he said, 'as long as we entertain the crowd. Otherwise, they won't bother to watch again.' He seemed haunted by the prospect of appearing at Wembley while the threat of relegation rumbled ominously in the background.

His fears eased three days later as form continued to improve. At Luton, an Aldridge penalty and Charles's strike brought Oxford's third away league win in a row. Aldridge's goal cemented his selection in Jack Charlton's first Republic of Ireland squad, to face Wales at Lansdowne Road alongside Houghton.

Wembley brought other challenges, with bookings and dismissals threatening suspension from the final. Newcastle manager Willie McFaul tested Gary Briggs's resolve by targeting him with Tony Cunningham and Billy Whitehurst. While Briggs stood firm, Neil Slatter had to be replaced by Dave Langan as the rough-housing brought its reward. Another Aldridge goal couldn't prevent a 2-1 defeat with spectacular goals from Paul Gascoigne and new England cap Peter Beardsley.

In west London, the Milk Cup Final narrative took another unexpected turn. QPR were at Chelsea and locked at 1-1 in the 90th minute. The explosive Jim Smith became involved in a pitchside altercation with Doug Rougvie and David Kerslake. The referee sent Smith to the stands, and with him the threat of a ban from Wembley.

John Aldridge was now in a dream state; over the next week the former Koppite who'd followed his team all over Europe was set to play against Liverpool at Anfield before making his international debut. Just one thing was missing: his Irish passport. Without his great grandmother's birth certificate and a £3 fee, nothing could be processed.

He eventually located it just before Oxford headed to Merseyside for their most daunting game of the season. Supporters were in a buoyant mood, under no illusions about the disparity between the two sides. Their only hope was that with the odds stacked so heavily against them, perhaps Liverpool would underestimate their opponents.

With Slatter's injury against Newcastle threatening to keep him out for some time, Dave Langan had an unexpected recall. Evans was delivered another crucial blow the day before the game when Alan Judge pulled out with a hip injury, meaning Steve Hardwick had to be recalled from his loan at Crystal Palace.

Anfield was a vast cathedral resonating with nearly 38,000 fans. It dwarfed Oxford emotionally, physically and mentally. The teams were led out by nine-year-old Liverpool fan and Oxford season ticket holder Jonathan Guiry, illustrating that for most the two clubs existed in different orbits.

Oxford were still getting used to their surroundings when, inside 60 seconds, Kenny Dalglish sent Ian Rush free to chip in the opening goal; Hardwick looked shell-shocked. Oxford tried to respond: Charles hit the bar and Ray Houghton was tigerish in midfield but in the 18th minute, Dalglish stepped up again to play Mark Lawrenson in for number two.

Seven minutes later Lawrenson was replaced due to injury, then Rush hit the bar twice in two minutes before Dalglish set up Ronnie Whelan for number three.

At half-time, Oxford received another blow when Briggs was replaced by Andy Thomas, forcing Charles into the fragile back four.

Jan Mølby took over in the second half with a 51st-minute penalty before Rush exchanged a one-two with the Dane to slam home number five. With a minute to go, the stars of the day, Dalglish and Mølby, combined for Mølby to score the sixth. The crowd were sated, aroused only briefly by the news that Everton had lost.

The Kop calmed to a satisfying hum; Oxford fans struck up a self-deprecating chorus of 'We only sing when we're losing'. In response, 'Aldo is a Scouser' rang out from the

Kop, filling the air. Aldridge headed for the tunnel, gazing into the stands that for years had been his home; perhaps there was a world for him beyond the Manor.

Maurice Evans could only marvel at Dalglish's performance and feebly accused his team of being pre-occupied by the Milk Cup Final and players' pool, but he knew they'd been outclassed.

The following Wednesday, despite outstanding debuts by Houghton and Aldridge, the Republic went down 1-0 to a Wales team featuring Jeremy Charles. An Ian Rush goal after a quarter of an hour was enough, although Aldridge, partnering QPR's Michael Robinson up front, hit the post with three minutes to play and Houghton cemented his growing reputation with a man-of-the-match performance.

Needing a calming influence in the squad, the Liverpool defeat re-energised Evans's interest in Steve Perryman. Tottenham's defeat to Everton in the FA Cup had seen Perryman dropped for the first time in his career. New contract negotiations stopped abruptly; his Spurs career was over.

Perryman went straight into the team for the much-anticipated return of Jim Smith to the Manor. Billed as a dress rehearsal for their Wembley encounter, both sides wanted to establish a psychological advantage.

After just 11 minutes QPR forward Leroy Rosenior's header was turned in by former Oxford schoolboy Clive Walker. Ten minutes later Houghton made up for a bad miss moments earlier by clinically converting a long ball from Rhoades-Brown, but Rangers hit back within a minute when Robinson's cross was chipped in by Martin Allen.

The start was breathtaking with both sides desperate to press home their advantage. But controlling the emotional flow was difficult. Allen, nicknamed 'Mad Dog' because of his reputation for aggression, flew into a shuddering tackle with Rhoades-Brown in the centre circle. It was a desperate, cynical and devastating challenge; Ken Fish wasted no time in ordering Rhoades-Brown off and insisting he go straight to hospital. It was a despairing but futile attempt to save the wingers' Wembley dream.

As Rhoades-Brown headed for surgery, transfer-listed substitute Kevin Brock made an immediate impact when he put through Jeremy Charles, whose shot was handled by Terry Fenwick, allowing Aldridge to convert the penalty. A minute before the break Fenwick made up for his error, converting his own spot kick after Gary Bannister was floored by Langan.

After the frenzied first half, Oxford controlled the second period and went closest when Houghton latched on to Brock's pass only to hit the post. With quarter of an hour to go, Rangers lost Warren Neill with a fractured cheekbone after a clash with Malcolm Shotton, putting him out of the final.

Oxford made it 3-3 when Aldridge was fouled by Alan McDonald, calmly slotting home the third penalty of the day, despite a lengthy delay while referee Neil Midgley fussed over the positioning of the ball.

While Rhoades-Brown sat in hospital ruminating at his lost opportunity, Evans was enthralled and frustrated by the spectacle. 'What a final it will be if it's anything like this,' he said. 'Much of the drama was supplied by the ref.'

Oxford headed to The Dell to face FA Cup semi-finalists Southampton. The distractions of Wembley and the fears of relegation did nothing to help the nervy and scrappy exchange. Aldridge's 34th-minute header opened the scoring but just before half-time, Mark Wright headed beyond Judge from eight yards from a corner.

The season was reaching its apex, Wembley and the realities of relegation consuming every nook and cranny of the Manor. Fear won the day the following Saturday against

Aston Villa as Charles's header gave Oxford the lead before Simon Stainrod brought about a draw.

Hoping for a place at Wembley, Billy Hamilton returned to the starting line-up for the first time since August for the visit of Watford. Oxford went a goal down after six minutes before Aldridge equalised six minutes after half-time. A fourth consecutive draw stretched Oxford's winless streak to six games. Their last chance to find some form before Wembley was a trip to title-chasing West Ham.

Evans introduced Steve Perryman as a sweeper to tighten up his defence. Despite their reputation as a pure footballing side, the Hammers walked a disciplinary tightrope as Mark Ward was booked after three minutes for throwing the ball at a linesman and Frank McAvennie narrowly avoided being sent off for a challenge on Hebberd.

On 13 minutes, Houghton put Oxford ahead after latching on to a long ball from Briggs. Awakened by the goal, West Ham laid siege with McAvennie's header hitting the bar and Judge denying Ray Stewart.

Things went wrong after the break and West Ham equalised after Tony Cottee's strike was deflected in by Trewick. Perryman then conceded a penalty for a foul on Alan Devonshire, which even the England international found harsh. Perryman was, however, given a reprieve when Stewart ballooned his kick over the bar.

McAvennie then put West Ham ahead before Stewart got another chance from the spot after Perryman fouled Dickens, this time making no mistake. The 3-1 reverse brought Wembley into view with the most curious dynamic. Jim Smith and Maurice Evans were like two duellers fighting over a woman neither truly loved. Evans seemed ambivalent to Oxford's success, saying only that he wanted the game to represent the best football could offer. Smith agreed, wanting both teams to play to their shared philosophy of entertaining crowds. He seemed reluctant to dent his legacy at Oxford, which he realised had come to define him. Many cup finals had teams who were happy to reach Wembley, but few had two teams more reluctant to win.

Despite nine months in charge, Evans still wanted to hide from the publicity and would have been happy returning to scouting, shielded by Smith's naturally outgoing exuberance. The final would expose both men like never before.

The Friday before the final, Smith, whose appearance on the bench had been threatened, was fined £500 and banned from the touchline for the rest of the season for his altercation against Chelsea. Diplomatically, the league said the ban would start the day after the final.

Rangers, unbeaten in eight games were hot favourites, but for Oxford United, was this their destiny?

Chapter 17

Trevor Hebberd

TREVOR HEBBERD knew that for players like him, the opportunity to play at Wembley was like passing through the eye of a needle. Being good enough was one thing; to be discovered another. To have the players around you to navigate through a competition was something else. In an age where, at most, four clubs made it to Wembley each year, and just 12 players from each side were selected to play, the opportunities for players like him were a rare and precious thing.

Hebberd wasn't complacent about being a professional footballer; he was the fittest player in the squad, a willing trainer, self-critical and dedicated. At just 21, and a regular in Southampton's starting eleven, the 1979 League Cup Final at Wembley should have been just reward for his commitment, but rather than being on the cusp of achieving his greatest ambition he wasn't even allowed to step on the turf.

Hebberd was discovered as a teenager by Southampton's chief scout Tom Parker at Alresford, the small Hampshire market town where he was born. Parker's judgement was well respected at The Dell, refined over a 50-year association with the club. He'd discovered Southampton's greatest player, England international Mick Channon.

While Hebberd was an apprentice cleaning the boots of Southampton skipper Peter Rodrigues, Channon was part of Southampton's 1976 FA Cup-winning team; the local boy became a legend. When Channon moved to Manchester City a year later, each emerging hope was burdened with the label 'the next Mick Channon'.

Hebberd was a homebody who thrived in the comforting surroundings of the club. Stability was deeply rooted in its culture; manager Laurie McMenemy had taken over in 1973 after a spell as assistant to his predecessor Ted Bates, who had been in charge for 18 years.

Playing in Channon's number nine shirt, Hebberd's ranging style and slight physical frame brought inevitable comparisons. His full debut came in 1976 against Hull, and by the end of the season he'd scored twice in his 12 appearances. His quiet, unassuming demeanour and versatility meant he rarely settled into a position he could claim his own.

Promotion in 1978 encouraged McMenemy to push the club beyond its modest ambitions. Hebberd was 21 and emerging as an integral member of the Southampton squad. When Scottish international striker Ted Macdougall unexpectedly quit for Bournemouth, his opportunity to cement a place in the starting 11 finally came against Maurice Evans's Reading in the second round of the League Cup. He scored in the second leg as Southampton eased through.

As Wembley came into focus, Hebberd scored against Channon's Manchester City, setting up a semi-final against Leeds United. In the first leg, Southampton came back from two goals down to draw 2-2 and sealed a place in the final with a 1-0 win at The Dell, Hebberd supplying Terry Curran's 11th-minute winner.

While the cup run was thrilling, Southampton were falling short of their manager's ambitions in the league. The semi-final sat in the middle of a four-game winless run. Southampton needed goals and Hebberd's return of four left McMenemy unconvinced so he turned to Irish youngster Austin Hayes.

In the four weeks before Wembley, Southampton returned to form. Hebberd could only watch as they beat Everton, Bristol City, QPR and Arsenal without conceding a goal. For the final, McMenemy retained his winning formula and Hebberd didn't even make the bench. As a non-playing member of the squad he watched from the stands, his dream dissolved in front of him.

Hebberd reflected on that lost opportunity seven years later as he stood in Wembley's long, cavernous tunnel. In front was the shining bald head of Jim Smith, the man who'd resurrected his career by bringing him to Oxford.

Wembley was all-consuming, and since the semi-final win over Aston Villa, a tidal wave of excitement, mania and opportunism crashed through the club, sweeping away the team's form.

The first challenge was tickets. The Manor's offices were overwhelmed with enquiries scrambling for the 30,000 available. Jim Hunt tried to manage the deluge, offering the first batch to season ticket holders, shareholders, lottery agents and people organising coaches. After ten days, they'd distributed over 8,000. Hunt's plan was to sell the remaining tickets at the turnstiles before the league game against Aston Villa. But with names and addresses needing to be recorded, he pivoted to offering vouchers with a priority to ticket stub holders from the semi-final.

Hunt assumed most fans would opt for £5 terrace tickets, but when most bought seats, those organising coaches could no longer be guaranteed tickets.

Issues came to a head when distributing vouchers before the Villa game. Operators ran out in the London Road terrace, forcing fans to head to the Osler Road terrace. Some season ticket holders arrived at half-time having watched the Grand National and were moved into the Beech Road stand. One demanded a refund for the previous five games, another unleashed a barrage of abuse at staff in the office. Hunt was dismayed, particularly at the abuse directed at women. As the game came to an end, two season ticket holders arrived expecting to get in. Finally, Hunt put his foot down and wouldn't let them pass.

With ten days to go, 25,000 tickets had been sold, an enthusiasm not shared across the game. Despite goodwill towards both clubs, sales were slow with some northern clubs sending their allocations back.

The Top Gear shop on the corner of London Road was stripped bare of merchandise as the club scrambled to re-stock. The Co-op on Cornmarket Street opened a special Top Gear department, taking thousands of pounds for mugs, scarves and a popular novelty cap with a pair of horns stitched on. For philatelists, the Post Office issued a special Milk Cup Final first day cover.

For a club that a few years earlier had been making pennies selling badges and programmes in a cupboard-like shop under the London Road terrace, commercial manager Nick Johnson was now having to go toe-to-toe with a new adversary: pirates. Opportunists stationed across the city sold scarves and flags, forcing Johnson to create an official Wembley logo, taking to the programme to implore fans to avoid buying cheap alternatives.

The club released two cup final records: 'A Yellow Road to Wembley' by Mick Brown (not the ticket office manager by the same name), and a reworked version of the Slade hit 'My Oh My' by local band Prism, featuring the squad singing the chorus. It was eventually released on legendary reggae label Trojan but didn't trouble the charts.

Maurice Evans was an oasis of calm. 'I'd love it to end up about five-each', he said, 'and the crowd really enjoy it, then we'll settle it in a replay.' Jim Smith, too, was looking forward to an open game which would give hope to other teams.

On the Tuesday before the final, QPR's confidence grew with a 4-1 win over Leicester. Apart from the injured Gary Waddock they would be at full strength, leading Smith to break the collegiate spirit, predicting his side would win 3-1.

The final was a paradox: it lacked the glamour of finals involving Manchester United, Liverpool and Arsenal, but it also illustrated football's wider appeal. Maurice Evans and Jim Smith were great friends who'd been rewarded for being among the most popular men in the game. Oxford represented a dream that all clubs retained: to navigate from obscurity to the top of the tree. 'A good game for everyone,' reasoned Smith. 'Apart from the ticket touts.'

With Bradford, Heysel and the Luton riot obscuring football's appeal, the game was dubbed the 'friendly final'. So friendly that it seemed like neither manager wanted to win the cup. 'We're a bit fed up with the league,' Evans said. 'Let's just go to Wembley and enjoy the day.'

Malcolm Shotton, too, felt the change of focus would benefit the team, 'Every week we run out to play in the league, the boys are tense and anxious. Tomorrow we go to Wembley for a one-off match, and will probably be so relaxed we'll play above ourselves.'

The day before the final, Evans took the players involved to Wembley, leaving the rest of the squad at home. Peter Rhoades-Brown, still reeling from his injury, confronted his manager, throwing a chair at him as the argument escalated. Evans was unrepentant, and the squad players travelled to the game with their families.

To distract the team, Evans took them to see Tottenham's goalless draw against Manchester United at White Hart

Lane. He also had one eye on Reading's game at Hartlepool, where another goalless draw secured them promotion.

Saturday night came and Evans finally settled on his starting line-up. There were two big decisions to make: although Neil Slatter's injury had cleared up, he opted for Dave Langan, and with Billy Hamilton's injury record, Jeremy Charles was selected to partner John Aldridge.

Cup finals were long associated with blazing-hot days which drained energy from the fittest players but on the morning of the game, fans and players drew back the curtains to find it was pouring with rain. For some athletes waking up on the biggest day of their sporting lives this was welcome news: the fifth London Marathon was being run on the morning of the final.

All over the county, fans boarded their coaches; from Gloucester Green, Banbury and Bicester, Witney, Wallingford and Wantage cars decorated in yellow and blue began their pilgrimage south. The motorway filled with fans, and every few miles a minibus would pull over on the hard shoulder to give its passengers a toilet break, their excitement and a morning of drinking getting the better of them.

The rain eased and the sun came out as Rangers departed from the Royal Lancaster Hotel opposite Hyde Park and Oxford left The Bell in Beaconsfield under police escort. The short journey was slowed as the coach weaved its way through the traffic, horns blaring as fans realised the cargo of the Heyfordian coach easing through the jams. The players, trying to remain focussed, smiled sheepishly, but it was hard not to be overwhelmed.

Jim Smith, aware of the tension in his players, turned to an unexpected tactic to relieve the pressure. Approaching Wembley Way, he produced a monkey glove puppet, and adopting a strange, croaky voice, he interviewed his 'colleague'. 'Three-nil today boss, it'll be easy,' predicted the puppet in front of his bemused squad.

On arrival, fans were consumed by Wembley's vastness: a panoramic vista, swathes of blue and white giving way at the halfway line to a great wave of yellow and blue. As kick-off approached the morning's rain cleared but the pitch started to cut up after a pre-match charity game featuring Jimmy Tarbuck's Rangers and David Frost's Oxford Dons.

High in the TV gantry overlooking the game sat presenter Jim Rosenthal, with Ian St John, Jimmy Greaves and Mick Channon. As the programme went on air, Oxford-born Rosenthal pinned a giant Oxford United rosette to his lapel.

Greaves summed up the mood of the nation, and perhaps even the managers, when confessing, 'To be honest, Jim, I don't give a monkey's who wins it.'

Below them, the players, in their light grey suits, stepped on to the pitch to absorb the atmosphere, but far from being overawed, they seemed to be relishing their opportunity to achieve something special.

Returning to the changing rooms, Ken Fish cleared a space to take control of the warm-up before handing out brandy, whisky and Mars bars to the squad.

The sun was shining as the teams emerged from the tunnel, Oxford wearing their silver tracksuit tops. The day's downpours had left puddles around the sandy perimeter track, forcing Evans to take evasive action to avoid getting a wet trouser leg.

Dignitaries were introduced and the national anthem sung before the game got under way. Hebberd danced impatiently with the ball at his feet, his eyes darting around, building a mental model. The opportunity he'd been deprived of seven years earlier was now in his hands. On the referee's whistle, John Aldridge rolled the ball into Hebberd's path and he immediately launched a fearsome attack deep into Rangers territory before being stopped by a crunching tackle. It was quite a statement.

Despite the relaxed pre-match routine, nervous energy coursed through the Oxford players as they competed for every ball. Alan Judge got his first touch, his heightened sense of awareness meaning he was distracted by a giant yellow balloon that drifted across his goal, casting a shadow across the pitch.

QPR opened with an aerial bombardment into the Oxford box, but it was easily absorbed by Malcolm Shotton and Gary Briggs. As Rangers tried to wrestle some control and slow the play down, Charles offered the first moment of quality when stealing the ball and laying it off to Ray Houghton to release Langan.

The early action encouraged a chorus of 'Come on you Yellows' to cascade from the east end of the stadium but despite the backing, the heavy pitch, blustery wind and nervous energy made the game disjointed and staccato.

Oxford tried to play football but Rangers, who seemed heavy-legged, countered with a series of robust challenges. Houghton nearly got behind the QPR defensive line, forcing Ian Dawes to concede a corner before Les Phillips screwed a shot so badly it went for a throw. A long free kick into the Oxford box was claimed by Judge while slightly off balance; for a second he fumbled it, but he caught it at the second attempt. The jittery opening flowed with energy but contained little quality.

It wasn't pretty but Oxford were encouraged by their opening few minutes, pinning Rangers into their defensive third with Houghton and Aldridge chasing down every ball.

After the frantic start the action lulled, and a blare of air horns filled the void. Petty fouls and offsides raised fears that the teams were becoming overwhelmed by the occasion and their responsibility to put on a show.

The drift was only jolted by a kung-fu kick from Terry Fenwick to Briggs's shoulder, but the defender didn't flinch as the referee waved play on.

After just half an hour, the players' shirts were smeared with mud, the sodden turf swamping the spectacle. Shotton patrolled the threat of Gary Bannister while Briggs dominated John Byrne, giving a platform for Phillips to pick up loose balls and release Hebberd and Houghton to push on. The game needed more finesse, someone to take ownership.

With the heaviest turf on the wings, Oxford sensed opportunities through the middle. As the sun appeared from behind a cloud, bathing Wembley in bright light, Houghton's header dropped to Hebberd.

Hebberd rolled his marker and played an exquisite pass with the outside of his boot to set Aldridge free. Suddenly he was one-on-one with Paul Barron, and the Oxford fans knew the script; Aldridge looked set to stroke the ball home but Steve Wicks lunged from behind, clipping the ball and sending the striker sprawling to the floor. Aldridge looked back at referee Keith Hackett hoping for a penalty, but Hackett waved play on.

The first pause in the game was to give Robbie James treatment. The Oxford bench looked concerned about the limping Jeremy Charles as a great noise rolled around the bowl of the stadium, supporters joining in glorious unison issuing their prophetic war cry, 'We're going to score in a minute'.

As Rangers hacked wildly trying to find a rhythm, Oxford's began to flow with Houghton and Langan making territorial gains. Hebberd looked on, knowing that if someone could take responsibility, it might provide the edge. Perhaps his clarity of thought, the self-reflection that often played against him, could be used to his advantage. He had the fitness and agility to take control of the game if he chose to.

By contrast, Rangers' spirit was draining away. Another ball was pumped forward and easily intercepted by John Trewick as, in the commentary box, Brian Moore, always the austere headteacher, read the final its last rites. There'd been so much hope and it had come to nought.

The crowded midfield left acres of space behind the defences for someone with the bravery to exploit it. The will to own an occasion was the difference between the good and the great. During another messy midfield skirmish, co-commentator Ian St John, like a parent trying to tell his excited children their birthday party was cancelled, diplomatically danced around the reality that the final was dying.

Down on the pitch, Phillips collected another knock-down and played it to Trewick to launch forward. Charles dropped deep to flick the ball on to Aldridge, who hopefully nodded it beyond the high Rangers defensive line.

Cast by the unseen hand of destiny, suddenly Hebberd burst free, and the crowd drew up to a singular roar as he loomed in on goal. The speed of the break entangled Barron in his own indecision – to take responsibility and close Hebberd down or trust his defence to scramble back.

Hebberd's first touch steered him wide and instinctively he looked up hoping for support, but Aldridge was still on the floor and Charles was deep in midfield unable to keep up with the break. He was alone with the glare of the spotlight bearing down on him.

Bringing the ball under control, he looked up; it was like he wanted to press pause and wait for support, to reset the norms, people like him didn't get opportunities like this. The whole world was watching, it was time to decide.

From the corner of his eye, Alan McDonald threw himself into view trying to block the path to goal. Instinctively, Hebberd steered the ball inside. He needed more time; had he frozen? Oxford fans willed him to shoot, but that primal moment was being overtaken by an interminable, unending sense of anticipation.

Hebberd assessed his options, recalling Maurice Evans saying he had to be more clinical after he'd missed a similar chance at Liverpool. He was surrounded by four Rangers defenders; his moment was fading.

Hebberd knew what it felt like to have opportunity ripped from his hands. Barron's own crisis of indecision had led to a tiny miscalculation, a gap at his near post. Hebberd saw it, this was his pathway out. McDonald lunged hopelessly to block the shot but the moment arrived, Hebberd finally engaged with fate, his shot snuck under the defender's leg, beyond Barron and into the deep Wembley goal.

Disbelievingly, Hebberd wheeled away one arm aloft like Mick Channon, but he was his own man, and this was his own moment. Oxford fans exploded with relief and joy, bodies piled on top of each other, flags waved furiously; a city divided by town and gown was united at a new frontier.

With just five minutes to half-time, Rangers tried to respond, knowing that going into the break a goal down would hand momentum to their opponents. Shotton and Briggs combined to guide a cross from Martin Allen for a corner. Judge flapped, but the kick was long and drifted safely out.

The goal seemed to double the speed of the play but halve the speed of the clock. Hebberd was everywhere, supporting the attack and covering at the back. Phillips ferreted away in midfield, while Charles retreated to combat the aerial threat.

As Rangers pressured, more spaces opened up. Houghton hooked the ball on and it broke to Aldridge on the halfway line but Dawes desperately crashed into the striker, winding him in the process.

Half-time came as a chorus of appreciation from the Oxford fans rolled around the stadium; their team had the initiative. Maurice Evans, who'd been watching from the stands, headed for the dressing room before being blocked by security. Eventually he got to his players with one message, 'Have you got the bottle?'

As Keith Hackett got the second half under way, Smith's concern grew; Rangers were leaden-legged and lacking ideas. Charles continued to justify his selection, channelling his experience and holding the ball up to win a free kick at the corner flag. The Oxford fans sang again, 'We're gonna score in a minute'.

Shotton and Briggs were having one of their most comfortable afternoons since entering the top division, absorbing the long balls and dominating Rangers' attack. Seven minutes into the second half, another emphatic defensive header from Briggs fell to Hebberd midway inside his own half. Hebberd laid it off to Houghton and set off in anticipation of a return ball. Houghton looked up, there was a gap; Hebberd's arcing run deftly beat the offside trap. Houghton threaded the ball into space, Hebberd burst through and was clear again.

Sparked by the dynamic attack, Houghton advanced into the QPR half, tracking the play. Hebberd closed in on the retreating QPR defence, fearful and flat-footed from the speed of the break; Hebberd was again in control of his destiny.

As Aldridge instinctively drifted to the back post, stretching the Rangers defence across the box, Houghton darted to the front post. Hebberd had options; with all the clarity of his goal, he paused, looked up and slid the ball into Houghton's path, then the tigerish midfielder lifted it over Barron and into the net; 2-0.

Two. Nil.

It was becoming real. Consumed with joy, Houghton sprinted down the flank in front of the jubilant Oxford fans.

It had been a goal of the highest quality; fluid and devastating in its speed and accuracy.

Where the first goal was a dream, the second brought into focus the reality of the cup. Houghton, surged with adrenaline, was struggling to concentrate as QPR tried to strike back, forcing Phillips to concede a free kick on the left.

Fenwick's cross to the back post was met by Steve Wicks who, for the first time, beat Charles. Judge tried to collect under pressure from McDonald, but he dropped the cross and fell to the floor. Panicked, Briggs cleared from Robinson with his knee, but it fell to Byrne, who looped a header goalwards. Judge sprung acrobatically, clutching the ball in both hands before remonstrating with the referee that he had been pushed. Robinson and Judge squared up before others intervened to quell his rage. They needed clear heads. In the chaos, the Oxford fans sang out 'Two-nil, two nil'; a reminder to the players not to lose what they had.

Rangers responded but Briggs and Shotton stood firm and Hebberd, Houghton and Langan were primed to strike on the counter-attack. As Byrne fired over while off-balance, Jim Smith looked lost. The Rangers fans quietened. 'You're not singing any more' goaded the Oxford fans; Rangers responded with 'Going down'. Bruised and beaten, they were retreating.

Nothing Rangers tried worked, and even with territorial advantage they couldn't create chances. Oxford fans were roused again. 'You should have stayed at the Manor' filled the air as much in affection for their former manager as derision. Smith could only agree.

As Oxford probed with menace, Smith brought on Leroy Rosenior for Martin Allen to chase the game, a sign of his growing desperation.

With 25 minutes to go, Houghton picked up Briggs's clearance and the space opened again. He released Phillips, who guided the ball across the box to Aldridge. This was it, the deadliest striker in the country with an open goal at Wembley – there was only one outcome. The ball rolled across but Aldridge's instinct deserted him, and with the goal at his mercy he sliced his shot wide for a goal kick.

Rangers' lack of imagination played into Oxford's hands. Each break had more finesse, more patience. The ball pinged between Brock, Langan, Houghton and Hebberd; they were now utterly dominant.

Only fatigue could let them down. As Rangers desperately resorted to hopeful long balls, Oxford slowed the game down; Aldridge rolled his socks down to his ankles. Langan, who'd been told by Maurice Evans to smarten up for the final, looked bedraggled. Hebberd, the player they called Nijinsky, looked like he could play all night.

Oxford relaxed, which invited pressure. Dawes's drive stung Judge's hands before Robbie James's header forced another corner which Judge punched away through a crowd of players.

The threat of counter-attack always loomed; Brock's impish back-heel sent Houghton free to cross to the far post where Aldridge scooped the ball high into the box. Brock won it, giving Charles the opportunity to lash it towards goal. Wickes cleared off the line, but it rebounded to Aldridge for his second chance of the day; this time Wickes scrambled to his feet and blocked the shot.

Rangers grappled with their crisis of confidence and even when they counter-attacked, there was no end product despite Michael Robinson driving them on, facing his fifth Wembley appearance without a win.

Oxford fans grew more confident; they couldn't quite believe what they were seeing. Oxford United, dominating at Wembley, where had it gone so right?

With four minutes to go, Aldridge dropped to pick up a Houghton clearance. With his insatiable appetite for goals, he advanced on the Rangers defence, who retreated furiously, knowing their effort was futile.

The striker squared the ball to Hebberd who was arriving to join the attack, sucking the defence in and leaving Aldridge free. With a clarity like it was the opening minutes of the game, Hebberd calmly pushed the ball back into Aldridge's path.

He needed no invitation to shoot despite the distance; Jeremy Charles knew he wasn't going to pass. Barron parried his fierce drive with both hands, praying that someone would arrive to clear the loose ball.

He looked up but his defenders hadn't reacted, and all he could see was the looming figure of Charles. This was to be the final confirmation; even before Charles made connection, Aldridge's arms were aloft in celebration. Barron scrambled to recover, Charles took a split second to compose himself and placed the ball side-footed into the empty net.

'That's three, and that's victory,' called Brian Moore.

The players were released from their concentration. Freed of their endeavour, the bubble popped and the enormity of their achievement seeped in. They had just a few moments to absorb it. Hebberd looked dazed, the disappointment of 1979 lifting from him with each passing second.

As the giant scoreboard showed the 90 minutes were up, Hebberd finally allowed himself a wry smile with Houghton. The midfield had won the day; the misfits and rejects, the underdogs and no-hopers were on top of the world.

On the bench, Evans impassively turned to his old friend Smith and graciously shook his hand with a solemnity he felt befitted the occasion. It wasn't his nature to rub it in. Smith embraced Ken Fish and Ray Graydon; his team, and yet he might as well have been on another planet. He looked haunted, torn between the success of the team he'd created and the failure of the one he led.

The players climbed the 39 steps towards the royal box; Shotton, Judge, Trewick, Langan, Phillips, Brock, Charles, Hebberd, Aldridge, Briggs, Houghton, Thomas. Only two players would lift major trophies at Wembley that season: Liverpool captain and Scottish international Alan Hansen, and former factory worker and ex-Nuneaton Borough defender Malcolm Shotton. Wearing a horned cap stolen from BBC Radio Oxford's Peter Baker, he hugged his chairman, whose presence, for once, had been overshadowed. Shotton kissed the cup and lifted it aloft for the banks of Oxford fans to see.

The mix of never weres, could have beens and has beens had been reassembled into a machine capable of winning a major trophy. The only time those 11 players ever took the field together. But whose success was it? The irrepressible Robert Maxwell whose money had funded it? The avuncular Jim Smith, whose vision and drive had catapulted the club through the divisions? Or Maurice Evans, who'd steered Oxford on the glide path to glory?

Evans knew; among the players was Ken Fish, a mother hen and sergeant major. The headmaster enforcing uniform rules on the last day of term. For Mr Fish, Oxford United wasn't a job, it was a way of life. He'd been a coach, physio, groundsman; he instilled a discipline in apprentices, insisting they painted white stripes on the players' boots when they faded; he'd run generations of players up London Road to the punishing Shotover Hill to hone their fitness; he and his wife would babysit for players with young children. He was the club and the club was in him.

Evans turned to Mr Fish and invited him to collect his medal. The 72-year-old coach – the oldest man ever to sit on a cup final bench – climbed the stairs with Smith, a moment of humanity as below Shotton danced on to the pitch with the trophy on his head.

The players set off for their lap of honour, pausing for a team shot bouncing excitedly while Rangers navigated the perimeter apologetically. They'd been deserted by their disconsolate fans, so it was left to Oxford supporters to applaud their efforts. As Houghton was surrounded by photographers, the team jogged around the track, full of energy. Noticing he'd been left behind, he scuttled to catch up, like a duckling who'd been left behind by his flock.

The celebrations started back in the changing room; Evans refused to do his press conference because he wanted to stay with the players. Once he was persuaded, the jubilant Maxwell offered him a contract for life. In the melee of the dressing room, the door opened and in walked Jim Smith, who just wanted a few moments with his players. It would never get better than this.

Chapter 18

Les Phillips

AFTER 14 games and just one win, Jim Smith couldn't avoid the pressure. Birmingham City had started the 1981/82 season well but poor form had seen them slip to just above the First Division's drop zone.

Smith had built a squad full of stars including his record signing Dave Langan, former PFA Player of the Year Colin Todd, Scottish international and World Cup star Archie Gemmill and the tabloid darling Frank Worthington. It was a team that should have been doing better.

But Langan's injury problems were deepening and at 35, Gemmill's celebrated career was winding down. Worthington's legendary excesses off the pitch were finally catching up with him. The formula that looked so promising on paper was failing.

Smith needed a new plan but he was running out of ideas. It was February, there was plenty of time to pull away from the relegation zone, but if the run continued much longer, his team could be sucked into a battle they weren't equipped for.

Birmingham's next opponents were West Ham and Smith decided he needed to add some youthful confidence. Les Phillips had these qualities. An England youth international in 1981, his performances in the reserves as a busy, battling midfielder were hard to ignore. Lambeth-born Phillips was small and aggressive with a large mop of curly hair which covered his eyes, making him look slightly unhinged. He was just what Smith needed.

Phillips had a nasty streak; in October 1981 he'd been sent off for the reserves at Reading before making a rude gesture as he left the pitch which led to an FA disciplinary hearing.

Phillips had replaced Gemmill for the game at Upton Park, injecting a freshness and playing without fear as the Blues secured a 2-2 draw. Giddy with the success of his debut, he told the press that he wasn't impressed with his opponents. 'I didn't rate [Trevor] Brooking at all,' he said. '[Billy] Bonds is a bit past it now.' It was exactly the bravado Smith liked; perhaps he'd found a solution to his problems.

But it was too late and three days later Smith was fired. Ron Saunders' brand of disciplined aggression suited Phillips and his impressive displays helped drag Birmingham to safety, earning the teenager rave reviews.

But, as the new season got under way, he was shocked to find he was transfer-listed, a victim of Saunders' brutal cost-cutting.

He dealt with it the only way he knew, head on. Birmingham continued to struggle, but Phillips's versatility meant he always had a role to play. Despite spending most of the season in the relegation zone, the Blues were saved by a final-day win at Southampton.

With the squad trimmed back, Saunders offered Phillips a contract, despite a court appearance after a violent argument with his girlfriend. Already banned from driving, he'd taken the keys to her Mini and driven off in a rage before police pulled him over ten miles from the house.

Despite the drama, the season started well, but a slump in November pushed Birmingham back towards the relegation zone. Phillips was edged to the margins of the squad again and as the transfer deadline neared, Jim Smith pounced.

By the time he arrived at the Manor, Phillips had played 43 First Division games. He thrived at Oxford in combination with Trevor Hebberd in midfield, propelling the club to promotion. The First Division held no fears. He'd scored three times in the Milk Cup campaign – only John Aldridge scored more – and now he was a Wembley winner.

After their momentous achievement, it was reasonable to question what the club wanted next. Robert Maxwell knew, using the civic reception the following day to press home the need for a new stadium. The 38,000 fans lining the streets of the city showed the club's potential.

The morning after the game there'd been a panic: the trophy was missing. Jim Hunt phoned around the players. Malcolm Shotton thought Peter Rhoades-Brown had it, but when Hunt phoned his house, nobody answered. During the celebrations Rhoades-Brown had lost his keys when Brian McDermott took his jacket, so he stayed with Kevin Brock in Abingdon. Eventually Hunt phoned Brock to be told that Rhoades-Brown was asleep with the cup upstairs.

As the team boarded the open-top bus to take them into the city centre, the heavens opened. Trevor Hebberd, so dominant at Wembley, looked like he was on a wet family day out. The driving rain and hail meant most players wisely chose to wear their team-issue double-breasted raincoats as the bus crawled down the high street; only Rhoades-Brown gallantly stood at the front in a jumper and shirt, holding the cup.

For most of the journey, the rain seemed to dampen the enthusiasm of the crowds, and the winger was left waving at a smattering of supporters while shaking his hands to try and get some feeling back.

But as the bus approached Carfax Tower in the city centre, the numbers increased, and a vast bank of yellow flags came into view. Shops and restaurants emptied, the road teemed with fans in celebration, the committed and the disinterested were swept along and the bus, engulfed in a sea of yellow, came to a halt.

It crawled through the crowds stopping outside the Town Hall where the team slipped inside. Thankful for the warmth, they mingled with dignitaries as Maxwell headed to the balcony with Ghislaine to show the cup to the crowds.

Immediately after the game, Jeremy Charles had told reporters he was pulling out of Wales's friendly against Uruguay due to a groin strain he'd suffered in the last 15 minutes of the final. But when he hadn't phoned manager Mike England the following day, the Wales boss branded Charles 'unprofessional', assuming he'd been caught up in the post-match celebrations.

Kevin Brock left the celebrations to join the England under-21 squad for the first time in two years to face Italy in the semi-final of the European Championship at Swindon.

He'd missed Italy's 2-1 first-leg win but was recalled to add pace and width to the attack. The Italians, though, were experts in containing teams and were dangerous on the break with Roberto Donadoni forcing Bobby Mimms to make a smart save before having a penalty appeal waved away.

Just before the hour, a corner from Brock went long to the back post for Stewart Robson to volley home. The goal brought brief hope, but as England pushed forward, Italy threatened again and Mimms was forced into two excellent saves before Gianluca Vialli ended all hope with a last-minute equaliser.

Wembley had felt like another planet where Oxford's worries were wiped away. But even most post-match interviews touched on their precarious league position.

Maxwell, Maurice Evans and the players were adamant that they could survive if they could recreate the form they'd shown to lift the cup.

It took a few days to refocus on the league and the fight for survival. The weekend's results had been kind with Birmingham, West Brom and Ipswich all losing. Oxford were in 20th, two points behind Ipswich, their next opponents, with a game in hand. With Nottingham Forest, Everton and Arsenal still to play, the visit to Portman Road looked like a must-win game.

The Suffolk club were now almost entirely held together by their captain Terry Butcher; a warrior built for a relegation fight, even though he was rumoured to be looking to leave at the end of the season.

Oxford replaced Brock with Steve Perryman in an otherwise unchanged team. Portman Road was bathed in a bright spring sunlight. The mood, though, was of unresolved tension; Aldridge had scored more goals than the entire Ipswich team, who hadn't found the net in seven and a half hours of football.

The hard surface caused the ball to bounce erratically and with both sides packing their midfield, neither was able to gain control. Nonetheless, Dave Langan engineered some space on the wing, presenting early chances for Aldridge and Charles. In response, Jason Dozzell brought a smart save from Alan Judge.

The breakthrough came after 29 minutes, moments after Aldridge headed narrowly wide from Phillips's cross. Constantly alert, Phillips caught Ian Cranson with a thundering block tackle as he casually dribbled out of defence. He looked up and played a simple ball to Aldridge on his left, who slotted beyond Paul Cooper for 1-0.

Despite losing Charles five minutes later when his groin injury flared up again, Oxford felt in control. Ipswich, low on confidence and in poor form, launched desperate punts into the box that were easily cleared by Malcolm Shotton and Gary Briggs. To add to their woes, Phillips's free kick into the box was attacked by Briggs whose elbow and forehead crashed into Butcher's face, opening up a large, deep cut. Butcher grabbed a sponge from his physio and battled on.

Ipswich opened the second half brightly, and on 54 minutes Judge came out to collect a hopeful ball from Parkin on the edge of his six-yard box. With the goalkeeper focussed on picking the cross out from the sunny sky, Kevin Wilson barged into him and the ball dropped to Dozzell to volley into the empty net. Oxford called for a foul, pleading for common sense. The referee awarded the goal.

The equaliser lit up Portman Road, injecting Ipswich with momentum. Within minutes a long free kick from the centre circle dropped to Butcher, who beat Briggs to the ball. McCall's shot was scuffed back into the path of the England defender, who controlled with his left foot and volleyed into the corner with his right. Having not scored in nearly eight hours, they'd registered two in two minutes. Butcher's primal celebrations, the release of his relentless will to win, whipped the crowd into a frenzy.

Butcher defended with animalistic fervour but an elbow from Hebberd opened the head wound again. Play continued and he recovered to head Langan's cross clear for a corner. Finally he was bowed; unable to stand, blood poured from the gash and for once he was forced to leave the field for stitches.

As Butcher headed down the tunnel, Perryman pushed his short corner to Brock, whose swinging cross dropped to the near post. Paul Cooper's weak punch fell to Phillips, who gratefully accepted the gift on the volley to ram home his first league goal of the season.

Once again Ipswich looked defeated, their brittle confidence shattered by the loss of their captain. With the away fans noisily roaring on their team, the anxiety around

Portman Road gave way to a wave of collective relief as Butcher reappeared heavily bandaged. The emphasis shifted again; Judge collected at the feet of Wilson before Houghton danced through the defence to fire wide and Hebberd went close with a header.

With fatigue and pressure growing, both teams resorted to long balls; a draw looked inevitable, the relegation battle unresolved.

Two minutes into injury time Ipswich desperately launched another ball towards Dozzell on the edge of the box. The striker backed into Shotton, trying to engineer some space to bring it under control. The Oxford captain stood firm, his arms aloft appealing to the referee. Obligingly, the whistle went, but to everyone's disbelief he awarded the free kick to Dozzell inches from the edge of the area.

On the bench, Maurice Evans watched on. A lifelong student of the game, he'd spent hours watching trialists looking for a break. It was an obsession where he'd watched thousands of players, but signed just one: Ian Atkins for Shrewsbury Town.

Evans looked out at Mark Brennan standing over the ball, and next to him was Atkins watching the Oxford wall assemble looking for a weakness. The crowd hushed, a sense of calm descended; the game had reached its crucible.

Brennan rolled the ball to Atkins, whose drive was straight and true. As Shotton charged out it clipped his ankle, directing it through a gap in the wall and ricocheted off Wilson's hip into the net with Judge stranded.

Portman Road erupted as Oxford players tried to claw back time, remonstrating at the referee, but the game had gone. There was nothing they could do. Six days after their finest hour, they were on the brink of total failure.

There was just time for Judge to launch the ball forward before the referee blew his whistle to signal a cruel and

Mild-mannered footballing man Maurice Evans (pictured in 1986), who took over from Jim Smith as the club prepared for the First Division.
Steve Daniels

Gary Briggs makes his mark on the First Division by putting Garth Crooks out of the first game of the season after just 20 minutes.

Les Phillips secures Oxford's place in the Milk Cup Final with a goal against Aston Villa in the semi-final.

Trevor Hebberd, man of the match for the Milk Cup Final, scores Oxford's first against QPR.

After a scintillating move, Ray Houghton secures Oxford's second.
Steve Daniels

Malcolm Shotton celebrates with the cup wearing his famous horned baseball cap.

Ken Fish, the oldest man to sit on the bench at Wembley, salutes the Yellow Army after Maurice Evans insisted he collect the manager's medal.

Steve Daniels

John Aldridge and Dave Langan let it all sink in.
Steve Daniels

Alex Ferguson was the centre of attention for his first game against Manchester United at the Manor. A 2-0 win for Oxford was a humbling start.

Dean Saunders, signed from Brighton as replacement for John Aldridge who'd gone to Liverpool.
Steve Daniels

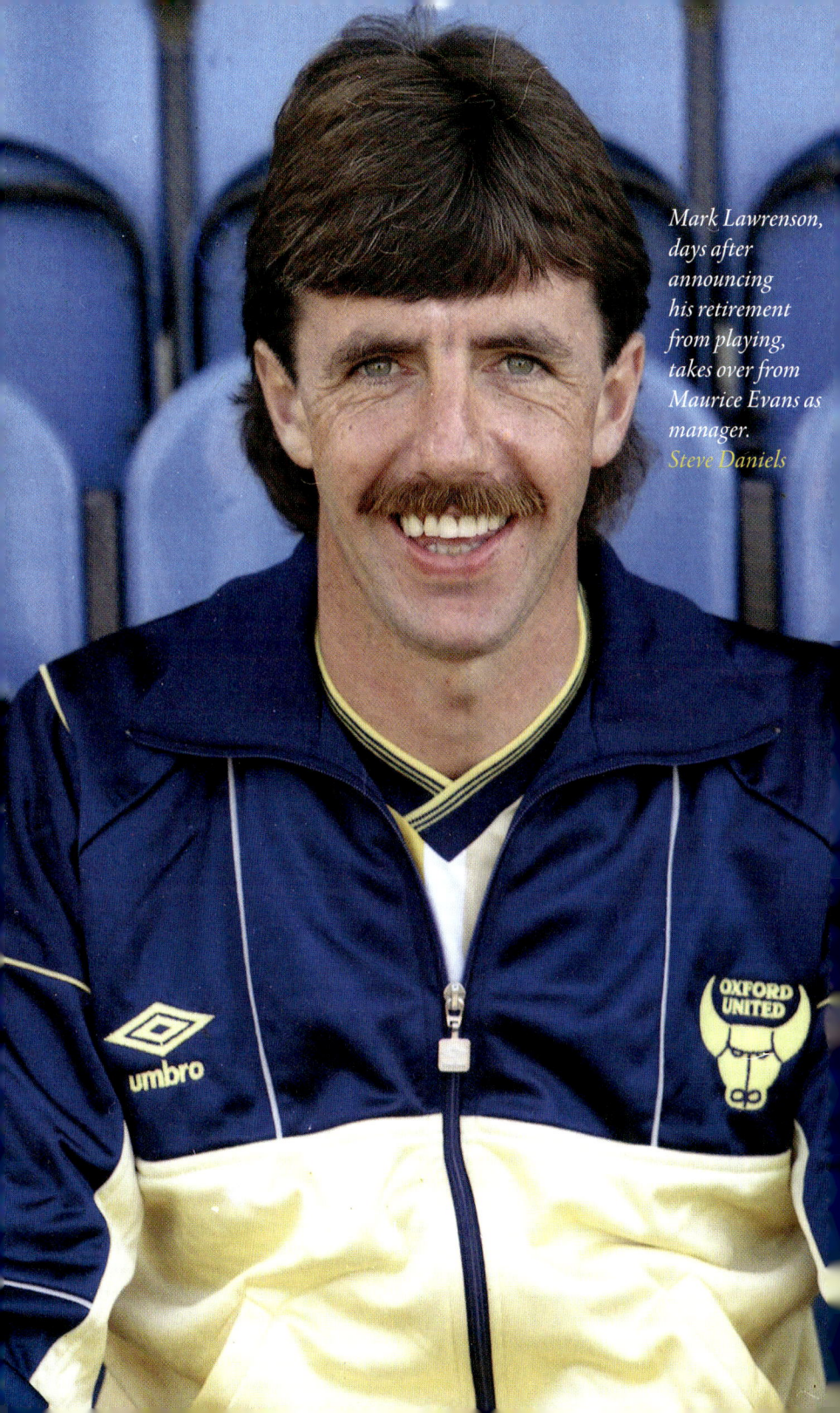

Mark Lawrenson, days after announcing his retirement from playing, takes over from Maurice Evans as manager.
Steve Daniels

The Manor, pictured during Oxford's final First Division game at home against Manchester United in 1988.

Martin Foyle gets his shot away as Oxford say farewell to the First Division away to Nottingham Forest. *Steve Daniels*

crippling defeat. Ipswich fans streamed on to the pitch convinced they were safe from relegation. The Oxford players were lost in their own world. Evans was crestfallen. 'And you wonder why I don't want to be a manager,' he said.

The relegation dial was moving. Oxford were now three points behind Leicester with a game in hand, but they had to face Nottingham Forest, Arsenal, and first champions Everton, all three at the Manor.

Since Adrian Heath's interception from Kevin Brock's back-pass two years earlier Everton had been transformed. The goal had been a springboard to reach the Milk Cup Final, then later that season they won the FA Cup against Watford and followed it up with the league title and Cup Winners' Cup after beating Austria Wien in 1985. Now, like their rivals Liverpool, they were chasing a historic double.

The evening was pivotal at both ends of the table, with all three title-chasers facing relegation-threatened sides. Leaders Liverpool were at Leicester, second-placed Everton headed to the Manor, while third-placed West Ham hosted Ipswich. A defeat and a Leicester victory would leave Oxford six points from safety with just two games to play.

Everton, with one defeat in 26 matches, were two points behind Liverpool with a game in hand. With home encounters against Southampton and West Ham remaining, a win at the Manor would all but secure the title.

Before the Heysel ban and anticipating an assault on the European Cup after their title win in 1985, Everton had sold striker Andy Gray to Aston Villa and spent £800,000 on Leicester City's Gary Lineker. The step up for Lineker was daunting; after seven years at his hometown club he was moving to the champions of England as their marquee player. He was so at home at Filbert Street that on his Everton debut – at Leicester – he walked into the home dressing room by mistake.

Everton fans were incensed by Gray's departure, ladling more pressure on their new striker to overcome his imposter syndrome, particularly after his old club opened the season with a comfortable 3-1 win over the champions.

Lineker gradually pulled the Everton fans around, scoring 25 goals immediately prior to the game at the Manor. Unable to fully accept that his poacher's instinct was down to ability, he attributed his success to one thing: a lucky pair of Adidas boots.

He'd worn the boots all season, insisting that they were taped up whenever a hole appeared. With the title race tightening, Lineker left nothing to chance. Whatever it took, the boots would see him through.

On arrival at the Manor, Lineker and the rest of the team got off the coach and bustled their way into the cramped changing rooms under the Beech Road stand. The backroom staff unloaded the kit, but to the striker's horror, his boots were missing.

His blood ran cold as the search for another pair began. An Oxford apprentice was dispatched to the boot room for a replacement. On his way back with a new pair, Peter Rhoades-Brown intercepted him, sending him back to get an old, battered pair a size too big. Lineker was crestfallen. His poise deserted him; the boots felt like clown shoes.

Jeremy Charles's injury against Ipswich meant that Maurice Evans had to recall Billy Hamilton for only his third start since September. Determined to establish a psychological advantage, inside a minute, Briggs picked up his 12th booking of the season, clashing off the ball with Graeme Sharp.

The tension at the Manor increased after 20 minutes as news filtered through from Filbert Street. Ian Rush had given Liverpool an early lead, then eight minutes later Ronnie Whelan added a second, turning the games at Upton Park and the Manor into must-wins for the other championship hopefuls.

The pressure grew; John Aldridge and Kevin Ratcliffe were booked for dissent before Everton coach Colin Harvey was sent to the stands. The game was just 37 minutes old.

Despite the intensity, Oxford were more than matching the champions. Houghton had a shot saved when both Aldridge and Hebberd were better placed to score. Everton keeper Bobby Mimms then prevented a breakthrough, saving from Ray Houghton and then Phillips.

At the other end, Everton had a penalty appeal turned down when John Trewick appeared to bring down Lineker. It wasn't Lineker's only dose of bad luck; he spurned numerous chances, silently cursing his boots.

At Upton Park, free-scoring West Ham were all over Ipswich with Frank McAvennie, Tony Cottee, Alan Devonshire and Mark Ward being repelled single-handedly by Terry Butcher.

The sun dipped as half-time came with Liverpool winning and the two other games goalless, leaving relegation and the title on a knife-edge.

Just after the hour, there was news from Upton Park where Kevin Wilson had outmanoeuvred the West Ham defence to shoot directly at Phil Parkes, but with the keeper prone on the floor, Wilson collected the loose ball and slotted in for 1-0, putting Ipswich on the verge of safety.

Back at the Manor, Judge saved from Lineker again, his confidence seeping away with every fluffed opportunity. In response, with 22 minutes to go, Hamilton bounced the ball off the bar. Time, chances and luck were slipping away.

Seven minutes later there was more news from Upton Park; Paul Cooper's goal kick was intercepted by West Ham defender Alan Dickens, whose header sent Paul Goddard away down the left. Devonshire picked the ball up and played it into the feet of Frank McAvennie, who relayed it back to Dickens and set off in anticipation of a return pass. The space allowed Dickens to scoop the ball beyond Cooper and into the net. It was the news Oxford fans had hoped for, although it didn't ease the tension; a goal for Everton would leave Oxford needing a miracle.

With nine minutes remaining, Everton ominously introduced Adrian Heath in place of Kevin Richardson. Liverpool were cruising to victory, putting the title firmly in their grasp, so securing three points was Everton's only option.

Rather than signalling a turnaround, Oxford nearly broke through when Houghton fed Aldridge, who chipped to Hamilton, leaving Mimms stranded. Hamilton's effort looked certain to go in but it was cleared off the line by Gary Stevens. Undeterred, the home side pressed again. Phillips crossed for Houghton only for Mimms to save.

The games entered their final minute. At Upton Park, West Ham surged forward looking for a winner. Ward wriggled into the Ipswich box where, sandwiched between Nigel Gleghorn and Mark Brennan, under pressure he went to ground. It looked like Gleghorn had got the ball but the air was pierced by the shrill of the referee's whistle. Ipswich despaired as he pointed to the spot. Penalty to West Ham.

While Ipswich surrounded the referee in angry protest, back at the Manor the frenzy peaked, and there wasn't time to acknowledge what was happening to their rivals as Trewick swung a cross in from the left towards the tiring Hamilton.

The ball dropped from the night sky in front of the London Road terrace and the Irishman strained, deftly bringing it under his control. His touch took the ball away from the Everton defence, giving him a moment to glance up. Into his line of sight came Les Phillips charging from the gloom into the box, so Hamilton rolled it into his path.

Without a second thought, Phillips unleashed a ferocious drive beyond Mimms, the first goal Everton had conceded in six games. Oxford were back in control of their destiny and Liverpool were a point from the title.

The ball hit the back of the net and London Road reacted like a wasps' nest being hit by a stick, dissolving into pandemonium as Phillips leapt into the air; the pressure cooker had blown. The Everton bench looked on in disbelief, their championship hopes disappearing into the chaos of this magical little ground. It was a cruel but delightful revenge.

There was more to come at Upton Park and the ever-reliable Ray Stewart slammed home West Ham's winner from the spot, sucking Ipswich back into the relegation fight. Oxford's survival was firmly back in their hands.

Everton's loss put the title in the hands of Liverpool, which was too much for one Toffees fan, who sent death threats to John Aldridge which were so explicit that the striker reported them to the police.

The final scheduled weekend of the season left four teams competing to avoid the last relegation place. Above Oxford were Coventry by a point and Ipswich by two. Below were Leicester on goal difference. A win against Forest would secure Oxford's survival.

After a patchy season, Forest were finishing with a flourish and now 11 games unbeaten, a strong contrast to Oxford with just one league win in ten. After the manic joy of the Everton win, Oxford set to work with admirable purpose, but they seemed anxious and rigid. John Metgod, Colin Walsh and Nigel Clough pressured Briggs and Shotton while Trewick and Langan's attacking instincts left vulnerabilities down the wings.

Houghton tested Steve Sutton in the Forest goal early on but with just 15 minutes gone, Franz Carr's cross from the right was flicked on by David Campbell. On the edge of the box, Nigel Clough met the ball as it dropped, smashing it past Alan Judge for 1-0. His father Brian leapt from the dugout in celebration.

The early goal pushed Oxford back into the relegation zone. But they wouldn't surrender, and on the half-hour mark Gary Fleming's weak back-pass allowed Charles to pick up the ball, turn Metgod and beat Sutton for the equaliser.

A minute later, news filtered through that John Byrne had put QPR ahead against Coventry while Ally Mauchlen had scored for Leicester against Newcastle. Nine minutes before half-time, Coventry equalised through Brian Kilcline before David Bennett gave them the lead. Oxford were two points adrift.

Things became worse moments later. Back at the Manor, with Oxford gaining the upper hand, Briggs went up for a high cross with Des Walker. As the two players landed it was clear Briggs was hurt; his cheekbone fractured by Walker's wayward elbow.

Brock replaced Briggs, meaning Charles was moved into defence. The attacking dynamic changed immediately as Oxford conceded territory. With 20 minutes to go, news came through that Leicester had doubled their lead through Banks.

The opportunity to confirm survival slipped away and with nine minutes remaining, Clough fed Carr down the right, who drove into the Oxford half and returned the ball to the forward to fire home with his left foot.

A minute later, there was news of another goal: Brian Marwood had put Sheffield Wednesday ahead against Ipswich, leaving them just above the relegation zone. From celebrating on the pitch at Portman Road, Oxford could now relegate Ipswich by winning their last game.

Maurice Evans, who'd resisted the Oxford job because he loathed the pressure, retreated to his office. He faced the daunting prospect of one game to survive with Jeremy

Charles, Billy Hamilton, John Trewick, Les Phillips, Dave Langan and Gary Briggs all injured. It had been two weeks, but the Milk Cup Final felt a lifetime away. Brian Clough came in for a drink but Evans didn't have the appetite. 'Why are you worried?' Clough asked. 'All you've got to do is beat Arsenal.'

Evans knew how difficult it would be to be patient with a feverish Oxford crowd willing them to safety. 'We know what we have to do but the crowd will be a problem,' he lamented. 'They'll want us to score in the first few minutes but if we don't the crowd's reaction could have us chasing around like idiots. We know what we've got to do. Now we'll have to see if we have the courage to do it.'

The team was selected based on who was the least injured. Although Evans lost Trewick and Phillips, others picked themselves up for the final push. Langan wasn't going to miss this one and Hamilton was ready to risk his World Cup to play. That would leave a gap in defence into which Gary Briggs, the old warhorse, would partner Malcolm Shotton despite his shattered cheekbone, exactly where he'd been for the whole adventure.

Oxford's whole season was concentrated into 90 minutes and a simple objective. Three more points.

The Manor was full the following Monday, the sunshine signalling the coming of summer. But it couldn't disguise the tension that sat heavily over the stadium. From the tunnel emerged the enormous figure of Robert Maxwell lumbering on to the pitch with one final rallying call. 'Don't be a burden to the players,' he warned. 'They are doing their best.'

If there were nerves in the stands it wasn't evident on the pitch. This was cup football, winner takes all, something Oxford had excelled at for three years. Arsenal's unremarkable season was over, their players' minds on the World Cup and their summer holidays.

Oxford played with an unexpected freedom, fluid and connected, and after just nine minutes Hebberd's through ball found Aldridge, who laid it off for Houghton to drive beyond John Lukic for the opening goal. Nerves settled, they set about confirming their safety; Paul Davis headed off the line from a Houghton shot that threaded its way through the Arsenal defence before Mark Jones nearly connected with crosses from Hamilton and then Houghton.

With 18 minutes to go, Viv Anderson and Aldridge tussled, competing for Hamilton's pass into the box. Cleverly, Aldridge went down under Anderson's light touch. The referee pointed to the spot as Anderson protested his innocence. Aldridge got to his feet, placed the ball on the spot and stepped back. The London Road terrace prepared itself; Aldridge, forever reliable, rolled the ball into the corner beyond Lukic for his 31st goal of the season.

That was the buffer, the pressure release, and survival came into focus. With eight minutes remaining Hamilton picked up Houghton's pass in acres of space and slid the ball under Lukic for the clincher. It suddenly seemed so easy.

The final whistle confirmed that Oxford were safe and Ipswich relegated. The Manor roared in relief; the tensions of the previous months blew gently into the spring sky like petals from a dandelion. As Maurice Evans sat quietly in his office, the players were joined by Maxwell as they paraded the Milk Cup to a jubilant support.

Ten months after he'd been offered it, Evans finally succumbed to Maxwell's peresuasion and signed a contract. 'I've been a fool for too many years,' he reflected. 'Maybe it's the right time to take what's been offered.'

Summer was here and Oxford had survived, and there was just time for Maxwell to announce his latest plans for a new stadium. Some things never change.

Chapter 19

Billy Hamilton

TENSION HUNG in the air heavier than the oppressive heat as a coach weaved its way towards Guadalajara in the west of Mexico. From the roadside, few could doubt the ten-vehicle motorcade contained a precious cargo.

Each intersection is blocked by police ensuring safe and swift passage through the city. Inside, next to the driver, a man runs his fingers over the loaded rifle. Dark glasses and weak smiles betray a nervousness, a thin line of protection against bandits and kidnappers.

Skittishness and uncertainty are everywhere, but one thing is for sure: Billy Hamilton wouldn't have it any other way.

Since the draw for the 1986 World Cup finals in the previous December, Hamilton had maintained a razor-like focus on one fixture, Northern Ireland's final group game against Brazil. 'Playing against Brazil is the big prize for any international,' he said. 'If I could get my hands on one of those famous green and yellow shirts it'd be my proudest soccer trophy.'

Hamilton hadn't played for his country for nearly two years; three cartilage operations and countless painkilling injections had left his World Cup prospects bleak.

The draw also paired Northern Ireland with Spain and Algeria, but Brazil on 12 June gave Hamilton renewed motivation to fight on. Manager Billy Bingham, a genius at serving feasts from scraps, knew he'd need all the quality he could find to survive the group; even a partially fit Hamilton would be on the plane to Mexico.

Another setback in January reminded Hamilton to respect his injuries as previously he'd rushed back, brushing them off like an elbow from a centre-back. 'I'm erring on the side of caution,' he said. 'I can't afford to go daft and rush back into training even though now I'm treading a tightrope.'

He wasn't idle. Injury had sparked his entrepreneurial spirit; his board game *Billy Hamilton's Football Academy* promised fans the opportunity to experience the life of a footballer from apprentice to World Cup winner. When Toys R Us agreed to stock it, Hamilton thought he'd struck gold.

By March, he was back in training, appearing in a 9-1 reserve team demolition of Reading, but he was negotiating a minefield. He knew there was a game, tackle or divot of turf that could end his hopes, and he needed to avoid them all.

Bingham had two friendlies to finalise his squad. Before facing Denmark, he challenged Hamilton, Martin O'Neill and Paul Ramsey to prove their fitness before their final friendly against Morocco.

In April, Bingham was in the Beech Road stand watching Hamilton's return to first-team action after seven months for the draw with Watford, then he played again three days later against West Ham. The intense return after so long out meant he faced an unenviable decision.

With Bingham announcing his squad ten days later, Hamilton had to sacrifice his place in the Milk Cup Final. As potent as Hamilton and John Aldridge were, Maurice Evans wanted Jeremy Charles's reliability. Wembley was a risk too far.

Hamilton watched from the bench before flying to Belfast for Northern Ireland's final friendly against Morocco. Starting as a substitute, he watched his rival Colin Clarke score after 15 minutes. With 35 minutes to go, Hamilton got his chance for the briefest trial in a 2-1 win.

He'd done enough; Hamilton was selected in the provisional squad despite rating his chances as 50-50.

Happy to sit out the rest of the season, he missed the defeat to Ipswich, but Charles's injury meant he had to play in the win over Everton. Charles returned against Nottingham Forest but wasn't fit, forcing Hamilton's scoring comeback against Arsenal, his first goal since August.

Even as the season ended, doubts remained. Bingham wanted his team to be the fittest in the tournament. Ignoring the altitude and heat, intense training sessions would leave the squad sprawled across the turf; it was the last thing Hamilton needed.

Sitting on the coach among the sirens and ceremony of a World Cup, Hamilton had made it. After just eight league games and three goals he was among the world's elite footballers. The ache in his knee reminded him of his uncertain future, but for now, he was happy.

The opening fixture was a noon kick-off against Algeria. Bingham opted for Hamilton's experience up front and Ireland looked composed, taking a fifth-minute lead through Norman Whiteside. They nearly doubled their advantage when Hamilton set up O'Neill to head wide before having a header cleared off the line and screwing a shot wide when he should have scored.

Ireland consolidated in the second half, slowed by the 90-degree heat and an ageing team. The Algerians increased their pressure and intimidation. Just before the hour, Hamilton conceded a free kick and Djamel Zidane thundered the ball through the Irish wall and past Pat Jennings for the equaliser. The draw meant the Irish had to beat either Spain or Brazil to avoid elimination.

Bingham blamed Hamilton for the goal, claiming he'd left a gap in the wall. The manager was criticised for playing Hamilton at all. With quibbles about payments and rumours that Bingham was quitting for club football in Saudi Arabia, the camp was unsettled, despite being seen carrying an ITV recording engineer with a broken foot into a local disco.

Against Spain, Hamilton made way for Colin Clarke. After conceding a goal from Emilio Butragueño in the opening minute and a second from Julio Salinas, Northern Ireland faced elimination. Clarke pulled a goal back a minute into the second half before Hamilton replaced Nigel Worthington with 20 minutes left. But there was no way through and Ireland were on the brink. Needing a handsome win, Bingham left Hamilton on the bench as he focussed on containing the Brazilians in their final match.

The packed Irish midfield sat deep, inviting their opponents to pepper Pat Jennings' goal from range. The breakthrough came after 15 minutes when Müller crossed for Careca to fire home. Four minutes before the break, right-back Josimar launched an audacious 35-yard drive over the veteran keeper's head for 2-0. Hamilton finally fulfilled the dream that had kept his recovery on track for eight months, replacing Norman Whiteside with 23 minutes remaining. It was too late; the Irish had run out of steam and a beautifully worked move saw Zico back-heel the ball into Careca's path for their third with three minutes to go. The Northern Irish World Cup adventure was over, as was Hamilton's international career.

At home, Maurice Evans prepared for the new season. Oxford weren't a novelty; the Milk Cup had put them on the map, and despite their brush with relegation no opponent would be complacent, particularly visiting the Manor.

With Hamilton's fitness and the growing reputations of Kevin Brock, Ray Houghton and, above all, John Aldridge, Evans knew that keeping his squad together would be difficult.

Among those circling the club was a familiar bald eagle. Jim Smith's QPR had finished the season in 13th place, an improvement on their previous campaign, but the Milk Cup defeat was considered a missed opportunity.

He made little secret of his best signing for Oxford; Trevor Hebberd's performance at Wembley confirmed that he'd matured into one of the most underrated midfielders in the country. Hebberd was coming to the end of his contract and Smith, holidaying in Florida, was ready to pounce.

After the World Cup, clubs scrambled to assemble their squads for the new season. The stars of the tournament were fought over but a new financial crisis faced English clubs paralysed by hooliganism and with little prospect of returning to European football. Everton striker Gary Lineker – top scorer at the World Cup – took his lucky boots to Barcelona along with Manchester United's Mark Hughes, while England internationals Chris Woods, Graham Roberts and Terry Butcher were lured to Glasgow Rangers.

The biggest prize was Liverpool striker Ian Rush and Italian giants Juventus made a bid of £3.2m, a record for a British player, to strong-arm the Welshman out of Anfield. Liverpool relented; Rush was offered a £2m three-year contract he couldn't ignore. With Italian clubs only permitted two foreign players, Juventus had to move either Michael Laudrup or Michelle Platini to make space. With Platini retiring at the end of the season, Juventus wanted to loan Rush to Napoli. Rush resisted, saying he'd sign if his loan could be back at Liverpool. Juventus agreed, giving the Reds a year to find Rush's replacement. There was one name on everyone's lips – John Aldridge.

While Evans's strikers and midfield were being tracked, his real problem was in defence. Few players were more revered than Dave Langan, Malcolm Shotton and Gary Briggs, but they'd conceded 80 league goals, the second-worst in the division. Aldridge's goals kept them up: the team had scored 30 more than relegated Ipswich but finished above them by just one point. Dismantling the back line risked unbalancing the squad; these were the players who embodied its spirit.

Evans's solution came from the World Cup where the heat and altitude favoured patient teams. The English game was physical and direct, which was exposed by Diego Maradona and Argentina, while Scotland and Northern Ireland were outmanoeuvred by more technical opponents.

English managers were turning to the sweeper system favoured by many continental teams, and Evans wanted Hebberd to give the team some backbone.

When Hebberd's contract expired at the end of July, he flew to Sweden to join Jim Smith on QPR's pre-season tour. Knowing the fee would be decided by a tribunal, Smith offered £200,000 and included him in their next friendly. When Jim Hunt rejected the offer and protested at Hebberd's involvement, he returned home an Oxford player.

Hebberd's personal terms and fee weren't the only obstacles facing Smith; Robert Maxwell was returning from holiday. Evans left Hebberd out of the squad for a friendly against Brentford to allow the two to meet. By the end of the 2-1 win, rumours began circulating that the QPR deal was on the verge of collapse.

Although Hebberd rejected Maxwell's second offer, Rangers couldn't improve on it, and he was cornered. White smoke rose from Headington as Oxford announced that the midfielder had signed a new three-year deal.

With Billy Hamilton's career in decline, Evans needed a target man to support Aldridge. He'd long admired the

Newcastle United centre-forward Billy Whitehurst, missing out when the striker moved from Hull City. Whitehurst's time at St James' Park had been difficult; he hadn't scored for three months and was blighted by injuries. Against a backdrop of talents like Peter Beardsley and Paul Gascoigne he seemed out of step with the club's direction of travel.

The appeal for Evans was the aggression that Whitehurst would add to the squad, but this wasn't limited to the football field. His drinking and brawling was part of the package; you couldn't have one without the other.

Despite the speculation, pre-season was quiet, and a two-game tour of Bulgaria was followed by a trip to Northern Ireland while Maxwell made his son Kevin deputy chairman and invited Patrick Morrisey, director of Mirror Group Newspapers, to join the board.

The Football League announced their plan to introduce a new relegation play-off between the team fourth from bottom of the First Division and those finishing third to fifth in the Second Division. Jim Hunt called it 'the craziest scheme ever dreamed up in the history of the Football League'.

Following an open day where players signed autographs and held a light training session, a week before the start of the season, Oxford won the Oxfordshire Benevolent Cup against Stoke City while at Wembley double winners Liverpool played out a draw with Everton in the Charity Shield, a game Oxford felt they had the right to play in as Milk Cup holders.

The season opened with a sobering 3-0 defeat to Watford at Vicarage Road, the pace of John Barnes and strength of Luther Blissett exposing Oxford's defensive frailties. 'We concede too many goals away,' Evans despaired. 'I changed the system today, but the goals still went in. I'm afraid it's going to be a struggle.'

Evans introduced teenager Tony Obi in the second half ahead of Andy Thomas, who'd drifted to the margins of the squad. Rumours began circulating in the north-east that Newcastle were interested in Thomas's signature.

The home campaign opened at a rain-soaked Manor against Chelsea, whose combative reputation was an Achilles heel for Oxford. In anticipation, the home side started aggressively, with Aldridge forcing Chelsea goalkeeper Tony Godden into an early save and drawing a booking for Joe McLaughlin after a cynical foul when the striker broke clear.

Just before the half-hour point, Chelsea striker David Speedie kicked the ball at Gary Briggs as he lay injured on the floor – angry retribution for Briggs breaking Speedie's teeth in the Full Members' Cup. Speedie was booked alongside Les Phillips for retaliation. The incident inspired Speedie, who'd planned to fine himself £10 for each booking, with a friend matching it for every goal. Nine minutes later his diving header went between striker Kerry Dixon's legs and past the bewildered Alan Judge for the opening goal.

Chelsea failed to build on their lead with their new signing from Hibernian, Gordon Durie, having little impact. They were punished seven minutes after the break when Briggs headed an equaliser from a narrow angle following Dave Langan's free kick. Evans was left frustrated as Oxford laid siege to the Chelsea goal with only Godden standing between them and three points.

Jack Charlton included Aldridge, Houghton and Langan in his Republic of Ireland squad for their opening European Championship qualifying game against Belgium in Brussels. Aldridge, now a Wembley winner, proven top-flight goalscorer and established international striker, could see from the experiences of Ian Rush and Gary Lineker that Oxford were limiting him. 'Going abroad doesn't really appeal to me but money talks. You cannot turn your back on the sort of sums they [foreign clubs] are offering,' he said.

'But it would be nice to play for a big club in England and that's my ambition.'

Despite this, Aldridge was struggling for form as the month ended with the visit of West Ham. Hebberd slotted in perfectly to Evans's sweeper system, collecting loose balls and occasionally breaking the lines to join the attack. He and Shotton controlled Frank McAvennie while Tony Cottee was ably patrolled by Briggs. With Phillips holding in midfield and Langan pushing down the wing, even with a new defensive shape, Oxford looked threatening. Aldridge and Charles had chances while Shotton's ferocious free kick seven minutes into the second half hit Phil Parkes's left-hand post.

But they couldn't break through, and despite being the first team to take points off West Ham that season, they were disappointed not to secure their first win. Hammers manager John Lyall feared that Evans had stumbled on a system which would neutralise his title ambitions.

That evening, in the north-east, Billy Whitehurst's career took another twist. Driving back after Newcastle's draw at Luton, he was breath-tested by police after two pedestrians were knocked down. Out of form and grabbing the headlines, the patience of Newcastle's authoritarian manager Willie McFaul grew thin.

September opened with Oxford still looking for their first win and facing Everton at Goodison Park. Evans hoped Hebberd would again shore up his defence, but it was a rainy night and a difficult surface and after five minutes Hebberd slipped, letting Trevor Steven in for a chance that was blocked by Alan Judge.

Judge then saved from Adrian Heath and Kevin Sheedy. In response, Ray Houghton, Steve Perryman and Les Phillips battled to give chances to Jeremy Charles and John Aldridge before Houghton nearly broke through, firing straight at Bobby Mimms from point-blank range following

Aldridge's knock-down. Everton responded, Graeme Sharp heading Neil Adams's cross wide for the best chance of the half.

Oxford's dogged performance was undone six minutes after the break. Sheedy's pass sent Heath clear and Judge dived at the striker's feet, but the referee ruled he'd taken Heath before the ball and pointed to the spot. Despite Oxford's protests, Trevor Steven calmly opened the scoring.

Aldridge nearly equalised, shooting wide after breaking clear, but Sharp went closer before Judge was relieved to see Alan Harper's shot cannon off the post and into his hands.

A misunderstanding between Paul Power and Kevin Ratcliffe allowed Houghton to equalise, raising hopes for a point. But Harper regained the lead with 18 minutes to go and Kevin Langley shot through a crowd of players to make it three ten minutes later. Maurice Evans thought both sides were 'absolute rubbish', drawing the ire of Everton manager Howard Kendall.

The defeat dropped Oxford to second from bottom in the table, above Ron Atkinson's Manchester United, who hadn't registered a point, a stark contrast to their record-breaking unbeaten start the previous season.

Evans's spluttering defensive changes had only partially worked and the only team to concede more goals were the next visitors to the Manor, Aston Villa. There was another blow before the game when Malcolm Shotton failed a fitness test on his knee, forcing him to miss a game for the first time since the Third Division days.

In the commentary box, Radio Oxford's Peter Baker announced that Shotton had been dropped, infuriating the defender's wife, who nearly phoned the station to correct the reporter. Baker already had his 'prayer mat' out – a gimmick he used for good luck when Oxford needed a goal – he'd need it if Treda caught up with him.

In the opening exchanges, Aldridge threatened to tear Villa apart before Charles sustained a head wound and was replaced by David Leworthy. With 23 minutes to go, Aldridge finally headed his first goal of the season from Langan's cross before Leworthy doubled the lead from Houghton's pass. Simon Stainrod's penalty six minutes from time wasn't enough to stop Oxford from securing their first win of the season.

As Billy Hamilton made another tentative return for the reserves against Arsenal, Aldridge, Houghton and Langan flew to Belgium, securing a 2-2 draw in Brussels before Langan played in their 1-1 draw with Uruguay. Charles and Neil Slatter were in Helsinki as Wales faced Finland. Slatter was introduced at full-back with Finland a goal up. Fifteen minutes later, he met a Clayton Blackmore corner on the volley which ricocheted off Pekonen and the underside of the crossbar before going in.

In the league, a dour goalless draw with Manchester City forced Maurice Evans to address his striking problems. He offloaded Mark Jones to Swindon and had a £200,000 bid for Derby County striker Bobby Davison accepted. Despite their success in recent years, Oxford's appeal was still limited as Davison chose to stay in the Second Division.

The following Wednesday, Jim Hunt took a call from Newcastle's secretary with an offer of £75,000 for Andy Thomas. With a 5pm deadline and Evans unavailable, Hunt consulted Ray Graydon before contacting Robert Maxwell.

Maxwell, who relished transfer negotiations, got Newcastle's chairman Stan Seymour to phone him to agree the fee, securing an extra £10,000 plus £25,000 for 25 appearances.

Hunt and Thomas travelled to Durham to have dinner with Willie McFaul. The following morning, after a medical, the papers were faxed to the Football League to finalise the deal. Hunt left Thomas with his new club, returning home at 8.45pm.

'He needed to get out of this environment,' admitted Evans, who had agreed with Thomas that he'd be open to offers to allow the striker a fresh start following two injury-hit years.

The following Saturday, Oxford headed to Highbury to face Arsenal without Steve Perryman, whose thigh strain forced Hebberd into midfield with Slatter covering as sweeper.

After a goalless first half, Charles clashed with Arsenal's Graham Rix and was sent off for swearing at the linesman. Evans fumed at the official's lack of common sense; he could barely afford to lose Charles in the absence of Billy Hamilton.

Even with ten men, Oxford held out and nearly took the points when Aldridge outmanoeuvred Tony Adams to shoot narrowly wide. To come away from Highbury with a clean sheet and a point and still feel disappointed felt like progress.

In Newcastle, Andy Thomas made his debut against Wimbledon, but Paul Gascoigne's goal ten minutes after half-time was a moment of quality in an otherwise poor game. Billy Whitehurst extended his goalless streak to seven games with a bad miss that drew loud boos from the St James' Park crowd. Whitehurst was defiant. 'People talk about players losing confidence,' he said. 'Well, I don't think that's the case.' Unconvinced, Willie McFaul dropped the striker for their League Cup tie against Bradford City – the competition now sponsored by catalogue shopping company Littlewoods.

John Aldridge was also struggling for goals with just one in seven games. Evans decided a run in the reserves might help him find his range as they began their League Cup defence against Gillingham.

A successful cup campaign was about more than just the pride of being holders. The financial benefits of progressing were essential; despite record prize money of £250,000 for winning the cup, Oxford's first season in the top division had still resulted in a £166,000 financial loss.

Against Gillingham, fresh from the reserves, Aldridge surged back to form to open the scoring after just eight minutes. Mark Weatherley's own goal doubled the lead before Aldridge converted a 37th-minute penalty for number three. He completed his hat-trick on the hour and headed a fourth ten minutes from time.

There was still time for Ray Houghton to complete the thrashing with the sixth of the night, but the much-needed win was overshadowed by a serious knee injury to Jeremy Charles, adding to Evans's growing injury worries.

Off the field, there was good news from the county court. Portsmouth fan Michael Walker had sued the club for £200 for his obstructed view in the previous season's Milk Cup tie. Walker claimed breach of contract, arguing his £10 seat prevented him from seeing any more than a third of the pitch. Judge Clark, presiding over the case, visited the Manor Ground before ruling in favour of the club.

The week ended at home to Charlton, who led after five minutes when Colin Walsh pounced on Alan Judge's fumble. Twelve minutes later Dave Langan crossed for John Aldridge to head the equaliser.

Charlton goalkeeper Nicky Johns saved from Leworthy before Aldridge made it six goals in two games with a penalty after being fouled.

Langan then released Houghton down the flank to cross for Trevor Hebberd to head number three. Another Charlton goal made the final minutes nervy, but Oxford held out for a welcome win.

Jeremy Charles's scan revealed extensive cartilage damage, meaning he faced a lengthy spell out of the game. In the north-east, Billy Whitehurst was facing Derby County in the Central League watched by his old manager, Hull

City's Brian Horton. Willie McFaul admitted he would sell if the price was right, alerting Maurice Evans.

Oxford's optimism collapsed at Hillsborough, where eighth-placed Sheffield Wednesday had already hit the post and had a shot cleared off the line before Carl Shutt opened the scoring after three minutes. By half-time Oxford were three down and a minute after the restart, Shutt made it four.

Wednesday peppered Oxford's goal before Gary Shelton scored a fifth. Aldridge pulled one back on the hour, but Wednesday completed the misery four minutes from time to make it 6-1. Only teenager Sean Reck's debut from the bench and Ray Houghton's industriousness enlightened a dismal performance. Evans demanded the players return to Oxford the next day for extra training, admitting, 'The attitude of some of my players was terrible. We were out-run, out-fought, out-everything.'

Three days later they had an opportunity to shake off the defeat against Gillingham in the second leg of their Littlewoods Cup tie. With a six-goal cushion from the first leg, Evans felt confident enough to recall Billy Hamilton to the starting line-up. Despite having a shot cleared off the line, he looked far from fit and was eventually replaced by Leworthy. Oxford progressed into the next round when Aldridge scored his eighth goal in four games in an unconvincing 1-1 draw.

Things were coming to a head for Billy Whitehurst, and an hour into their second leg against Bradford, Newcastle were struggling to close their 2-0 first-leg deficit. Whitehurst, returning to the starting line-up in place of the injured Andy Thomas, failed to make an impression, forcing McFaul to replace him with Ian Stewart. Whitehurst trudged off to another hail of boos, and finally the striker's frustrations got the better of him as he rudely gestured to the crowd.

That was the final straw, and with 500 fans outside chanting 'sack the board', McFaul transfer-listed Whitehurst. 'It would take seven players to go down with flu or a bomb to drop for me to get another game,' Whitehurst conceded. The incident alerted Evans, who knew Maxwell could outbid Brian Horton for Whitehurst's services.

Maxwell was in a combative mood after Cherwell District Council threw out his latest stadium proposal and the Football League announced that a rival newspaper, *Today*, were to succeed Canon as league sponsors. He was also one of only five chairmen to support Luton Town's ban on away fans, which had led to their expulsion from the Littlewoods Cup.

Evans's own woes deepened as Les Phillips missed the home game with Coventry City. More troubling was a cartilage injury to Alan Judge. With Steve Hardwick struggling with a groin problem Evans signed Tottenham goalkeeper Tony Parks on loan.

With the team patched up, former Wallingford Town defender John Dreyer made his debut in place of Shotton and Hamilton started his first league game since May. A drab first half was enlivened when referee Brian Hill pulled a muscle and was replaced by Don Morgan, before Hebberd fed Houghton to cross for Aldridge to score in his fifth consecutive game.

Aldridge doubled the lead after 77 minutes when the referee gave a penalty for handball by Trevor Peake that only the replacement linesman, Roger Levick of Banbury, seemed to see. With the points secured, Maxwell left early with Ghislaine and a coterie of hangers-on, much to the annoyance of the Coventry board, who'd expected a more attentive welcome.

For Hamilton, the game confirmed something he'd known for more than a year: his career was over. 'I can hardly walk now, the pain is so bad, and it would be another month before I could even think about playing again,' he said. 'A specialist told me to quit 13 months ago but I desperately wanted to go to Mexico. Having done that sweetens the blow. But when I was out there, I was swallowing painkillers like smarties and I knew then that I had little chance of getting over the injury on a permanent basis.'

Hamilton was irreplaceable; in just 41 games he'd scored 20 goals, and with Aldridge he had formed the most potent strike partnership in the club's history. Evans responded with a £175,000 bid for Whitehurst. 'I like his aggression and determination,' he said, undeterred by the news that the police were passing a file to the Crown Prosecution Service for his accident in September. Newcastle accepted the offer, and after 12 hours of negotiations and a bombastic intervention by Maxwell, Evans had his man.

The following day, while Langan, Houghton and Aldridge featured in a drab goalless draw against Scotland in Dublin, Whitehurst arrived at the club and was approached by a stranger with a curious problem.

'Can you help me find my tortoise?' the individual said. The two started to search for the lost reptile before the players appeared laughing. Whitehurst had been pranked by Terry Gordon, a friend of Peter Rhoades-Brown, and a regular presence around the squad.

Whitehurst's eventful week continued the following day when he was summoned to court for another speeding offence from August, but he went straight into the team to face Liverpool at Anfield.

Mindful of their 6-0 thumping the previous season, the players sat in the dressing room preparing for Maurice Evans's team talk. As he started, Whitehurst interrupted him to describe a dream he'd had in which Oxford had won 2-1.

'What a dream that was,' said Whitehurst, leaving Evans dumbfounded.

Whitehurst was keen to make a good impression, forcing Bruce Grobbelaar into a scrambling clearance from Hebberd's early through ball. Despite that threat, Liverpool seemed to be playing within themselves with Alan Hansen and Gary Gillespie containing Langan's crosses with ease.

After 24 minutes, Whitehurst jumped for a high cross. As he landed, he felt a sharp pain in his back. Evans, fearing a curse which had struck Billy Hamilton and Jeremy Charles, signalled to Sean Reck to replace the stricken striker. Whitehurst's debut was over before half-time.

Four minutes later, Oxford buckled and Rush grabbed his 200th Liverpool goal, glancing home Steve Nicol's cross. Within four minutes it was two as Kenny Dalglish was played in by Rush. Tony Parks kept Liverpool at bay until John Dreyer handled in the box and Jan Mølby converted the penalty eight minutes into the second half. Rush completed the rout in the last minute.

Evans could only applaud. 'I was sitting with Steve Perryman and we concluded that Kenny Dalglish is the best thinker in football,' he said. 'You can almost hear the brain ticking over from the stand.' As for Evans, his big-name striker was in hospital, flat on his back in a plaster jacket, where he would remain for the next 48 hours.

Chapter 20

Ron Atkinson

BY FEBRUARY 1964 the British cultural landscape was shifting; the postwar generation was turning to adulthood. Its first celebrity, Elvis Presley, had hit a mid-career slump after being dragged through a relentless schedule of underwhelming films and soundtrack tie-ins that sacrificed the quality and vibrancy of his early releases.

Into the void stepped the Beatles, their impish charisma shining through in their debut LP and a procession of hit singles. It wasn't long before the news of their success reached an American public desperate to escape their mourning after the assassination of John F. Kennedy.

On 7 February 1964, following the release of their album *Meet the Beatles!*, the group flew out from Heathrow – waved off by 4,000 screaming fans – and landed in New York to be greeted by thousands more. An appearance on *The Ed Sullivan Show* – beamed to 73 million people, the biggest US TV audience in history at that time – propelled them into the consciousness of the nation's youth. By the time they flew back to England on 22 February, the Beatles were global superstars who had ignited a cultural revolution.

A week after the Beatles left for the US, the youngest Football League club, Fourth Division Oxford United, were preparing for their biggest ever game against double-chasing Blackburn Rovers at the Manor in the FA Cup fifth round.

The stadium was overflowing with a record crowd of 21,700 fans. Kicking towards the Cuckoo Lane End, Tony Jones gave Oxford the lead from eight yards. Terrorised by Peter Knight on the right wing, the minnows pressed Blackburn back.

Attacking down the slope in the second half, Jones added a second before Blackburn responded with a volley from outside-right Mick Ferguson. Unperturbed, in the last minute Pat Quartermain centred for Bill Calder to tap in for 3-1. At the final whistle, fans streamed on to the pitch from all sides. It was the shock of the round in an age when the FA Cup enjoyed primacy in the nation's consciousness, and the next day newspapers shone a light on the club like never before. If the Beatles' American odyssey framed the revolution, fleetingly, Oxford United were part of the zeitgeist.

In the glare of the spotlight, one Oxford player felt right at home: 24-year-old captain Ron Atkinson. Known to fans as 'The Tank' due to his angular build, Atkinson was gregarious and outgoing, awash with charisma.

He'd arrived at Oxford four years earlier. Starting as an apprentice at Wolves, where he'd been mesmerised by the exhibition game against Honvéd in 1954, he joined Aston Villa but was released in 1959 before making an appearance and was sent south to play for Headington United in the Southern League. It was a drop in divisions so far and obscure that he thought he was being sent to London.

Over 12 years he would accumulate a record 562 appearances, leading the team into the Football League. In 1962 he was joined by his brother Graham, who scored Oxford's first goal in the Football League, one of the 107 that made him the club's all-time leading goalscorer.

The win over Blackburn made Oxford the first Fourth Division club to reach the FA Cup quarter-final. Ever the opportunist, Atkinson set up a players' pool to maximise the commercial benefits of their success, a tradition usually reserved for cup finalists. The move attracted a stinging rebuke from the press at Atkinson's arrogance, despite the £15 they made from selling the match ball to a local bookmaker.

Although success was short-lived – another record crowd saw a narrow defeat to Preston North End in the next round – it gave Atkinson a taste for a high life that he liked.

In 1971, Atkinson left Oxford to become player-manager of Kettering. After promotion to the Southern League Premier Division and the title the following year, plus an FA Cup giant-killing over Swansea City, his success attracted Fourth Division Cambridge United, who offered him his first Football League appointment.

Atkinson's simple philosophy paid dividends; like his kindred spirit Jim Smith he treated players like he wanted to be treated. After three seasons Cambridge won the Fourth Division title and were on the verge of a second promotion when First Division West Bromwich Albion approached Atkinson to take over at The Hawthorns.

The successes of Bill Shankly and Matt Busby at Liverpool and Manchester United during the 1960s had helped to mythologise the cult of the football manager. No longer taciturn administrators, they were now genius witch doctors and media personalities. Colour television and mass media consumption brought the personalities to the fore. A generation of larger-than-life characters like Don Revie, Alan Mullery and Brian Clough dominated the game.

Atkinson was the apotheosis of that generation with his gift for one-liners, a taste for the champagne lifestyle, expensive clothes and outlandish jewellery. Decades later, parodies of football managers would lift directly from Atkinson's traits.

At West Brom, he created a team in his image, full of attacking vigour led by Laurie Cunningham, Cyrille Regis and Brendon Batson – labelled 'The Three Degrees'. West Brom were the first club to regularly feature three black players, a milestone for first-generation migrants in English professional football.

They fired West Brom to an FA Cup semi-final, a UEFA Cup quarter-final and a fourth-place finish in the First Division, threatening Liverpool's stranglehold as champions of England. But, before the project could be completed, Atkinson started attracting the attention of an even bigger name.

Manchester United were suffering an extended hangover after their stellar years under Sir Matt Busby. They needed someone to compete with Liverpool's winning machine and the mercurial Brian Clough at Nottingham Forest; Atkinson and Manchester United made sense.

Spending heavily, including the record-breaking signing of Bryan Robson from West Brom for £1.5m, Atkinson secured United's first silverware for six years with an FA Cup win in 1983, regaining the trophy in 1985. Hopes were raised that he would eventually bring the title back to Old Trafford.

Everything seemed to come together at the beginning of 1985/86. As Liverpool recovered from the Heysel tragedy and the unexpected resignation of manager Joe Fagan, United registered 13 wins in 15 unbeaten games, winning their first ten. By November, they were ten points clear at the top of the table.

Injuries to Robson, Jesper Olsen and Remi Moses disrupted their rhythm, and a secret deal to sell Mark Hughes to Barcelona killed United's momentum. A rampant drinking culture and ill discipline added to the sense of chaos. If Atkinson's personality was larger than life, the team he'd created had become a monster. Winning just nine more games, they finished the season fourth.

The following campaign was a disaster; during the World Cup Robson was injured before Hughes left for Barcelona. Rumours of ill discipline at Old Trafford grew and the European ban meant spending had to be reined in. The era of the ostentatious manager came to an end. With United in 19th, two places below Oxford, for the first time in his colourful career, Ron Atkinson was on the brink.

While Atkinson's troubles simmered ominously, back at his old club, after the sobering defeat to Liverpool, Maurice Evans faced league leaders Nottingham Forest at the Manor without his marquee signing, his captain or either goalkeeper.

To compound things, the day before the game he arrived at the Manor to find that John Aldridge had gone down with food poisoning. With ten goals in six games Evans could ill afford to lose him now. He was also becoming concerned about Dave Langan's form and pulled him aside at training to tell him he was at risk of being dropped.

By contrast, Brian Clough's men had started the season in blistering form, scoring 26 goals in their opening 11 games, providing the biggest test to Oxford's five-month unbeaten home record.

On the morning of the game, Evans was relieved when Aldridge declared himself fit to play. David Leworthy replaced Billy Whitehurst and Kevin Brock made his first start since the Milk Cup Final. The plan was to target Dutch playmaker John Metgod in midfield while doubling up on the threatening Franz Carr with John Dreyer and Neil Slatter.

There were ominous signs for Clough when their coach was held up in traffic and the team arrived barely half an hour before kick-off. A blustery autumnal wind swirled around the Manor, disrupting their rhythm, a timely reminder of the tiny ground's formidable powers.

After half an hour, Langan, stung by Evans's rebuke, intercepted Stuart Pearce's pass, breaking down the left and crossing for Aldridge to prod past Hans Segers at the second attempt. It was a deserved reward for Oxford, whose attacking was matched by a defensive steel against the league's most potent attack. Gary Briggs and John Dreyer went into the book as they limited Forest to one shot on goal. Moments before half-time, Aldridge turned provider, evading Des Walker to square for Ray Houghton, who chipped delicately for 2-0. As the half-time whistle went, the Manor bellowed its appreciation.

Evans knew he'd rattled Clough when five minutes before the end of the break the Forest players trudged past the home dressing room back on to the pitch. As he'd done at the City Ground the previous season, the league leaders were forced to shiver in front of the bemused crowd waiting for their opponents.

The humiliation had little effect until Oxford tired. With 20 minutes to go Pearce pulled one back from the penalty spot after Brock handled, and with four minutes left Dreyer picked up a second booking for a foul on Nigel Clough, departing to a standing ovation from the Beech Road stand.

'Ninety per cent of our lot ought to be embarrassed by their display,' Clough fumed before leaving the Manor without a word to Evans, who for once was happy to face the media. When asked why his team had won his answer was simple, 'Determination.' Beating the table-toppers gave Evans renewed hope; without Billy Hamilton or Malcolm Shotton, Aldridge's form had eased them to a comfortable 15th place.

Attention returned to the Littlewoods Cup and Sheffield United; set-piece goals from Gary Briggs and Neil Slatter put the tie beyond doubt before half-time. The irrepressible Aldridge made it 12 in eight with the decisive finish two minutes after the break. Only a late consolation dampened an otherwise comfortable 3-1 victory.

Following a disappointing goalless draw against Newcastle at St James' Park, Evans received another blow at the start of November when Steve Perryman opened talks with Brentford to become their assistant manager.

As Evans battled to maintain stability, Manchester United were a rolling soap opera. Having lost five of their first seven games, a defeat to Chelsea, including two missed penalties in a minute, heaped more pressure on. Off the field, the rabid tabloid press had a field day when Remi Moses punched Jesper Olsen in training, leaving the Dane with a black eye.

A 4-1 defeat to Southampton in the Littlewoods Cup finally put paid to Atkinson's tenure with United sitting fourth from bottom.

In Scotland, three days before United's visit to the Manor, Aberdeen manager Alex Ferguson was preparing his side for a league game against St Mirren when Manchester United chief executive Martin Edwards phoned to offer the Scot Atkinson's job. Ferguson had built Aberdeen to be a dominant force in Scottish football, winning ten trophies in eight years. He'd been Scotland's caretaker manager during the World Cup in Mexico after Jock Stein died after a qualifier against Wales. Before his death, Stein told Ferguson his biggest regret had been turning the United job down when he was Celtic manager. When Edwards called, Ferguson didn't hesitate to say yes.

The Manor became the backdrop to Ferguson's arrival in English football. He was mobbed by both sets of fans while getting off the coach as his team eased their way through the throng.

Ferguson was without Gordon Strachan and Colin Gibson for the game while Evans had the benefit of Shotton returning to the starting 11, allowing Slatter to move to left-back.

The fixture attracted a full house with the Beech Road and London Road areas filling early, forcing fans into the Osler Road terrace. Before the game, Ray Houghton received the Player of the Month award for October while Danish Oxford speedway star Hans Nielsen paraded the world championship trophy he'd won in Poland a couple of months earlier. Oxford had become an unlikely nexus of sporting success.

Ferguson sat in the Beech Road stand for the first half as Oxford dominated the opening exchanges while attacking the Cuckoo Lane End. Houghton and Phillips overpowered Paul McGrath, playing in midfield after being moved out of defence by Ferguson. The territorial advantage allowed Oxford to target United's defensive frailties, a product of Ron Atkinson's preference for extravagant attacking over defensive assurance.

After 16 minutes, Aldridge pounced on a loose ball on the left, cutting inside to wrong-foot Kevin Moran. The defender's trailing leg sent Aldridge crashing to the floor. The striker made no mistake from the spot kick, giving Ferguson a nightmare start.

Aldridge almost doubled the lead minutes later but was thwarted by Mike Duxbury from three yards out before a third chance went narrowly wide. Oxford continued to press and were disappointed to go into the break with only a one-goal lead.

Ferguson, frustrated at his team's lacklustre display, unleashed his fury in the away dressing room before heading to the bench in the second half. The roasting had some effect as his new charges showed some fighting spirit with Frank Stapleton clipping the top of the bar.

Nonetheless, attacking down the slope towards the London Road terrace, Oxford were a constant threat. With ten minutes to go Brock's corner was cleared to Houghton, whose long looping cross fell back to Brock on the back post. He drove the ball low into the six-yard box for Neil Slatter to poke home the crucial second goal.

Ferguson watched on, frustrated by his team's lack of fitness and drive. Throughout the half, next to him sat a bespectacled man in a casual jacket, not someone Ferguson recognised from the coaching staff who were in tracksuits.

'Who are you?' he said eventually. 'Derek,' the man replied. Derek 'Sooty' Sutton drove the Manchester United team coach. Under Atkinson, he'd become a regular fixture in the team's dugout. For Ferguson, it illustrated the depth of the problems he'd inherited at a club intoxicated by its own hubris. Derek was never seen on the Manchester United bench again.

The result reignited memories of the great nights at the Manor; a win over Manchester United, a prize scalp regardless of their ineptitude. Afterwards, Evans joked about the anticlimax of Ferguson's debut in the cramped Manor with its 13,000 fans. Ferguson, surrounded by reporters, admitted he was glad it was over, remaining calm even when one local radio journalist asked for his views on calls from the London Road terrace that he should resign.

John Aldridge's scorching form had put Oxford back on track; the win had catapulted them to tenth in the table. Maurice Evans finally seemed to be enjoying his success, joking that his team were so high up the table, he was getting a nosebleed. For Aldridge, though, thoughts were beginning to turn elsewhere.

Chapter 21

Bogart's

WHEN JIM Smith arrived at the Manor, his infectious influence spread across the club. He was quick to ingratiate himself with Ken Fish, Robert Maxwell's secretary Jean Baddeley and groundsman Mick Moore. It gave him ears and eyes in every corner of the club. When Maxwell appointed Brian Dalton in 1985, threatening to break these bonds, it convinced Smith to resign.

The camaraderie spread across the squad; amid the broken teacups and tears, Smith tapped into the psyche of the players, developing a pack mentality they craved. Bobby McDonald was integral to implementing a 'no blame' culture when the team reached the top flight, which was cemented by an active and tightly bonded social scene, nights out for the squad and a coffee club for the wives and girlfriends.

Win or lose, Saturday socials would often start in the supporters' club at the Manor or the Britannia pub across the road where the club was originally founded. It would invariably progress to Bogart's nightclub, which was owned by Oxford fan Steve Winstone.

Bogart's was on The Plain, a roundabout which acted as an intersection between the suburbs, the working-class area of Cowley and the university quarters in the city centre. As students, including future prime ministers Boris Johnson and David Cameron, enacted their entitled debauchery on the other side of Magdalen Bridge, Bogart's was the meeting point of town and gown.

As the unofficial clubhouse for the squad, it often attracted those looking for confrontation. Anyone picking a fight with Malcolm Shotton or Gary Briggs would be quickly put in their place but occasionally the trouble would spill over. One night, the squad were drinking in the club when a local invited Bobby McDonald outside for a fight. McDonald, concerned that he might be outnumbered, asked John Aldridge and Les Phillips to provide reinforcements.

As McDonald and his opponent set about sorting out their differences, Aldridge decided attack was the best form of defence and swung a wild punch. He missed and caught Phillips full in the face, laying him out on the floor.

Mishaps aside, nights in Bogart's helped get the squad through the toughest times. But as 1986 came to an end, the bonds were becoming brittle and started to fragment. One tempestuous decision would threaten to tear it all apart.

Although it was bright and sunny outside, in a hotel room in Manchester the day had yet to begin. Daylight fought to make itself known through the cracks in the curtains. Those inside stubbornly refused to stir; they wanted to sleep for as long as the adrenaline and nerves would allow.

The phone punctuated the silence and Aldridge opened his eyes, his brain dragging him back to sleep. Still orientating himself, he sensed movement in the room; on some subconscious level, he'd been aware of it all night. A shadow reached out, reacting to the din.

Nobody calls at 10am on a matchday. In a half croak Aldridge's room-mate McDonald picked up the phone and uttered his first words of the day. 'OK, I'll send him down, boss,' he said, before replacing the receiver as Aldridge woke with a jolt.

Recent weeks had been like this: disorientating and unsettling. Players usually lived in a bubble, scrutinised and judged, detached yet constantly in the spotlight. Their response was to play; as they acclimatised to their curious existence, they evolved from being a person to being a player.

John Aldridge hadn't fully completed that journey. He'd played in the lower leagues, worked in factories, now he was famous; people talked about him. Recently they'd talked about him a lot. The person inside him was still catching up.

'John,' McDonald said. 'The boss wants to see you in his room. You know what that means, don't you?'

He did, he'd thought about little else, talked about little else, read about little else. His only escape was on the pitch, where he could let the troubles flow from him and allow his instinct to take over. His mind was racing, ideas and thoughts flying past like a fruit machine spinning with the tantalising prospect of a jackpot.

Bobby McDonald stood by him, 'That's your move to Liverpool.'

Liverpool was almost too perfect. When Ian Rush announced his move to Italy, Aldridge was the obvious replacement; they looked identical and shared a similar style. To many Liverpool fans, scarred by the loss of their record goalscorer, it would mean little adjustment, a seamless transition, almost as if Rush hadn't left at all.

But Aldridge was three years older, he thought he had one more contract before his career would begin its downward trajectory. Would Liverpool really sign an older, unproven version of what they had before?

Aldridge was now a dominant striker in English football. Maurice Evans knew it, and even before the win against Alex Ferguson's Manchester United he'd fielded an enquiry from

Arsenal and warned them off with a £1m price tag. Evans knew it was only a matter of time before there'd be a bid he couldn't refuse, or more specifically, one that Aldridge wouldn't.

Aldridge was comfortable at Oxford; he scored goals and knew the fans would pull him through barren runs and poor form. He'd already achieved everything he thought was possible.

Immediately after the win against United, he headed off on international duty, along with Dave Langan and Ray Houghton, losing 1-0 to Poland in Warsaw before rejoining their team-mates to face Queens Park Rangers at Loftus Road in a rerun of the Milk Cup Final.

For years, cold winters and hot summers had left the Loftus Road pitch without any grass. During the wet winter months it would churn up and during the summer it would become hard and dusty. Looking for a solution, Rangers officials had visited Houston Astros in the US to look at their artificial Astroturf but opted for the cheaper Omni Turf: a carpet laid over a slab of concrete.

The pitch offered another advantage as balls would bounce freakishly, slide tackles would give nasty burns, and goalkeepers had to wear tracksuits to protect themselves. The unique surface helped Rangers to the FA Cup Final, promotion to the First Division, a place in the UEFA Cup and the Milk Cup Final. But they were out of form and fans were becoming restless with Jim Smith.

The surface gave ball players like Ray Houghton and Kevin Brock the opportunity to attack. Surviving an early scare, when Malcolm Shotton cleared off the line after half an hour, Les Phillips sent David Leworthy clear to square the ball to Houghton, who mis-hit his shot into the ground. The force caused the ball to bounce up and over David Seaman's head and into the net. The stadium was consumed by an eerie silence. The home support were stunned; the visiting fans seemed unaware their team had scored. Oxford had benefited from the strange surface, but they deserved their lead.

Leworthy and Brock had opportunities in the second half and Oxford were denied a penalty when Houghton was brought down. Entering the final moments, they were set to heap more misery and pressure on Smith.

With two minutes to go the game became stretched and Aldridge broke clear, pulling the ball back for Houghton, whose shot hit the post. The play grew more desperate. Oxford fans readied themselves to celebrate a rare away win as Rangers pumped the ball forward, John Trewick misjudged the freakish bounce, Robbie James was free, and he fed John Byrne to score a barely deserved equaliser.

It was cruel luck and even Jim Smith offered his condolences. After a curt interview with the press, the usually placid Maurice Evans fumed in the dressing room. The anger flowed through him uncontrollably, demanding the players were back on the team bus by 5.30pm, much earlier than normal.

The tightly bonded group decided there was just enough time to drown their sorrows in the bar. After their drink, John Aldridge, Kevin Brock, Jeremy Charles, Steve Hardwick, Les Phillips, Peter Rhoades-Brown and Malcolm Shotton headed to the pick-up point but were briefly held up by autograph hunters. When they reached the car park, the coach was gone. A few Oxford fans were milling around and one told Aldridge it had left a few minutes earlier. The players were stranded and had to get a lift back with some Oxford directors.

For Aldridge, the fragments of doubt, hope, ambition and fear calcified; what was he worried about? Why should he be limited? Ian Rush's replacement at Liverpool? If not him, then who and if not now, then when?

Evans's pettiness was out of character, but it highlighted what was holding Aldridge back. He would always be beholden to the club's character flaws in the way an institution like Liverpool and Arsenal never could.

Aldridge contacted his agent Eric Hall, a music promoter who'd drifted into football after bumping into Steve Perryman in a nightclub. Hall knew little about football, but as a promoter of the Sex Pistols, he knew how to manipulate the media. He contacted *The Sun* with an exclusive: Aldridge wanted out. 'I can't see Oxford chasing honours,' he was quoted as saying. 'This latest incident sums up how small they are.'

Except that's not how Aldridge saw it; he was angry at the petty decision to leave the players at Loftus Road, not at the club. The misreading suited Hall and *The Sun*, and the Liverpool hierarchy sensed an opportunity.

The following Monday, Aldridge handed his transfer request to the crestfallen Evans who was contrite, apologising and admitting he'd acted in haste. The players apologised for being late, but it did little to soften Aldridge's resolve.

Robert Maxwell phoned later that day. Aldridge expected to be offered a new deal, money often being Maxwell's answer to problems. But the chairman was just angry that Hall had gone to *The Sun* with the exclusive, telling Aldridge, 'If you need to do these things, they need to be done in the *Daily Mirror*.'

Maxwell used his newspaper to respond. 'Aldridge's transfer request has been made in such a rude and improper manner that no notice will be taken of it,' he announced haughtily. 'His agent must realise that this lack of professional conduct has diminished his chance of getting away.' There were no formal bids, so no basis on which to request a move, he argued. Maxwell planned to ignore his player's tantrum.

The following day, Aldridge hit back, 'I expected him to say something like that. I'm sticking to my guns. I still want away.'

Maxwell responded, 'The fact that he chose to inform his agent of the transfer request before informing the club will prove to be a stupid and disastrous move.'

While the feud intensified, Oxford travelled to Upton Park to continue their defence of the Littlewoods Cup against West Ham. Already burdened with injuries, United lost Trewick on the morning of the game with a broken nose after a collision with reserve goalkeeper Brian Vasey during training. Surprisingly, Evans gave teenager Sean Reck his first start in defence.

In wet and windy conditions, Houghton nearly opened the scoring after a minute before Brock's lob clipped the bar midway through the half. Just before half-time Aldridge raced into the box but slipped while preparing to shoot. Oxford went into the break looking the stronger side, but an Achilles injury forced Evans to replace Gary Briggs with John Dreyer.

After the break, Frank McAvennie drew a solid save from Hardwick as West Ham dragged themselves back into the tie. With ten minutes to go the Scottish international burst into the Oxford box and appeared to stumble in the mud. To Oxford's amazement, referee Howard Taylor pointed to the spot for a foul by Shotton. Despite the protests, Tony Cottee blasted his kick into the roof of Steve Hardwick's goal.

Oxford's grip on their trophy was slipping with every passing second as the game descended into chaos. Two minutes later, Taylor sent Les Phillips off for dissent for sarcastically clapping his erratic display.

Oxford were out. Shotton insisted he hadn't touched McAvennie, Evans describing the decision as a joke but stopped short of commenting on Phillips's sending-off for fear of FA reprisals. He signed off by saying that he was so frustrated, he was walking home.

Four days later, Oxford defended their impressive home record against Tottenham Hotspur, featuring goalkeeper Tony Parks just two weeks after returning to his parent club. Spurs were just above Oxford in tenth with their striker, Clive Allen, in similar form to Aldridge.

After three minutes, Ray Clemence parried Aldridge's shot into the path of David Leworthy to prod home against his old club. The lead lasted for just over ten minutes when Spurs sliced through the Oxford defence for Allen to side-foot the equaliser. After 25 minutes Houghton headed Glenn Hoddle's cross to Allen, who volleyed home for 2-1.

Houghton's error seemed to break Oxford and it wasn't long before Chris Waddle scored his side's third. Briggs pulled a goal back only for Ardiles to send Waddle away in the closing minutes to make it 4-2 and inflict Oxford's first home defeat for six months.

After a bruising week, Ray Graydon took a strong squad to defend their national five-a-side title backed by over 1,000 fans, including Maurice Evans, who sat with his wife in the stands. With Oxford City loanee Paul Richardson in goal, they beat Aston Villa 2-0 but were defeated by Southampton in the second round with a goal from teenager Matt Le Tissier, a former trialist at the Manor.

With the month turning sour, Oxford hosted Norwich City without Houghton and Shotton but with Phillips back from suspension and Bobby McDonald returning for the first time since January. Billy Whitehurst had also recovered from the back injury he picked up on his debut against Liverpool.

Thick fog didn't help the spectacle and it was no surprise when Norwich went ahead from Kevin Drinkell's header after 13 minutes. Nine minutes later, Hardwick failed to hold Ian Crook's free kick, allowing Dale Gordon to prod in for 2-0. Eleven minutes before half-time Aldridge headed in Leworthy's cross for his first goal since the furore over his transfer request.

After the break, Whitehurst had a header cleared off the line, but a late tackle on Mark Seagraves drew a second booking and a sending-off. Whitehurst had played two games and hadn't finished either.

Five minutes from time, Norwich striker Wayne Biggins was taken off with concussion, coming round in the dressing room to ask if he'd scored. He hadn't, but his side had secured three points.

Four games without a win, Aldridge agitating for a move, poor discipline and injury problems; Evans was forced to defend his side from accusations they were a dirty team, despite Sean Reck being booked in each of his first six professional games.

Another shuffle was required for the home game against Luton; Phillips was suspended and Shotton injured but Houghton, Trewick and Trevor Hebberd all returned. Luton had Les Sealey in goal four days after his brother had been killed in a car accident. Mercilessly, Briggs charged into the keeper in the opening minutes to test his resolve.

Minutes later, Sealey recklessly pursued a diagonal pass from Aldridge as Houghton closed in. The midfielder got to the ball first and touched it around Sealey, crossing for Aldridge to score from eight yards. Houghton followed it up with a world-class chip for number two before Brock made it three with a thunderous volley on the hour.

Oxford eased off, allowing Brian and Mark Stein to score in a four-minute burst to bring it back to 3-2 with 15 minutes to go. Mike Newell forced a smart save from Hardwick before Aldridge completed his hat-trick on the stroke of full-time. 'I have been feeling a little poorly in the last few days,' Evans said, 'but he has cheered me up a bit.'

Two days later, heading to Truro for a friendly to celebrate the non-league side's new floodlights, Oxford drew Fourth Division Aldershot Town in the FA Cup. For all the struggle resulting from Heysel and Bradford, it was nothing compared to clubs further down the divisions. Aldershot were £250,000 in debt and their Recreation Ground reduced to a capacity of just 3,000, so the draw offered a lifeline they were keen to make the most of.

Direct from Truro, Ray Graydon led Lee Nogan, John Dreyer, Paul Swannack, John Trewick, John Aldridge, Bobby McDonald, Eddie Denton, Steve Hardwick, Kevin Brock and David Leworthy to Manchester for the annual Guinness Soccer Six tournament.

Featuring on the BBC's *Sportsnight*, the tournament was held in the newly opened GMEX Arena, a converted railway station. Despite being seeded as Milk Cup holders, the draw against Chelsea and Manchester United in Group D meant Oxford were very much underdogs. 'I wondered what reaction I would witness from the senior players,' said Graydon. 'Any doubts were soon dispelled, however, when the players heard the roar of the crowd in the first match versus Manchester United.'

In front of a partisan Manchester crowd, Oxford kicked off and the early pace was fierce with rolling substitutes draining the players' energy. Aldridge had the first chance before Hardwick saved from Mike Duxbury after Gibson had darted in from the substitutes' bench to cheekily rob McDonald of possession. With 90 seconds of the first half to go, Brock skewed a shot off the boards and Aldridge tapped in the rebound past Chris Turner.

Sensing humiliation, United's competitive pride took over. Gibson had the ball in the net but Dixon was inside the goalkeeper's box, one of the many idiosyncratic rules the players had to get used to. Peter Barnes rattled the bar before Peter Davenport's shot hit the inside of the post and ricocheted into Hardwick's arms. With a minute to go Duxbury's drive was finally steered in by Davenport for 1-1.

With seconds remaining, both teams attacked furiously; Gibson was sin-binned for breaking a rule which stated at least one player had to stay in the opposition's half. McDonald rolled the free kick to Trewick, who fed Leworthy to stun the home crowd with the winner.

Oxford's draw against Chelsea put United out of the tournament and left the Londoners needing to win their last match to reach the final. With Alex Ferguson watching, United had pride to play for which encouraged a free-flowing game. Davenport scored in the first half before John McNaught equalised, then Gibson volleyed in Liam O'Brien's crossfield ball for 2-1.

In the second half, Jesper Olsen waltzed through the Chelsea defence to make it three, putting Oxford on the verge of the final. Confirmation came when Gibson made it four and Billy Garton scored the fifth. Late goals from Micky Hazard and Roy Wegerle weren't enough to prevent Oxford from making the final.

Facing the league leaders Arsenal, Oxford would have to muster some of the spirit of their great cup wins if they were to have a hope.

Early on, Brock fired wide before Hardwick parried Ian Allinson's shot and Aldridge hit the post. After the furious start, the game settled into a cagier affair before Graham Rix attacked down the left, slipping the ball under Hardwick. John Dreyer instinctively tracked back to clear, stepping into the box and conceding a penalty which Michael Thomas thundered into the back of the net for 1-0.

Searching for a way back, Aldridge was reintroduced, giving Oxford hope. They continued to press, but Arsenal's tight defence kept them at bay. With three minutes remaining,

Trewick's quick corner allowed Aldridge to ghost in at the near post to poke in the equaliser.

Arsenal's response was instant, but Hardwick confirmed his Player of the Tournament award by saving a stinging drive which dropped to Aldridge to clear. From the sidelines, Graydon sent teenager Paul Swannock on to the field as Arsenal retained possession preparing for penalties. As the seconds counted down Arsenal were penalised when a long ball didn't bounce in the central section of the pitch, leaving Oxford one last chance.

Knowing there was no time, the ball was worked back to Dreyer, whose only option was to shoot. John Lukic parried, but the ball fell to Swannock, who poked in the winner to give Oxford the Soccer Six title. Trewick lifted the trophy and received a £10,000 cheque in front of an increasingly disinterested Mancunian crowd; nonetheless it was more silverware for the trophy cabinet.

Oxford hoped to take that momentum into their trip to Filbert Street to play Leicester City, who were struggling in 20th with just two points from nine games. The morning kick-off, an experiment to boost crowds, left frost on the pitch, making the conditions treacherous.

John Dreyer's early dipping free kick was tipped away by Ian Andrews before a five-man move sliced through the Oxford defence to allow Alan Smith to open the scoring. Aldridge nearly equalised a minute later but his contribution was limited by the lack of a physical presence offered by the suspended Billy Whitehurst. With 17 minutes to go Ian Wilson combined with Andy Feeley to slide the ball past Steve Hardwick for 2-0, leaving Oxford 13th.

After much deliberation, the following day, Aldershot revealed their plans for the cup tie. Having rejected a switch to the Manor, they decided to increase their prices by 300 per cent with terrace tickets costing £9 and seating £11 –

more than the FA Cup Final itself. Fans flooded the local newspaper to complain, and an FA spokesman summed up the sense of shock, 'Good god, I am amazed.'

Five days before Christmas, before the home game against Aston Villa, players and officials were told that chief executive Brian Dalton, whose arrival had triggered Jim Smith's departure, had left the club, another victim of Maxwell's endless reshuffling.

The match started brightly as Garry Thompson put Villa ahead after seven minutes. When Nigel Spink was penalised for time-wasting after just quarter of an hour, Briggs equalised from Houghton's free kick. Villa restored their lead after 25 minutes when Mark Walters hooked the ball spectacularly into the far corner.

The game pivoted in the second half when referee Keith Miller pulled a muscle and was replaced by linesman George Pearson. Les Phillips returned from suspension to replace Bobby McDonald. Six minutes later Aldridge equalised from the spot, after Pearson judged that Gary Williams had brought down Phillips in the box, a decision so ludicrous that even Phillips laughed at it.

Phillips led the search for a winner but in his eagerness he was booked for dissent, then another foul on Williams five minutes later led to a red card. His return from suspension lasted 16 minutes.

On Boxing Day, Oxford travelled to Wimbledon with striker Alan Cork setting the tone for a game high on farce and low on quality, appearing from the tunnel wearing a set of Mickey Mouse ears.

John Fashanu unsettled Oxford's defence, although one foul on Steve Hardwick seemed so harsh that even he appealed the decision. After half an hour Fashanu finally beat Hardwick to a cross, the goalkeeper bringing the big striker crashing to the floor, allowing Glyn Hodges to convert the penalty. Ten minutes after half-time, Oxford lost Billy Whitehurst to concussion before Aldridge volleyed home Houghton's cross for the equaliser with six minutes to go.

The following day, Oxford were back at the Manor for the return of Jim Smith. It allowed Maurice Evans to reflect on working with his old friend – the happiest time of his career. Oxford started well, nearly taking the lead after 25 minutes from Dreyer. Five minutes later Aldridge headed Dave Langan's cross just wide.

The game flared up just before the hour when Briggs floored Ian Dawes near the corner flag. Already booked, the referee had little option but to send the defender off. Almost immediately, Dreyer sliced the ball into his own net under pressure from Leighton James for QPR's winner. As the players headed for their Christmas party, Evans lamented the team's lack of discipline: 'Don't ask me any questions about the sending-off. We work hard all week and now get this.'

Despite the frustrations, the turn of the year saw Oxford sitting comfortably in 14th and welcoming injury-ravaged Southampton to the Manor. McDonald returned to replace Trewick, who was ill, as Oxford took control early on. After half an hour Gerry Forrest brought down Aldridge for a penalty. Forrest's protests led to a red card before Aldridge converted from the spot, making him the second-highest scorer in Oxford's history. Three minutes later Whitehurst scored his first for the club to double the lead. Despite Jimmy Case hitting the bar for the visitors, Oxford's numerical advantage allowed Houghton to score the third with 15 minutes to go.

Evans was content that his side had become hard to beat. If he could maintain a goal threat, he was sure he could avoid relegation, though he was under no illusions as to how difficult that would be.

Oxford travelled to Manchester to face City at Maine Road on 3 January when the call finally came from Liverpool with a £750,000 bid for John Aldridge. Even Maxwell accepted the price was good and there was little they could do to stop the striker.

Evans knew the news would soon be in the press and that he couldn't risk reopening old wounds, so he phoned Aldridge's room and asked him to come down. Aldridge took 20 minutes to arrive, wanting to play it cool, but his head was spinning. As soon as McDonald told him, mentally he was already walking through the Shankly Gates at Anfield.

The disruption at Maine Road wasn't limited to Aldridge; Sean Reck replaced the suspended Phillips and teenager Lee Nogan joined the squad due to an illness for David Leworthy.

After 20 minutes, Hardwick reacted slowly to a City through ball, taking Paul Simpson's legs and conceding a penalty. Despite the keeper's protests, Neil McNab converted the spot kick for the only goal of the game.

Aldridge's mind was elsewhere, but he still had to face Robert Maxwell. Wisely, he ditched the antagonistic Eric Hall, offering Maxwell an exclusive story on the deal to the *Daily Mirror*. Maxwell seemed resigned to losing his star player. 'We would rather have Aldridge than the money,' he said, 'but we appreciate he's getting to an age where he needed to join a bigger club.'

But Maxwell rarely conceded so easily. Two days later Aldridge failed to arrive at Anfield as planned. Liverpool chief executive Peter Robinson, manager Kenny Dalglish and chairman John Smith left the ground to meet Oxford officials at a secret destination to hear Maxwell's latest proposition; he would sell Aldridge if he could be loaned back for the rest of the season.

The Reds countered that he could stay until Oxford were out of the FA Cup, and eventually the clubs agreed he would move on 2 February. Through clouds of frustration, his dream edged closer.

As well as Aldridge's imminent departure, Malcolm Shotton's persistent back injury threatened to end his season and both Neil Slatter and Jeremy Charles were long-term absentees. Charles lasted 12 minutes against Southampton in the reserves before being carried off with an abductor injury. With suspensions to Les Phillips and Gary Briggs forcing them to miss the upcoming FA Cup tie against Aldershot, Evans needed players.

He used Aldridge's fee to rekindle his interest in the Arsenal defender Tommy Caton, who he'd missed out on at Christmas, and he also made a bid for Northampton's Richard Hill, which was rejected.

After the majesty of Anfield, Aldridge returned to the half-empty Recreation Ground in Aldershot. Their pricing decision had backfired; they'd described ticket sales as 'steady' but Oxford confirmed they'd sold just 200 of their 750 allocation. The ticket office offered an explanation: 'They're a bit expensive, aren't they?'

When Oxford arrived, it felt like going back in time. Aldershot had sold just 1,966 tickets, the lowest crowd ever recorded for an FA Cup third round tie. The players could hear the individual shouts from the crowd, something they hadn't experienced at the Manor for years. For Aldridge, it reminded him of a past he was desperate to push beyond.

Disillusioned and in brutally cold conditions, Oxford were sluggish from the off, falling behind after six minutes to Colin Smith's header. A 30-yard drive by Glen Burvill made it two on the hour. With 20 minutes to go, Evans replaced Aldridge with Leworthy, admitting the transfer speculation had affected his performance. Bobby Barnes completed the humiliation with Aldershot's third. When Maxwell was told of the score, he assured everyone that Oxford would claw the deficit back in the second leg.

For Aldridge, the embarrassing exit opened the door for him to leave. As a precaution, he was left out as Oxford conceded twice in the last ten minutes to lose 4-3 to Blackburn in the Full Members' Cup.

As Billy Whitehurst avoided prosecution for his car accident the previous September, Maxwell flexed, allowing Aldridge to leave after the upcoming game against Watford at the Manor.

Before kick-off, Aldridge was presented with a silver salver for his contribution to the club's remarkable rise. Symbolism and emotion ran high but Watford were quick to capitalise as Nigel Callaghan steered the ball home after just two minutes. Half an hour later Briggs missed Callaghan's cross to allow John Barnes to bury the ball past Hardwick for number two.

Five minutes after the break, the London Road terrace took their frustrations out on Steve Hardwick after Mark Falco held off two defenders to slip the ball beyond the keeper for the Hornets' third. Despite Houghton's consolation, Evans admitted, 'I'd prefer if John wasn't remembered for the last two games.'

The following Monday, Aldridge left the Manor for the last time after 114 league appearances and 72 goals. Oxford had lost just five times when he'd scored. He travelled north with Jim Hunt to complete the formalities as his wife arranged a party to celebrate their homecoming at Hunts Cross Snooker Club. The tension of the last month seemed to get the better of him, and as the drink flowed, Aldridge punched a window, hitting a brick wall and breaking his hand. The following day, heavily bandaged, he was finally a Liverpool player.

Chapter 22

Dean Saunders

OXFORD'S SUCCESS was built on a dynasty of great strikers. Keith Cassells had fallen one short of the club's season goalscoring record when he left for Southampton, Steve Biggins broke it, then John Aldridge surpassed that to become the best striker in English football.

Could Maurice Evans top that? He prided himself on finding strikers, but he and football were changing; rather than prowling the touchlines of parks and reserve fixtures unearthing gems, he was a First Division manager with money to spend. Jim Hunt worried that Aldridge's fee would add a premium to any target.

Football was divided between the haves and have nots; Liverpool could spend nearly £1m on John Aldridge, while other clubs were on the brink of extinction with debts totalling a fraction of that.

Brighton & Hove Albion had fallen from grace since Oxford had beaten them in 1982. They'd made the FA Cup Final the following year while being relegated from the top flight. Attempts to bounce back failed and by 1987 their financial predicament had grown to such an extent they were struggling to pay players' wages. It was clubs like this where the normally genial Evans would go hunting.

As Aldridge headed north, his old team-mates were in Bermuda for an invitational tournament with Germany's Kaiserslautern, Swedish side Malmö and a Bermuda National XI. Oxford opened with a 5-2 win over the Bermudans with goals from Billy Whitehurst, Ray Houghton, Brian McDermott, John Trewick and David Leworthy, before losing the final 1-0 to Malmö in the last minute after Whitehurst was sent off.

Early rumours of Aldridge's replacement focussed on Terry Gibson at Manchester United and renewed interest in Derby's Bobby Davison. Evans was keen to raid his old club for Trevor Senior. 'I know him personally,' he confirmed. 'I've still had him watched since I've been at Oxford.' He also revitalised interest in Northampton's Richard Hill. Rumours he was looking at Lincoln's Gary Lund proved to be off the mark despite manager George Kerr claiming Lund was better than Aldridge and worth £1m. 'I saw on Teletext last night that we were interested in Gary Lund,' Evans said. 'It was the funniest programme on TV all night.'

Despite an encouraging opening half to the season, Evans was still concerned about his defence, and his assessment after the Watford defeat was brutal, 'People say I should spend the fee to replace [Aldridge]. I reckon we need some defenders, some of our defending was hilarious.'

Malcolm Shotton had been ruled out for the season, so Evans secured Tommy Caton from Arsenal for £180,000, paving the way for Bobby McDonald to move to Leeds on loan.

A knee injury to Alan Judge forced Evans to spend another £100,000 on QPR's Peter Hucker, who arrived on the morning of the visit to West Ham. Seemingly inspired, Steve Hardwick pulled off a string of saves as Caton made a stylish debut to secure Oxford's first away win in five months after Leworthy, Robert Maxwell's preferred replacement for Aldridge, miskicked his shot into the net after three minutes.

In the commentary box, former England international Trevor Brooking was less than impressed with Whitehurst, suggesting he might consider switching to become a rugby player.

Oxford stayed in London to face Chelsea at Stamford Bridge hoping to repeat their stunning win of the previous season. Despite four consecutive home wins, Chelsea were in a slump with several players negotiating their way out of the club. The crowd was 6,000 below average, meaning the game was played in an eerie silence punctuated by the odd shout and jeer. Chelsea opened the scoring when John Dreyer pulled down Gordon Durie, allowing Micky Hazard to score from the spot. After half an hour Hazard released Kerry Dixon, who held off Caton to square the ball to Durie for number two.

Nine minutes into the second half, Dave Langan sliced a clearance to Dixon, who nodded into an empty net for 3-0. Revenge was complete when Pat Nevin slotted home the rebound from John Bumstead's drive. Fans listening to Radio Oxford were thankful that a British Telecom strike caused the second-half commentary to be abandoned. Maurice Evans described the performance as 'pathetic'.

The first of a quartet of games against the top four was the visit of league leaders Everton on Valentine's Day.

Without Graeme Sharp or Kevin Sheedy, Everton struggled and went behind after 25 minutes when Stevens fouled Leworthy in the box, despite their claim that Langan had fouled Pat Van Den Hauwe in the build-up. Trewick fired the spot kick past Neville Southall, but the referee called for it to be retaken after a player encroached into the box. Trewick kept his cool, converting the second attempt.

Despite Briggs and Caton working well together, after the break Everton fought back and forced Hardwick to make saves from Ian Snodin, Gary Stevens and Paul Wilkinson. With Oxford fans willing the final whistle, Whitehurst was penalised for a foul in the centre circle. Kevin Ratcliffe's free kick was helped on by Adrian Heath and Wilkinson darted in to equalise from close range.

The Everton curse had struck again. Tempers flared and the referee had to break up a furious argument between Whitehurst and Everton captain Ratcliffe before Leworthy pushed Southall down the tunnel after the whistle.

Afterwards, Ratcliffe walked into the club bar to instruct his players to 'shut up and say nothing'. Southall, sporting a black eye, complied and said, 'I know nothing about what happened.' Howard Kendall offered an official comment: 'Anyone with character would react in those circumstances, but it should be done nicely.' As tensions simmered, the fire alarm went off and cleared the stadium.

Despite the defender not playing for two months after a cartilage operation, Evans reluctantly released Neil Slatter to the Wales squad while Houghton was watched by Evans, Ken Fish and director John Devaney as the Republic of Ireland faced Scotland. Three days later, Jeremy Charles's latest comeback was cut short when he lasted until half-time for the reserves against Brighton.

Following the international break, Oxford hoped to benefit from a bout of flu that had swept through Charlton's camp. The Londoners' successful appeal to the Football League to postpone the game didn't impress Evans, who thought that football was going soft. In retaliation, Jim Hunt resisted rearranging the match until Billy Whitehurst returned from suspension.

As light relief, Ken Fish, Malcolm Shotton, Alan Judge and Jim Hunt went to a luncheon for the Variety Club of

Great Britain in Birmingham. The highlight was the award for sportsman of the year but the Milk Cup holders lost out to a horse, the Grand National winner West Tip. Hunt bristled at the decision, particularly after a special award was given to Denis Howell MP for Birmingham's failed Olympic bid. Suspicions of a Midlands bias weren't helped when Stoke City defender George Berry won a £5,000 cruise in the raffle.

In the league, second-placed Arsenal visited the Manor. After a dour first half, the game pivoted when Hebberd put Perry Groves out of action with ligament damage. The loss of Groves, plus Hardwick's inspired form, meant the match ended goalless despite Arsenal claiming a challenge by Hebberd should have been a penalty; Maurice Evans reluctantly agreed.

With just two goals in four games, Oxford were feeling the loss of John Aldridge, whose departure inspired Rangers to test Maxwell's resolve with a £400,000 bid for Ray Houghton. When Celtic made a similar enquiry, Evans knew he couldn't resist forever.

The post-Aldridge baptism of fire continued against Nottingham Forest when two goals from Nigel Clough sent Oxford down to 16th, raising fears they were being sucked into another relegation battle.

The gloom lifted briefly when Billy Hamilton returned to the Manor for a testimonial against a Northern Ireland XI. Star turns John Aldridge and George Best didn't show, but Pat Jennings, Norman Whiteside and Sammy McIlroy made up a strong Irish team. Although marred by a Dave Langan injury, the game ended 6-4 with a Hamilton hat-trick and goals from Les Phillips, Langan and Kevin Brock.

If Hamilton was Oxford's past, in the Beech Road stand was the man Evans hoped was its future. Brighton striker Dean Saunders was the son of former Swansea and Liverpool wing-half Roy Saunders. He'd grown up around the club when his dad was assistant manager. 'I used to kick a ball around on the sidelines and dream of playing for Swansea,' Dean once said.

He became an apprentice in 1980 as Jeremy Charles was helping fire Swansea through the divisions. An equally rapid fall from grace saw the club in the third tier by 1983, when Saunders made his debut, ending the season with 12 goals in a struggling team.

Despite this, Swans manager John Bond, who'd offloaded Billy Hamilton to Oxford from Burnley, filled his squad with lower-league journeymen, allowing Saunders to go on loan to Cardiff City before releasing him on a free transfer.

Brighton manager Chris Cattlin signed Saunders, saying, 'I was amazed when the Welsh club let him go for financial reasons. He's young, quick and, if he works hard, he has a great chance.'

'Swansea just gave me away,' Saunders said. 'Despite the fact that I was top scorer in a team coming apart. I had every incentive to make the break from Welsh football and I joined Brighton.'

Saunders scored 19 goals and was Player of the Season. Wales manager Mike England handed him his first international cap away to the Republic of Ireland. His first goals came against Canada in Vancouver in 1986.

Brighton suited Saunders, who regularly played snooker with his team-mates and cricket for Haywards Heath in the summer. 'It reminds me of my hometown,' he said. 'I like living by the sea.'

Infamously, in 1986 he lined up for their team photo with new boss Alan Mullery in a kit featuring their new shirt sponsor, office suppliers NOBO.

Saunders sat with his legs apart on the front row with one of his testicles poking out of his shorts. Whether a prank or accident, the photo made it into the programme for Gerry

Ryan's testimonial match against Spurs, and also into *Shoot!* magazine, before it was discovered.

An uninspiring start led to Mullery's sacking in January 1987 with his assistant Barry Lloyd taking over. Lloyd dropped Saunders in favour of Richard Tiltman, a discovery from local football in a move rumoured to be about money more than ability. With Brighton struggling to pay their players, Evans took his opportunity to take Saunders to Oxford for £60,000, putting him straight into the side to face Liverpool at the Manor.

It had been a busy week. Tommy Caton visited his kit sponsors – Hairlooms Hairdressing Salon at the Moat House in Oxford – while Maurice Evans opened a new shopping centre in Grove. Back at the Manor, Jim Hunt received a letter from Mr Newton of Marston, suggesting the club hold a competition for new witty songs about the 'Town and Gown' divide to replace 'Who the fucking hell are you' and 'Who's the wanker with the flag'. Hunt thought it such a good idea that he published it in the programme and invited contributions.

Hunt resisted making the Liverpool game all-ticket but the Cuckoo Lane End was quickly full, leaving many Liverpool fans locked outside. Saunders made his debut alongside teenager Robbie Mustoe, deputising for the injured Dave Langan. John Aldridge – who'd only started one game since his transfer – watched from the Liverpool bench with Kenny Dalglish and Ian Rush playing up front.

The opening was scrappy, and Saunders' first notable contribution was a shot which cleared the London Road. After 36 minutes Craig Johnston was fouled by Caton on the right. Ronnie Whelan's free kick was flicked on by Johnston to John Wark, who headed beyond Hardwick for 1-0.

With Liverpool's fans still celebrating, a minute later Bruce Grobbelaar theatrically punched David Leworthy's header to Saunders, whose shot was parried into the path of Caton to equalise; a reward for their graft, if not their craft.

After the break, Oxford pushed forward hoping to snatch an unlikely win, but were punished eight minutes into the half when Dalglish sent Johnston away to cross for Rush to make it 2-1. The gulf in class told after 64 minutes when Dalglish combined with Johnston again to cross to Wark, who put the game beyond doubt. Afterwards, Dalglish admitted that Aldridge had been used as a psychological weapon against his old team-mates.

On Good Friday, Oxford headed to in-form Coventry City, managed by former Manor Ground scout John Sillett. The offer of tickets to the Sky Blues' upcoming FA Cup semi-final ballooned the crowd to nearly 24,000, their highest in seven years. The interest was a novelty for the home side, and it took most of the first half to find their rhythm, losing skipper Brian Kilcline to concussion when he was kicked in the face by Billy Whitehurst, who was returning from suspension.

A minute after the break, David Bennett's solo goal opened the floodgates. A David Burrows free kick, after a foul by Caton, was met by Cyrille Regis to head beyond the Oxford defence for number two before Bennett fed Regis to score his second with 20 minutes to go. Oxford had now won just once in 11, scoring only two goals. Being without John Aldridge was harder than they could have imagined.

Oxford next headed to London to face struggling Charlton Athletic, who were desperate to rekindle their season. With just one win between them since the turn of the year there was little quality on show, and only Saunders and Houghton set the visitors apart from their opponents.

Hebberd nearly broke the deadlock, forcing Bob Bolder to save from 25 yards, a momentary flash of quality in an otherwise poor goalless game. 'No guile, no craft,' concluded Charlton manager Lennie Lawrence.

As Oxford prepared to entertain Sheffield Wednesday, Evans took his spending since Aldridge's departure to £420,000 with the £140,000 signing of Martin Foyle from Aldershot.

Despite a collapse in Wednesday's form, they opened the scoring after just 40 seconds when Hardwick fumbled Gary Megson's shot and Lee Chapman poked home the rebound. Things went from bad to worse when Houghton hobbled off with a hamstring injury to be replaced by Foyle.

Despite the setback, Oxford rallied; Dean Saunders opened his account on 26 minutes, heading in Brock's corner. Eleven minutes from time Brock repeated the feat for John Dreyer to grab their first win in seven.

Since the win against Alex Ferguson's Manchester United at the beginning of November, Oxford had won four out of 23 games. Now they faced Ferguson again with the Scot seeking revenge.

With Foyle making his first start, Oxford opened brightly and after 18 minutes, keeper Gary Walsh stepped outside his box with the ball and the referee awarded a free kick for handball, giving skipper Caton a chance to crash home a shock opening goal.

The lead lasted for just seven minutes as Peter Davenport fired low for the equaliser. Oxford were forced into a reshuffle when Langan was replaced by Leworthy, allowing Liam O'Brien to feed Davenport for 2-1 ten minutes before half-time.

Despite United threatening to extend their lead, just after the hour Mike Duxbury, under pressure from Foyle, lobbed the ball into United's unguarded goal for 2-2.

Oxford pushed for a winner but paid the price in the last minute when Bryan Robson's sucker punch made it 3-2, leaving Oxford five points above the relegation zone, having played more games than most teams below them.

Meanwhile, Robert Maxwell's new project, Derby County, were top of the Second Division and 11 games unbeaten. With the prospect of Maxwell owning two clubs in the top division, the Football League were growing concerned by the motives of club owners, particularly with a spate of investors in football property in recent months.

Oxford entertained second-bottom Newcastle United, whose six-game unbeaten run had been inspired by their emerging teenage star Paul Gascoigne. Having scored his first professional goal against Oxford in October, Gascoigne ominously said, 'I would say they were my lucky team.'

Without the injured Langan or Charles and with Briggs and Whitehurst suspended, Oxford's weaknesses were exposed six minutes from half-time when Paul Goddard released Darren Jackson. Oxford paused, expecting an offside flag, as Jackson slid the ball under Hardwick for 1-0.

Caton prevented Gascoigne from increasing Newcastle's lead before Phillips, Foyle and Saunders all wasted good chances. With ten minutes to go the pressure told when Dreyer chested down Brock's corner and fired the equaliser into the roof of the net. The point, although welcome, left Maurice Evans lamenting the loss of Aldridge, who he thought would have given his team the edge to take all three.

A week later, Oxford travelled to Southampton, just five points above the relegation zone and two ahead of Leicester City in the play-off spot. Evans railed against the play-off innovation, arguing, 'These decisions are made by people who know least about football.'

Despite welcoming back Briggs and Whitehurst, wearing an unusual light-blue kit they rarely threatened the Southampton goal. With 20 minutes to go Glenn Cockerill punished their lack of punch with a low drive past Steve

Hardwick. Cockerill then turned provider, crossing to Gordon Hobson to score before George Lawrence punished his old club by setting up Danny Wallace for the third. Oxford dropped into the dreaded play-off spot.

Ninth-placed Wimbledon visited the Manor on the anniversary of the Milk Cup Final win. With little to play for, the normally aggressive Dons looked lethargic after rapid-fire goals from Saunders and Whitehurst made it 2-0 at the break.

Dave Bassett, Wimbledon's manager, was so incensed that he wouldn't allow his players into the dressing room at half-time, claiming that there was so much wrong with their display he wouldn't have time to go through it all. 'They thought they were on holiday, so I sent them out to do some sunbathing,' he said.

Improving after the break, Wimbledon pulled a goal back before Saunders sealed the points with his second. The win lifted Oxford above Leicester, who they were to meet on the last day of the season in a potential winner-takes-all shoot-out.

With just four games remaining, Evans took his side to third-placed Tottenham Hotspur, whose title aspirations had fallen away. Evans was in awe of their quality, particularly Glenn Hoddle who was returning to the starting line-up for his penultimate home game before joining Monaco.

Despite having the better of the opening exchanges, Oxford were baffled to find themselves 2-0 down after Chris Waddle headed in Steve Hodge's cross just ten minutes in and Paul Allen added a second.

Undeterred, Saunders reduced the deficit after 21 minutes when Ray Clemence missed Brock's corner before he and Whitehurst went close with the England goalkeeper making amends with some smart saves. The quest for an equaliser stretched into the last minute, when Langan's swinging cross was firmly headed away by Richard Gough and the ball dropped to Hoddle, who turned and drove at the beleaguered Oxford defence.

With acres of space and seemingly in control of time, Hoddle glided towards Caton. A deft acceleration easily beat the defender to go clean through on goal. Peter Hucker advanced, but Hoddle's dummy unbalanced the keeper and left him on his backside. The mercurial midfielder casually rolled the ball into the back of the net, taking the applause with a sheepish grin; a masterful talent above all others.

With three to play and just four points clear of relegation, a final-day showdown with Leicester looked likely. With Whitehurst and Foyle injured, Hebberd partnered Saunders up front at home to Norwich. The only goal of the game came after just two minutes when Dale Gordon cut in to shoot past Hucker. As the fans' frustrations grew, Evans snapped back, 'They started their groans and that made things worse rather than better.' The man who loathed pressure was feeling it like never before.

The dismal run since Aldridge's departure had taken Oxford from being comfortable in mid-table to the edge of the drop zone. A year to the day since their escape against Arsenal, Oxford travelled to fifth-placed Luton Town for their penultimate game of the season in a bid to avoid a relegation decider against Leicester.

Luton's ban on away fans and synthetic surface had turned Kenilworth Road into a fortress. Behind Liverpool, they had the best home record in the division with one defeat all season. Evans needed the players to think beyond the statistics. Sitting them down in the changing rooms, he asked a simple question: 'Do you want to be in the First Division or not? What do you want from life?'

Despite the partisan crowd, the surface suited Oxford's attacking strengths. With Luton missing Mick Harford,

Brian Stein, Ashley Grimes and Tim Breacker, the visitors dominated from the opening moments. After just five minutes Saunders out-jumped Stacey North to connect with Brock's cross to open the scoring. Oxford began to breathe.

Five minutes later it was nearly two when Trewick intercepted North's pass and sent Saunders through only for Les Sealey to race to the rescue. The save delayed the inevitable; after 22 minutes Hebberd's running header from Brock's cross doubled the lead, putting Oxford on the brink of safety.

The home fans booed Luton's feeble performance at half-time; the catcalls and jeers were a calming balm for the Oxford players. Once again, they could contemplate another season in the top flight.

Things barely improved for the home side after the break and their first shot on target took an hour to materialise. Oxford were cruising as Evans replaced Dreyer with Phillips to see the game out. The change seemed to upset the team's concentration, and with four minutes to go Mike Newell finally offered a telling response, making it 2-1. Oxford restarted knowing they just had to negotiate the remaining time to secure First Division football for another season.

Seconds later, Luton attacked again. Substitute Darron McDonough delivered a cross to Mark Stein and the striker headed the equaliser. With Leicester drawing at home to Coventry, in a matter of seconds, Oxford had gone from relative comfort to facing their date with destiny.

The clock ticked down as desperation and despair set in. Luton sat back and absorbed Oxford's pressure but with just 15 seconds to go, Hebberd launched a hopeful ball into the home side's box. Dreyer controlled it high on his chest and in a single movement chipped a cross for Saunders to dart across Sealey. Stooping to reach the ball, his header ricocheted into the net for the winner. Saunders turned, his head in his hands as the few Oxford fans who'd snuck in celebrated wildly around the ground. Amid the hollow silence of the home support, Oxford had survived without Aldridge.

The end-of-season dinner at Minchery Farm Country Club took a celebratory tone. Billy Hamilton returned as the guest of honour while Les Phillips picked up the Player of the Season award. The highlight came when Maurice Evans drew Peter Rhoades-Brown's raffle ticket to win a portable colour television.

The mood continued into the last day of the season with a jazz band entertaining the crowd before the game. Leicester, on a run of 17 consecutive away defeats, looked shaky as Brock hit a post in the first half. Just after the hour Saunders completed a theme of the season and was sent off seconds after being booked for a dangerous challenge on Morgan. Evans blamed his team's poor discipline on a breakdown in communication between referees and players, although the statistics spoke for themselves. Malcolm Shotton made a brief appearance off the bench after six months out as the game petered out to a goalless draw, sending his former club down.

As the season ended, Dave Langan joined up with the Republic of Ireland squad to face Brazil with Ray Houghton missing out through injury. Although Brazil were fading from their previous glories, they were still formidable opponents, even with an under-strength side. Liam Brady, Ireland's standout talent, struck after half an hour in a man-of-the-match performance for a famous win. Houghton returned days later with Aldridge and Langan to bring the season to a close with a goalless draw against Belgium.

Maurice Evans's mind turned to the new season. Could Oxford survive without John Aldridge or Billy Hamilton? With stalwarts like Malcolm Shotton and Gary Briggs getting older? With the vultures circling around Ray

Houghton, Trevor Hebberd and Kevin Brock? More than ever, Evans needed his owner's commitment, to rebuild and reinforce.

But, as May concluded, Robert Maxwell announced that he'd resigned as chairman of Oxford United.

Chapter 23

Kevin Maxwell

'PISS OFF, we don't get up for an hour.' Being a Maxwell offered many perks, but a simple life wasn't one of them.

Although Ghislaine was Robert Maxwell's favourite, his youngest son, Kevin, was groomed as the heir to his publishing empire. Kevin's childhood was overshadowed by his father's discipline, which he found both awe-inspiring and frightening. Maxwell was oppressively controlling and brutal, and on one occasion he locked his son in a boat after he refused to eat his dinner.

Kevin joined the family firm after graduating from Oxford, becoming chief executive of Maxwell Communications Corporation. Considered calmer and more financially astute than his older brother, Ian, Kevin held his counsel to avoid confrontation. Like his father he was a workaholic, sacrificing everything in pursuit of profit. His compliance gave him capital in the tyranny. Only when he planned to marry his university sweetheart Pandora did he find himself in opposition to his father, who reportedly objected to her lack of Jewish heritage and status. When Kevin followed his heart, Maxwell removed him from the business for a year.

Now it was early on 18 June 1992, his father was dead and the Maxwell empire was crumbling. Kevin's reward for his loyalty was that he was now being held accountable for Robert's many failings.

With the confidence of a life blessed with privilege, Pandora opened the window of their Chelsea home and shouted abusively at two men she assumed were reporters who had dogged them since Maxwell's demise eight months earlier. The two men pressed the doorbell persistently. The window shot up again. 'I'll call the police,' she warned.

'We *are* the police,' they replied.

The door opened as the two officers hid wry smiles from the paparazzi. Within minutes Kevin was being ushered into an unmarked police car, heading for arrest.

Unlike his father, Kevin seemed genuinely interested in Oxford United. In 1984 he cut short his wedding celebrations to attend the potential title clincher against Exeter. In court, he was accused of spending more time at the Manor than administering the Mirror Group pension fund that his father had plundered millions of pounds from.

In the summer of 1987, Robert's decision to succeed Ian as Derby chairman meant resigning from the Oxford board. He anointed Kevin as his successor, the youngest chairman in the country, though few believed he was more than a puppet.

A new chairman wasn't the only change at the Manor Ground; four years of breakneck progress meant the squad who'd inspired their rise were either ageing or restless. Malcolm Shotton hadn't started a game for eight months while Kevin Brock and Ray Houghton, inspired by John Aldridge's move, saw a world beyond the Manor. Maurice Evans needed to accelerate the pace of change at the club.

With a new membership scheme threatening attendances, Oxford announced that seat prices would increase to £9, making the Manor the most expensive place to watch football in the country behind Luton Town.

Capitalising on merchandising opportunities, their 25th season in the Football League was marked with a new Umbro kit featuring a striking design with three shades of yellow and white stripes.

The shirts again featured Wang Computing after Kevin signed a £500,000 sponsorship deal at the Savoy Hotel in London. The agreement was celebrated the next day when a Wang Celebrity XI, featuring Jim Rosenthal, Steve Perryman and Radio Oxford's Nick Johnson, were beaten 6-1 by the United All Stars at the Manor, with Ray Graydon scoring five.

But Oxford still found themselves trailing; transfer inflation spiralled as the market went into overdrive. Liverpool, aiming to break the resolve of champions Everton, spent nearly £3m on John Barnes and Peter Beardsley. Manchester United paid £1m for Viv Anderson and Brian McClair. Even Coventry and Wimbledon spent heavily.

Freedom of contract meant Evans struggled to retain and sign players. There were no such difficulties for Arthur Cox at Derby, where Robert Maxwell stated proudly he 'wanted only the best' for his new club, lavishing nearly £2m on England goalkeeper Peter Shilton and former Oxford defender Mark Wright from Southampton.

Shilton, at 38, was viewed to have had a poor season for the Saints but, for Maxwell, who'd been deeply involved in the negotiations, he was a marquee signing and a signal of intent to the rest of the division.

While Derby benefitted from Maxwell's money, Evans's problems began early when Billy Whitehurst received a three-month driving ban and £100 fine after being caught doing 104mph in his Ford Escort Ghia near Horsley.

Good news didn't come until late July when Gary Shelton signed from Sheffield Wednesday for £135,000. A week later, the squad headed to Sweden, setting up base in Trosa, south of Stockholm. Their first game was 80 miles away in Edsbro, and after pre-match entertainment of dog racing, Peter Rhoades-Brown and Billy Whitehurst put Oxford 2-0 up before another from Whitehurst and a fourth from Robbie Mustoe brought a convincing opening win.

Two days later, they travelled nearly 300 miles to Skärblacka, hammering a combined team of fourth- and fifth-tier players 9-1 with four goals from Dean Saunders, two from Whitehurst, then Shelton, Kevin Brock and Sean Reck completing the rout.

A 1-1 draw with IF Brommapojkarna preceded an 11-0 win over Trosa with four from Foyle, a Saunders hat-trick, a Reck brace and Brock and Whitehurst scoring. The final game saw a 9-1 win over Horfors with Whitehurst's hat-trick complementing goals from Rhoades-Brown, Houghton, Foyle, Saunders and Brock and an own goal. Four days later the team returned for Gary Briggs's testimonial against Swindon, losing 3-1.

Although signings were a struggle, the threat of players leaving was a bigger concern. Having slipped down the pecking order behind Alan Judge and Peter Hucker, Steve Hardwick asked for a transfer, immediately turning down an opportunity to join Wrexham. Dave Langan was also transfer-listed and John Trewick was lined up for a swap move with Ray Ranson at Birmingham. Meanwhile, Brighton wanted to take Dave Leworthy on loan.

Most concerning was that at the beginning of August, having snagged Brighton's Danny Wilson from under Oxford's nose, Luton were preparing to sell their midfielder Peter Nicholas to Aberdeen for £350,000. Manager Ray Harford planned to use the money to bring in reinforcements with Ray Houghton topping his shopping list.

Resisting Luton's interest was one thing, but Oxford couldn't ignore a £1.3m enquiry from Italian giants Inter

Milan. Any move depended on the departure of their Belgian midfielder Enzo Scifo or Argentinian defender Daniel Passarella, but it highlighted Houghton's growing market value. The approach was an attraction to the club and its finances, but a headache for Evans.

Two days before the start of the season there was another blow when Jim Smith made an offer to take Kevin Brock to QPR. Smith's low-ball bid of £135,000 threatened to take the deal to a tribunal, but the clubs eventually agreed a fee of £260,000. Evans despaired at the loss of Brock for £65,000 below Oxford's valuation.

Steve Hardwick headed to Sunderland on loan as the season opened at home to newly promoted Portsmouth. Despite a threadbare squad and difficult summer, Oxford seemed keen to prove the doubters wrong. Two Billy Whitehurst goals and one apiece for Dave Langan and Tommy Caton in a 4-2 win saw them take three points from their opening game in the top flight for the first time.

The following Tuesday, Oxford headed north to Sheffield Wednesday without Langan due to a leg injury. A new-found steel was evident against a notoriously robust side. Whitehurst floored Brian Marwood with a fierce tackle, forcing the winger off after just 15 minutes. Moments later, following a corner, the big striker appeared with blood pouring down his face; it was the kind of battle he relished.

Wednesday broke the deadlock two minutes later when Lee Chapman looped a header over Peter Hucker. Undeterred, Trevor Hebberd brought a good save from Wednesday keeper Martin Hodge before Martin Foyle headed his first goal for the club from Neil Slatter's deep cross. Ray Houghton apart, it was a point that lacked any real quality. Nonetheless, a satisfactory opening week finished with Oxford in sixth after a draw at Wimbledon and another goal from Foyle.

With Tommy Caton and Gary Briggs forming a solid defensive partnership, after eight months out with a back injury Malcolm Shotton knew that his prospects of returning to the side were fading. Alan Ball offered a three-year contract and £70,000 to take him to Portsmouth. At 30 years old, it was a deal too good to turn down. Shotton exited the Manor after eight unforgettable years and 336 appearances.

September opened with a trip to White Hart Lane to face Tottenham Hotspur, who were defending an 11-match home winning streak. Oxford looked solid in defence and threatening up front, but after 20 minutes Spurs' technical superiority told when Belgian Nico Claesen latched on to Paul Allen's pass to convert at the near post for 1-0.

Spurs started to take control; Chris Waddle's audacious 15-yard back-heel to Gary Mabbutt was one of many tricks that terrorised the Oxford defence. Five minutes before half-time Clive Allen picked himself up after being fouled on the edge of the box to fire a free kick beyond Hucker for number two. Claesen added his second after the break from John Metgod's cross as Oxford tumbled to their first defeat of the season.

On the eve of their home game against Luton Town, John Trewick became the third member of the Milk Cup Final team to leave in a matter of weeks when he joined Birmingham. Maurice Evans's programme notes were tinged with malice, suggesting Shotton and Brock were about 'to see if the grass is really greener on the other side'.

With Ian Greaves returning to the Manor for the first time since his resignation, spying for Mansfield's upcoming Littlewoods Cup tie, Oxford's defensive problems were exposed as Luton rampaged to a 5-2 win. In just two games the team had dropped to 16th.

With Houghton on international duty and anticipation of his move growing, Maurice Evans bid £400,000 for Derby

County winger Nigel Callaghan. But, with rumours that Callaghan's former club, Watford, were also interested, he rejected the offer.

It was poor preparation to face unbeaten Liverpool at Anfield. Evans's mood wasn't helped when John Aldridge opened the scoring after 13 minutes and John Barnes's goal put the game beyond doubt 25 minutes later.

One man having a very good start to the season was Jim Smith. QPR were the surprise league leaders with six wins from seven games, conceding just two goals. With Oxford in a slump, it was the perfect time to bring his side, including Kevin Brock, back to the Manor.

Immediately before the game, after a long and frustrating pursuit, Maurice Evans finally strengthened his threadbare squad with the signings of right-back David Bardsley from Watford and midfielder Richard Hill from Northampton Town for a total outlay of £400,000.

Bardsley's signing was ominous news for Dave Langan, who needed to retain his place in the side if he was to fulfil his dream of representing the Republic of Ireland in the summer's European Championship.

Before the game, Ghislaine Maxwell paraded the World Speedway trophy with Oxford rider Hans Neilsen, the title he'd retained in Amsterdam two weeks earlier. Oxford hoped it might bring good luck, having done the same before the Manchester United win the previous season.

QPR were torn to shreds by a masterclass from Houghton; his swift passing and endless energy exposed the visitors' statuesque sweeper system. Debutants Bardsley and Hill provided an additional edge, combining for the opening goal with Hill glancing a header beyond David Seaman after 15 minutes.

Although Rangers showed flashes of the form that had taken them to the top of the table, Hill helped Houghton clinch the game two minutes before half-time. Evans had secured another famous victory over his old friend.

Houghton's performance illustrated again how essential he was to the team. Evans was realistic about losing him, but angry about his invidious position; cashing in risked relegation, but if he let Houghton's contract expire, he'd leave for a fraction of his worth. Whichever way he turned he would lose.

The players celebrated at the Blenheim Fun Run the following day, Peter Rhoades-Brown finishing tenth and Billy Whitehurst 14th with Dean Saunders and Martin Foyle dawdling in 20 minutes after the winners.

Having narrowly avoided an embarrassing Littlewoods Cup defeat at home to Ian Greaves's Mansfield when Saunders equalised Kevin Kent's first-half opener two minutes from time, Houghton's transfer saga was threatening to boil over. George Graham, Arsenal's manager, angrily walked away after Houghton ignored his £750,000 bid for two weeks.

On the eve of their trip to Derby, Robert Maxwell tested his son's resolve with an audacious and perhaps facetious £800,000 bid of his own. Rather than feeling intimidated, the father and son boardroom clash excited Kevin. The game was a proxy war; he could face his father without retribution, promising a case of champagne to the first Oxford goalscorer. Robert Maxwell took his seat in the Baseball Ground directors' box for the first time to watch his new team face his old one. Neil Slatter's goal secured the champagne and saw Oxford take the three points with Maxwell leaving some time before the end.

With Briggs suffering a back injury, Evans's evolution of the squad neared completion as only Houghton and Les Phillips remained from the Milk Cup-winning team for a dominant 3-0 win over Norwich. Goals from Foyle, Hill and Slatter put Oxford tenth but despite their best start to a First Division season, a thick apathy was descending over the Manor with just 6,847 in attendance.

Membership cards, Maxwell's waning interest, Evans's dry pragmatism and the game's insurmountable inequalities combined to drain the enthusiasm from the Oxford public. Those with longer memories remained in awe at the club's achievements but those who'd been drawn in by their success were growing tired of the struggle to stand still.

Successfully navigating their Littlewoods Cup second leg against Mansfield with a 2-0 win, Oxford headed to Highbury to face fifth-placed Arsenal. Despite days of heavy rain threatening the game, driven by the creativity of Paul Davis and Steve Williams Arsenal used the slick turf to great effect. After 11 minutes Davis's deflected shot skimmed past Peter Hucker for 1-0.

Oxford threatened on the break, but Arsenal dominated with Alan Smith a constant menace. After two penalty appeals, a chance that crashed off the bar and another headed off the line by Bardsley, the win was confirmed late on when Williams drove home from 25 yards.

Ray Houghton headed off on international duty as another of the game's big bears took a swipe at the midfielder. Brian Clough had also grown frustrated after Oxford accepted Forest's £800,000 bid, but he felt snubbed when Houghton said he'd only talk to Liverpool, Tottenham or Arsenal. 'Let's face it,' Clough said with typical panache, 'meeting me would have been an experience in itself!'

With Houghton's transfer becoming rancorous, Oxford entertained struggling West Ham, who were yet to register a win on the road. After six minutes Tommy Caton's own goal put the Hammers on course for three points. A wild and mistimed challenge from Dreyer allowed Tony Cottee to cut inside for number two. Saunders got one back after 34 minutes to set up a siege on the West Ham goal, but with

Alvin Martin and Ray Stewart standing strong, Oxford fell to their second defeat in a row.

Evans was magnanimous, saying he was pleased for manager John Lyall while conceding that the substituted Houghton had been under-par.

His distraction was explained after the final whistle as he headed north to meet with Liverpool secretary Peter Robinson. Discussions went on into the evening until, just before 11pm, Jim Hunt's phone rang: the deal was done, and the details would be finalised the next day.

Liverpool unveiled their £825,000 signing the following day at a testimonial for Dundee full-back George McGeachie, a loyal if unspectacular performer. Star of the night was Houghton, who scored in a 4-0 win.

Back in Oxford, another member of the Milk Cup-winning side, Alan Judge, was loaned to Cardiff and there was further bad news when Gary Briggs and Neil Slatter were ruled out for weeks. Oxford's problems seemed to be mounting.

While Houghton's career was taking off, Dave Langan's was in trouble. In mid-October the Republic of Ireland confirmed their qualification for the 1988 European Championship. Langan, desperate to make the squad, missed their final qualifier having featured throughout the campaign. Losing his place in the Oxford starting 11 after the defeat to Luton, he knew he had to play so Maurice Evans allowed him to go to Leicester on loan.

Oxford returned to the Manor four days later, registering an encouraging 2-1 win against Charlton with goals from Foyle and Saunders putting them ninth. Despite the loss of Houghton, and much of the Milk Cup Final team, Oxford were in one of their best positions since arriving in the top flight.

Exiled in Leicester, Langan's frustrations got the better of him. When Oxford blocked him from playing in his new team's upcoming Littlewoods Cup tie at the Manor he protested. 'Why can't I play?' he said. 'I don't think I've been treated very well.' Jim Hunt hit back, quoting from the loan agreement that Oxford retained the right to prevent Langan from appearing.

A goalless draw against Leicester preceded a trip to seventh-placed Chelsea at Stamford Bridge, who were unbeaten since the beginning of April. For the first time, Oxford felt the loss of Houghton's energy in midfield, producing a sluggish display and relying on Hucker to save from Roy Wegerle, Colin Pates and Pat Nevin, while Trevor Hebberd cleared another shot off the line.

Despite the onslaught, after 24 minutes Hebberd beat the offside trap to lob goalkeeper Eddie Niedzwiecki for a shock opening goal. Oxford survived until five minutes into the second half when Wegerle beat Hucker from an acute angle before Nevin turned in the winner with 13 minutes to go. Even after Chelsea lost Niedzwiecki for the final six minutes, replaced by midfielder John Coady, Oxford couldn't prevent another defeat.

They returned to their favourite competition for their Littlewoods Cup replay at Leicester. But the visitors' lack of drive showed again when Gary McAllister scored after 20 minutes, adding another seven minutes later.

Sliding out of the competition, Oxford woke up just before half-time; Les Phillips's free kick found its way to Dean Saunders to head in at the far post. Six minutes into the second half, Peter Rhoades-Brown broke down the left and crossed to Saunders, whose knock-down was headed home by Gary Shelton. As extra time approached, with Leicester disputing a handball during the build-up, Shelton scored again to secure the winner in a stirring comeback.

Saunders' form continued three days later when he scored the winner against Coventry City at the Manor, and he was again on target against Crystal Palace in the Full Members' Cup. He was emerging as a potent replacement for John Aldridge, giving confidence that Oxford could survive in a world without the striker, Ray Houghton, Malcolm Shotton or Kevin Brock. Despite the good form, crowds stubbornly refused to increase.

A 3-0 defeat at Southampton brought the good run to an end as they prepared to face Wimbledon in the Littlewoods Cup. The Dons were keen to live up to their growing reputation with Andy Thorn cynically scything down Saunders as he was set to fire past goalkeeper Dave Beasant early on. The challenge went unpunished, but Thorn gave the referee no choice but to book him four minutes later when he clattered Saunders again.

The striker had already put Oxford ahead after four minutes, receiving a ball from David Bardsley and shooting into the far corner. Wimbledon's response was typically ugly with the battering ram John Fashanu heading over and Lawrie Sanchez firing wide before substitute Alan Cork equalised with 25 minutes to go.

Ten minutes later, John Gayle's mistake freed Les Phillips to play a one-two with Saunders and prod the ball past Beasant for 2-1. Despite their struggles with players, fans and their board, Oxford, unbeaten at home for eight years in the competition, were again starting to look towards Wembley.

Chapter 24

Elton John

THE DWINDLING interest in Oxford's progress was rekindled when the draw was made for the quarter-finals of the Littlewoods Cup. Four years after their epic trilogy of games, they would once again face Manchester United at the Manor.

So much had changed in the intervening years; the two clubs were now in the same division and it would be Maurice Evans v Alex Ferguson and not Jim Smith v Ron Atkinson. Kevin Maxwell's guidance and Evans's deep well of experience and knowledge meant the hysteria of those early days had been replaced by a calmer stability.

Smaller clubs like Luton and Wimbledon had benefitted from the legacy of debt, hooliganism and in-fighting that infested larger clubs. Oxford had navigated a similar path and were establishing themselves as a well-run club with moderate but sustainable ambitions.

The template for this new model had been Watford. In 1976 while in the Fourth Division, they were bought by rock star Elton John. Over the next six years they soared through the divisions, led by their pragmatic manager Graham Taylor. When Oxford faced financial peril, Jim Hunt talked about 'finding their Elton'.

Watford's success meant their best players were plundered by bigger clubs and Taylor eventually left to join Aston Villa, being replaced by former Wimbledon manager Dave Bassett. The changes destabilised the club and relegation was on the cards. Elton John, facing allegations about his private life and a lawsuit against *The Sun*, was under pressure from Watford fans as they negotiated the transition from Taylor to Bassett.

As Watford headed to the Manor, John announced his solution. He'd agreed to sell his controlling stake to Robert Maxwell's publishing company for £2m. Maxwell's empire continued to grow, making Oxford an even smaller piece of the pie.

Following the morning's announcement, in a moment of characteristic theatre, Maxwell and a sheepish-looking John squeezed into the Beech Road stand as the teams emerged from below. Photographers clamoured for the best angle, ignoring the game.

Maxwell would have controlling interests in Watford, Derby and Oxford even though BPPC chief executive John Holloran would become chairman at Vicarage Road. Few were convinced about Holloran's independence, although Football League secretary Graham Kelly, recognising Maxwell's volatility, wanted more details before commenting.

In an echo of the merger with Reading and the Manchester United takeover, secrecy surrounded Maxwell's deal. It was a surprise to Watford's vice-chairman Geoffrey Smith, whose relationship with John was strained after the singer had apparently leaked a story that he planned to sell the club before their FA Cup semi-final the previous April. John's unilateral decision to appoint Bassett and their poor start to the season did little to cool the tension.

Although Jim Hunt assured fans the deal would have no impact on Oxford, with problems finding a new stadium and the loss of Ray Houghton, Kevin Brock, John Aldridge and others, would Maxwell give Oxford the attention they needed? Without backing, they could slip back to where they'd been five years earlier: destitute and drifting.

More broadly, there were growing concerns about owners with interests in multiple clubs. Maxwell's vision was that football should be media- and family-friendly, popularised, and monetised like American sports. He'd failed to gain influence in the corridors of power at the FA. With a portfolio of smaller clubs, he could leverage their accumulated influence instead.

While also retaining shares in Reading, Maxwell was under pressure to be more transparent. He threatened to abandon the Watford deal if the Football League Management Committee didn't approve it. The committee had a choice – approve the deal and go against its principles or reject it and face the wrath of Watford fans, the Mirror Group and Maxwell himself.

Maxwell's largesse at Derby County left few doubting his commitment at the Baseball Ground. He'd meddled in a rights issue at Reading and was the face of the sale of Watford to BPPC. But what of Oxford? Maxwell argued, unconvincingly, that they were run independently. His rule-breaking was hidden in plain sight, but he was banking on the fact nobody would dare call him out.

Maxwell likened his involvement to the Moores family who had controlling stakes in Everton and Liverpool. The comparison was facetious; Sir John Moores hadn't been a director of either club for more than a decade, but by exposing apparent duplicity in other committee members, Maxwell thought he might shame them into allowing the Watford deal to go through.

To rule against him would result in fines and bans or maybe even the removal of one of his clubs from the Football

League. He was relying on the league's notorious indecision and its reluctance to expose its imperfections.

Elton John looked subdued in the Beech Road stand alongside Maxwell's menacing frame in a bow tie and baseball cap. A few years earlier he had overflowed with emotion as Watford took their place in the FA Cup Final. Now, he looked like he'd sold his soul.

Not for the first time football became a sideshow as the teams played out a diplomatic 1-1 draw. Afterwards, reporters clamboured for more detail; John explained that he'd retired from recording and touring and Watford were a financial burden, so he wanted to hand the club over before causing permanent damage.

Bassett looked beaten, half a stone lighter than when he joined Watford. John Holloran refused to back him, and only Maurice Evans offered any support, but even his patience wore thin at the barrage of questions.

Cornered, Bassett unleashed a torrent of abuse against the press. 'You decide to build up a boy from Wimbledon into a superstar and then you knock him down,' he shouted. 'At the end of the day you'll do me a favour and get me the sack. That's the best thing that could happen to me, for me to be paid off.'

Four days later, Elton John resigned from the Watford board while the Football League Management Committee debated the legitimacy of the takeover. Their deliberations slowed when paperwork they'd requested failed to arrive. Meanwhile, Maxwell set his newspapers on to Bassett, breaking a story that David Pleat was ready to take over at Vicarage Road.

Eventually, the committee announced they wouldn't sanction the takeover. Maxwell was furious and threatened to go ahead regardless. They were backed into a corner with only the nuclear option of an expulsion available.

Maxwell was banking on the fact they'd never be bold enough to press the button and went on the attack, labelling them 'the mismanagement committee'. 'We have a professional game dominated by incompetent, selfish, bungling amateurs,' he said. 'It's time those who loved the sport woke up to the fact and kicked them out.'

Legally, the league couldn't prevent the takeover and John was still keen to sell. The league knew their rules were ambiguous. To punish Maxwell would invite legal challenge and embarrassment. They called an extraordinary general meeting to discuss the crisis, raising the possibility of at least one of Maxwell's clubs being expelled.

Maxwell argued that he wanted to secure Watford's financial stability. John issued a statement supporting the deal and even Dave Bassett gave his backing. Would the committee rule against the much-loved pop star whose involvement in Watford seemed authentic and heartfelt? The league hoped Maxwell would blink and walk away, but he was too invested and gaining the upper hand.

Back at the Manor, Maurice Evans extended Alan Judge's loan spell at Cardiff and had a £125,000 bid for winger Andy Sinton rejected by Brentford, before the week concluded with a trip to fifth-placed Everton.

Everton were struggling to keep up with their free-scoring neighbours Liverpool since the departure of Howard Kendall to Athletic Bilbao the previous summer. Despite dominating, their strike force of Graeme Sharp and Adrian Heath looked jaded, and a brave defensive display ensured Evans's men returned south with a point in a goalless draw.

As the month concluded and Maxwell continued to wreak havoc, quietly, Dave Langan's time with the club came to an end as he moved to Bournemouth in a loan deal which would eventually become permanent.

With the aftershocks of the Watford takeover saga lapping at their door, Oxford welcomed Newcastle to the Manor. Even as fans were reading reassuring words by Jim Hunt in the programme, he was being summoned to an impromptu board meeting with Kevin Maxwell, who announced the club was up for sale again.

After a frustrating 3-1 defeat, hostilities resumed between Maxwell and the Football League when the league won an injunction blocking the Watford takeover. The hearing was held secretly because of their concern Maxwell would bring the deal forward from its proposed completion date of 8 December.

As with the merger of Oxford and Reading, the legal process was getting the better of Maxwell. The judge also blocked Maxwell's family, his companies, John Holloran and Watford from taking part in any deal for fear that Maxwell might find an alternative route to complete the takeover.

As Oxford conceded their Guinness Soccer Six title, drawing 0-0 with Newcastle before losing 4-0 to, ironically, Watford, Arsenal chairman David Dein brokered a meeting between Maxwell and the Football League president Philip Carter. Maxwell admitted he dictated the direction of Oxford despite public protests to the contrary. Afterwards, Carter announced the league would sanction the takeover if Maxwell disposed of his interests in Oxford within six months.

Maxwell was on the verge of abandoning Oxford United completely. Carter instructed the league's solicitors to withdraw its objection to the Watford takeover. Secretary Graham Kelly denied that the league had caved in.

Kevin Maxwell seemed relaxed about the announcement. 'We're in no hurry to pull out,' he said. 'The family spent six years building the club up. Whether we pass our interests over to an individual or a group, they'll have to show an intention to keep Oxford in the First Division, together with a new stadium.' It would be a high price to pay given Maxwell's failure to find a new home.

Oxford fans questioned why it was them who faced an uncertain future. They were innocent bystanders; it felt like they were being sacrificed so the league and Maxwell could solve a problem. The committee once viewed Oxford as the autonomous club, reasoning that Maxwell could hardly sack his son like he might do with John Holloran at Watford. Suddenly, out of convenience, they'd changed their minds.

The deal was set to go through, starting the clock for Oxford's disposal from the Maxwell portfolio, but the Football League's Management Committee refused to sanction Carter's instruction to lift the injunction, leaving their QC David Oliver stuck in a constitutional crisis. Sensing turbulence, Maxwell announced a 48-hour delay. Most of the eight-man committee opposed the agreement, and Crystal Palace's Ron Noades led the charge, arguing that Carter had acted without consultation.

Maxwell and Elton John issued a statement saying that nothing should prevent the Watford deal from going ahead and set a deadline of 10 December for its completion. They blamed Carter's lack of availability due to a trip to Dubai to watch Everton play Rangers in the Dubai Super Cup – a fixture that navigated around the European ban and had strained relations between the president and his committee.

Oxford headed into Christmas after falling to a 3-1 defeat to Manchester United at Old Trafford, leaving them five points above the relegation zone. They then faced a daunting double bill at home to Nottingham Forest before entertaining top-of-the-table Liverpool on Boxing Day.

If Maurice Evans was banking on his players being focussed on the battle ahead, he was sorely mistaken. Immediately after the game at Old Trafford, Billy Whitehurst was again arrested for drink-driving after crashing his car on the A34. This came shortly before captain Tommy Caton was banned from driving for three years for being almost four times over the legal alcohol limit. Caton told the court he'd driven home after a hoaxer told him his wife was ill. Alongside Gary Briggs and John Trewick, four players had driving bans.

Undeterred by his arrest, Whitehurst then got into a fight with three men outside a pub, gouging his assailant's eye with his thumb. One of the attackers hit him in the face with a cosh, breaking his nose, before a third landed a blow to the back of his head, opening a wound that needed 30 stitches. Evans was unimpressed and insisted Whitehurst play.

Meanwhile, the Football League's Management Committee met near Manchester Airport to discuss the Maxwell stalemate and review their regulations. It was unlikely that they'd sanction their president's agreement or block it completely, which risked opening a split. There'd long been discussions about a breakaway super league so the saga had the potential to do irreparable damage.

The most likely outcome was that the issue would be handed to the other Football League chairmen where there would be strength in numbers. Oxford United's future was now in the hands of the rest of English football.

Following a four-hour meeting there was another twist as the committee overruled its president and recommitted to its rules but also accepted that Maxwell could proceed with the Watford takeover if he disposed of not only Oxford, but Derby and Reading as well.

Maxwell issued a statement reiterating that Carter had agreed he could buy Watford – if he sold Oxford and his shares in Reading by the end of the year – and that David Dein had counter-signed the agreement. In his view, the president's decision was final.

Two days later, Maxwell threatened to walk away from football altogether, taking his family with him, before it was reported that he'd bought a ten per cent stake in Marler Estates, who owned Queens Park Rangers, Chelsea's Stamford Bridge and Fulham's Craven Cottage. Maxwell appeared to now have interests in six clubs.

The report widened the divide between Maxwell and the Football League. The normally taciturn Graham Kelly said it reinforced the committee's decision to force Maxwell to reduce his influence. Maxwell admonished Kelly for speaking without the facts at hand.

As the arguments raged on, Oxford entertained third-placed Nottingham Forest. Despite a buoyant crowd due to free admission for OAPs and junior members, Oxford were quickly on the back foot. Forest played fast, attacking football with standout players Calvin Plummer and Tommy Gaynor replacing Paul Wilkinson and Franz Carr. After half an hour Peter Hucker saved Nigel Clough's penalty, but it was only a matter of time before the breakthrough came.

In a rare Oxford attack, Forest keeper Steve Sutton went up for a challenge with the patched-up Whitehurst. Sutton mistimed his punch, catching the striker and opening the wound from his fight a few nights before. At half-time Ken Fish removed his stitches and stapled the gash.

On the hour, a slick move between Clough and Neil Webb fed Brian Rice to score the opening goal, and the second came 14 minutes later when Plummer finished off an interchange between Webb and Clough.

Afterwards, Maurice Evans commiserated with Jim Smith in his office. He was growing tired of trying to bridge the gap between his side and those at the top, tired of the pressure, tired of the drama; when asked what was wrong with his team's performance, he simply said, 'Everything.'

The following day, during the televised game between Derby and Tottenham, news broke that the sale of Watford was off and Oxford were no longer on the market. One month from Maxwell's announcement, Elton John, exhausted by the power struggle and damaged by the arguments, asked that the deal be left to die. Once upon a time Oxford had been saved by its biggest rivals, now it'd been saved by one of the world's biggest rock stars.

The relief was short-lived. Liverpool were the visitors on Boxing Day; after 19 games they were chasing a club-record unbeaten start and there were whispers they could complete the whole season undefeated.

There was little to suggest that Oxford would halt their progress as the growing gulf in class was laid bare. Ray Houghton and John Aldridge in the Liverpool starting line-up was a further reminder that smaller clubs were prey to those greedy for success.

Where the Manor had once been a place to fear, it was now homely and welcoming. Five home defeats had seen its reputation shredded. Houghton showed what Oxford were missing and was integral to Liverpool's best work. After 41 minutes, Aldridge scored after Ronnie Whelan's header had been blocked on the line.

Peter Hucker denied Steve Nicol and Peter Beardsley before John Barnes made it two from Beardsley's pass nine minutes into the second half. Steve McMahon completed the rout with a 30-yard swerving drive into the top-right corner before Beardsley nearly made it four by hitting the post.

After 80 minutes Liverpool were cruising, their ability to keep possession infuriating Billy Whitehurst. As his frustration grew, he went up for a challenge with goalkeeper Bruce Grobbelaar, the resulting clash causing Whitehurst's stitches to burst open. 'It's bad Billy, you have to come off,' Ken Fish insisted. Whitehurst looked him in the eye, blood streaming from his face. 'You try to take me off and I'll fucking kill you!' he growled.

Four consecutive defeats became five two days later as Oxford visited QPR, who'd slipped to sixth after 11 games without a win.

As bad as their form had been, Oxford's was worse. Mark Falco opened the scoring just before the half-hour mark then Gary Bannister's header looped into the roof of the net five minutes later when Peter Hucker fumbled Alan McDonald's effort. He nearly made it three before the break, but Hucker redeemed himself with a comfortable save.

Two down at half-time, Oxford rekindled some fighting spirit in the second half and David Bardsley's 53rd-minute cross dropped to Dean Saunders, who beat Paul Parker to head beyond Nicky Johns for 2-1.

Three minutes later, Warren Neill's low cross was met fortuitously by David Kerslake, who placed the ball beyond Hucker to reclaim their two-goal advantage. In response, substitute Peter Rhoades-Brown picked up the ball from Hebberd, turned Neill and drove home emphatically from the edge of the box for 3-2. Despite the dogged second-half display, Oxford ended the year 17th, two points off the relegation zone.

As 1987 ended, the Football League announced their plan to restrict Maxwell's influence by tightening their regulations and preventing anyone from using relatives, employees or associates as proxies. The one remaining question was whether the rule would be applied retrospectively; if it did Maxwell would be forced to sell either Oxford or Derby.

Maxwell responded aggressively, calling the proposal unfair and unworkable, but for many it was a tediously familiar threat. Almost as if Maxwell, and perhaps Oxford, had overstayed their welcome.

Hopes that the new year would bring better luck were quickly dashed after a 5-2 defeat to Wimbledon at the Manor, their sixth consecutive loss. Since their last league win, Oxford had dropped from ninth to 18th, picking up just two points. At the final whistle Maurice Evans left the dugout to a cacophony of boos.

A week later they faced Leicester City in the FA Cup third round. Steve Hardwick was pelted with coins by the visiting supporters, who ripped away the fencing on the Cuckoo Lane terrace. Three Leicester fans scaled the floodlights, with one jumping 35 feet into the crowd. Goals from Martin Foyle and Dean Saunders saw Oxford through. Jim Hunt described the trouble as the worst the club had seen. Once Leicester fans had left the ground, they broke windows and threw bricks in a grim spectacle.

Four days later, Billy Whitehurst was in Woodstock Magistrates' Court where he was banned from driving for 18 months after crashing and abandoning his car before Christmas. Whitehurst admitted being over the limit but blamed his erratic behaviour on concussion. The misery continued that night when Oxford went out of the Full Members' Cup 1-0 to Reading.

The following night, the club were devastated to hear that 18-year-old Oxford fan Dean Golding had been hit by a car, leaving him in a coma. Doctors gave him a ten per cent chance of survival; his mother contacted the club with a desperate plea for help. Jim Hunt sent a tape of Dean Saunders, Gary Briggs, Tommy Caton and David Fogg with commentary from the Milk Cup Final in the hope it might return the teenager to consciousness. As the club scrambled to help, all anyone could do was wait.

Oxford picked up their first point in six games when Saunders and Gary Briggs scored in a 2-2 draw at Portsmouth. Keen to address his defensive frailties, Evans's next target was Dynamo Kiev defender Volodymyr Bezsonov. Evans insisted on seeing the Soviet, who had appeared in the World Cup finals, in the flesh before deciding whether to offer him a contract. The prospect of Bezsonov travelling to England was remote. It was like Evans and modern football were parting ways.

Despite difficulties on and off the pitch, Oxford again reported healthy profits of £226,055 for the year ending 30 June 1987 and £114,606 in the six months to June 1986, although the figures were boosted by the sale of John Aldridge; the club was still not sustainable.

At their EGM, the Football League's club chairmen reconfirmed their resolve to protect their principles around club ownership, denting Robert Maxwell's ambitions. Maxwell still wanted to buy Watford as BPCC were the biggest employers in the town but Stuart Webb, Derby's managing director, vowed to sue the other 91 chairmen for damages if Maxwell was forced to pull the plug at the Baseball Ground.

Following an impassioned plea from Jim Hunt and Oxford director Paul Reeves, the chairmen voted to block the Watford deal unless Maxwell sold his interests in Derby, Oxford and Reading. They voted to allow multiple shareholdings of under ten per cent and to not apply the tightened regulation retrospectively, giving Oxford some breathing space. Defeated, Maxwell called for the management committee to be replaced by a 'supremo'. One could only imagine who he might have in mind.

Chapter 25

Gary Briggs

FOR A player who wasn't good enough, only Trevor Hebberd played more top-flight games than Gary Briggs for Oxford. The last man standing from Ian Greaves's first game as manager, nearly 500 appearances later he was as commanding and demanding as ever.

He'd have played more if it wasn't for the concussions, shattered cheekbones and suspensions.

Briggs was on the verge of joining the police when he signed on loan from Middlesbrough in January 1978. The application remained in his drawer as the deal was made permanent via English football's first transfer tribunal. By the end of his first full season he had been named Player of the Year, picking up the award at Oxford's final home game against Lincoln before ending the day in hospital with concussion.

Initially playing alongside Ian Stott, a part-time civil servant from Wallingford, in central defence, it was his partnership with Malcolm Shotton that was at the heart of Oxford United, according to Jim Smith.

Nicknamed 'Rambo', the vigilante 'one-man army' Hollywood action hero, off the field Briggs was quiet and likeable; a loner, the players teased him about his frugality, particularly when buying drinks at Bogart's.

He denied he was a dirty player, describing himself as a 'traditional stopper'. The First Division should have been beyond his ability, particularly with the league's modernisers outlawing the physicality he relied upon. Nonetheless, he outlasted Shotton, was named Player of the Year in 1987 and awarded a testimonial which, with typical understatement, he chose to play against Swindon.

A back injury against Liverpool meant he hadn't played since September 1987, but he returned for the FA Cup win against Leicester and scored in the draw with Portsmouth. Even if Oxford were creaking at the seams, Briggs remained resilient.

The realpolitik of the Watford takeover wasn't ideal preparation for the Littlewoods Cup quarter-final against Manchester United. Alex Ferguson, returning to the scene of his humiliating debut, had steered his side to fifth, although fans remained unconvinced. Securing his first piece of silverware was crucial; he called it the most important game of the season. Many things remained from their titanic tussles five years earlier, including Jim Hunt's ticketing problems. Touts re-emerged around the Manor, leading Hunt to declare them the most despicable people in society who he wanted to 'decapitate'.

More had changed; the pitch was greener, the stadium cleaner, the fences higher – even the corrugated iron roof seemed more uniform. Yet, the Manor remained charmingly dilapidated, its magic kindling in the embers of the season's struggle.

Protecting a nine-year unbeaten League Cup home record, fans filled the ground, a mosaic of 12,600 familiar faces swaying in the gloom; this was their home and their competition.

With the glow of the floodlights warming the chilly evening, Oxford opened attacking the Cuckoo Lane End, groaning under the weight of 3,500 United fans. Peter Rhoades-Brown foraged down the left wing looking for an early opening, but it was Brian McClair who nearly broke the deadlock, forcing Alan Judge into a smart save. In only his second game of the season, moments later, Judge showed little rustiness when collecting a dangerous cross from Jesper Olsen.

The tenacity of Dean Saunders was a constant threat. A foul on the striker by Clayton Blackmore allowed Rhoades-Brown to launch a free kick towards Les Phillips, who was bundled over by three United defenders in their clumsy eagerness. Rhoades-Brown reset his sights, but his low drive was saved by Chris Turner.

Another long ball allowed Saunders to break free; Kevin Moran chased before pulling up sharply. Bryan Robson bulldozed Saunders out of the way before Rhoades-Brown exacted revenge, crashing through the England captain for a free kick.

Moran's injury forced Ferguson to introduce substitute Graeme Hogg. From the restart, Blackmore and Phillips exchanged high challenges as the ball bounced awkwardly. Briggs stooped unflinchingly to clear, taking a stray boot from Blackmore in the face.

This time Hebberd took the free kick from just outside the centre circle. Briggs and Saunders drew the United defence to the near post, leaving Martin Foyle free with Hogg.

Still getting used to the pace of the game, Hogg crumpled as Foyle leapt to meet the ball. His header bounced tantalisingly across the box; Turner scrambled but Saunders reacted first. With United's defence frozen, he side-footed home at the back post.

With a goal in every round, Saunders thrust his finger into the air, a broad grin stretching across his face as he sprinted in front of the disbelieving United fans. The familiar

Manor roar that had haunted their dreams was back. Was history repeating itself?

United were keen to respond as Olsen threatened and Gary Shelton was booked before Viv Anderson headed wide under pressure from Briggs.

Weathering the storm, ten minutes before the break, Saunders drew on his bottomless well of energy, pressuring Mike Duxbury to concede a throw. John Dreyer scooped the ball up and found Saunders, whose neat header gave the left-back a moment to launch a hopeful ball inside the box between two United defenders who froze as a flash of yellow flew through the gap.

The statuesque Gary Briggs, stony-faced, stoic, focussed, a block of defensive granite etched with the battle of the decade, launched himself like a missile through the night sky. Scything the United defence in two, his header propelled the ball goalwards like a rocket beyond the helpless Turner for number two.

Gary Briggs. It was always Gary Briggs. If the story of Oxford's rise was distilled down to one player, it was him. A survivor; brave, unflinching, blooded, embattled, physically broken, psychologically unbreakable.

Oxford's glorious past reignited as the Manor erupted, the squally sea of the London Road terrace washing around in a vat of joy, imprinting a lifetime memory on to those who were there. Few could deny the dream was dying, but while it lived, so did they.

Within minutes Phillips, Foyle and David Bardsley combined to create a chance for Saunders to clip past Turner, but Duxbury cleared desperately off the line. Half-time was greeted with a cacophonous roar; Oxford were 45 minutes from improbable glory.

After the break, Olsen and Strachan tried to ratchet open Oxford's defence. Norman Whiteside rolled a chance into

Judge's hands before combining with McClair, only for the Scotsman to fire wide.

With no option but to attack, United grew more threatening, and Bardsley conceded a corner which was delivered to the edge of the six-yard box by Olsen. Robson swooped like a hawk attacking its prey but his header was directed into the ground and the ball bounced up, clipping the bar before going over to safety.

Minutes later, Olsen found Robson free at the back post. Stretching every sinew, the United captain directed his header across the Oxford goal. Judge was wrong-footed but, twisting in mid-air, he reached out a giant hand and plucked at the ball mid-flight, killing its momentum, allowing the defence to clear. With one miraculous touch, United's hopes turned to ash.

The Manor grew tense as the game edged towards the end, and United carved out another chance when Davenport robbed Bardsley and crossed to Olsen to fire wide.

With the blast of the referee's whistle, it was over. And yet it felt like it did when it all began. Oxford United, this riotous mess of a club, had navigated the rubble of a sport in crisis to produce another heroic victory. As it had been so often, the Manor in the League Cup was their place of sanctuary.

Although Wembley was back in their sights, the undeniable, relentless passing of time ploughed onwards. Two days later the euphoria was punctured by Jeremy Charles's decision to finally concede to his injuries and retire. He'd started just one game since the Milk Cup Final, but his legend was assured.

Standing between Oxford and another trip to Wembley were Luton Town. After trouble at Luton's quarter-final with Bradford City there were concerns the police might switch the game to a neutral venue, but despite a stabbing incident when Luton had visited the Manor in September, the good record of Oxford fans meant the authorities were happy to let 3,500 members and season ticket holders travel to Kenilworth Road for the second leg. The two-legged tie meant the sides would face each other three times in as many weeks.

Relegation and the Luton trilogy weren't Maurice Evans's only concern. Peter Hucker had put in a transfer request after being dropped against Wimbledon and was lining up a loan move to West Bromwich Albion. From the safety of The Hawthorns, Hucker lashed out at Evans, branding the club 'amateurs'.

Oxford hoped to continue their cup form at Second Division Bradford in the fourth round of the FA Cup, but they were quickly overrun, conceding three in the opening half an hour in a 4-2 defeat, poor preparation for their first trip to Kenilworth Road, a First Division match ahead of the two League Cup legs.

Despite their 100 per cent winning record on Luton's artificial surface, Evans was facing a defensive crisis with Neil Slatter's long-term injury and John Dreyer's suspension leaving a gap at left-back. A £250,000 bid for Tottenham's Mitchell Thomas was rejected, meaning Peter Rhoades-Brown had to deputise.

As advertising boards featuring Melka, Tylo Sauna and Chark Delicatessen enticed a European audience reported to be around 200 million watching live at home, the shouts of the players could be heard over the subdued hum of the lowest First Division crowd of the day. With the pitch an expanse of monotone green carpet and no away fans, the lack of tribal tension resembled an over-inflated game of five-a-side at a local leisure centre. You'd be forgiven for thinking that football had finally sacrificed its soul.

Evans dropped Trevor Hebberd back to sweeper, but it was evident early on that his brittle back five would be little match for the imposing front line of Mick Harford and the brothers Brian and Mark Stein, who ran Briggs and Tommy Caton into a world of confusion.

In a game with the tension of a midweek trip to a shopping centre, after six minutes Rob Johnson's long ball was knocked down by Mark Stein for Harford to bend his shot with uncharacteristic panache beyond the static Steve Hardwick for the opening goal.

Oxford's response was enthusiastically erratic: Hebberd and Bardsley ballooned speculative shots over the bar before Saunders stabbed wide from eight yards.

After 20 minutes, another moment of quality extended Luton's lead when a six-man move across the pitch allowed Tim Breacker to cross for Mark Stein to head number two. Oxford's defence seemed to collapse with every raid.

Despite the two-goal cushion, Luton's high defensive line left an expanse of space behind it. After having a goal disallowed, Foyle finally summoned the guile to spring their offside trap and cross towards Saunders. As Saunders and Breacker tussled for possession, the referee signalled for a penalty for handball against the Luton defender. Saunders placed the ball on the spot with the precision of a snooker referee re-spotting a black and drove past Les Sealey for his 17th goal of the season.

The impetus for a comeback lasted for a minute as Rhoades-Brown's attacking instincts left a gap for Breacker to loop a long cross towards Harford, who beat Briggs and allowed Darron McDonough to make it 3-1.

With Oxford's defensive incontinence, their best hope seemed to be occupying Luton's back line with erratic long balls and using Saunders' puppy-like enthusiasm to chase lost causes. Five minutes before half-time, his industry stretched the Luton defence, allowing space for Bardsley to cross for the unmarked Foyle to fire home for 3-2.

Evans was desperate to get his team into the dressing room, but still had to endure Hardwick fumbling Brian Stein's shot before the referee blew for half-time.

Oxford started the second half brightly and Rhoades-Brown fired narrowly wide, then won a corner which nearly fell to Saunders from Briggs's flick-on. With Oxford still processing the miss, Sealey's long clearance was flicked on by McDonough to Mark Stein, whose first touch took him clear and second slotted the ball in the back of the net for 4-2. Seconds after the restart, Hardwick conceded a corner under pressure from Harford and Ashley Grimes crossed to Steve Foster to head on to Mark Stein, who nodded his second in two minutes.

The game then spiralled into another dimension; Briggs's shot screwed out of play on the opposite side of the pitch before the Stein brothers combined to play McDonough in to hit the inside of the post.

With Luton encamped in the Oxford half, Gary Shelton picked up the ball in midfield and found Richard Hill, whose one-two with Foyle gave him time to make it 5-3. Sixty seconds later Brian Stein attacked down the right and pulled the ball back to his brother to make it 6-3. Even the scoreboard stubbornly insisted for several minutes it was still 5-2.

With half an hour left, Oxford were simultaneously chasing the game and facing a thrashing. Shelton freed Hill in the barren wasteland behind Luton's back four and Sealey raced from his goal, but his stray clearance fell to Phillips, who chipped home for 6-4. But for Sealey's desperate save from Hill and Rhoades-Brown skewing his follow-up drive across the goal, Oxford could have made it five moments later.

Then, just beyond the hour, Danny Wilson tapped a free kick to Breacker, whose deep cross found Harford with an abundance of time to head Luton's seventh.

There was still a third of the game to play when the bemused Evans replaced the injured Caton with Billy Whitehurst, whose first flat-footed contribution let Mark Stein in on goal only for Hardwick to collect. Although Luton could have made it eight, Oxford had chances for a fifth, and the BBC Radio Sport team were relieved neither side could add to the score, having promised to donate £1 for every First Division goal to Comic Relief, a fitting cause.

At the final whistle, the players trudged off the pitch without a stain of mud or bead of sweat, like the game was almost a complete fiction, like being drawn into a collective madness that nobody could now recall.

Despite the humiliation, no opposing team had scored more on Luton's synthetic surface. Evans assured fans, 'We didn't come out to concede seven,' before describing it as 'Sunday morning stuff, unreal.' The gentleman of English football, who promised to give the players 'the rocket of their lives', had come face-to-face with his new and unwelcome reality.

After 18 goals in their two league games that season following Luton's earlier 5-2 win at the Manor, the teams reunited in Oxford for the first leg of the Littlewoods Cup semi-final four days later. In contrast to the synthetic perfection of Kenilworth Road, a light dusting of snow across the turf disguised a pitch sodden after a heavy downpour. With two defeats in 17, Luton relished the conditions, consolidating the psychological advantages they'd inflicted days earlier and took the initiative, throwing themselves into challenges and skidding along the turf like children knee-sliding across a wedding dancefloor.

The Oxford defence quaked; Wilson fired over after 13 minutes and the Stein brothers and Harford combined threateningly. Luton were so dominant that after 20 minutes, the snow had been cleared from Oxford's final third while the area behind the visitors' defence remained untouched.

Despite the return of Dreyer, and with Hebberd in front of the back four, Luton's uncomplicated tactics, though familiar, dominated the first half. Judge saved from Mark Stein as Foster and Harford provided the aerial assault. Five minutes before half-time Brian Stein broke on the left, turned brilliantly, advanced to the edge of the box and unleashed a fierce drive beyond Judge into the net. The ball cannoned off the stanchion before resting next to the stricken keeper, and but for the delayed roar from the Cuckoo Lane End, a silence descended on the Manor.

Although Les Phillips headed Caton's long free kick narrowly wide, when the half-time whistle went Oxford could have no complaints.

Hope, as always, came from attacking the London Road terrace. Within seconds of the restart, a long clearance from Judge set Saunders racing down the slope in pursuit of Mal Donaghy. Despite giving his opponent a ten-yard head start, Saunders skated across the turf, making the 31-year-old Irishman look like he was ploughing the field. Darting across his path, Saunders brushed Donaghy's shoulder before theatrically throwing himself to the floor. As he slid through the slush, referee Keith Hackett pointed to the spot.

Fuelled by the confidence of a goal in every round, Saunders placed the ball. His run-up was long and purposeful, his strike was clean, and when it hit the back of the net it was his eighth goal in as many games.

Despite the equaliser, Luton continued to threaten. Wilson drove narrowly over before Mark Stein and McDonough missed chances. Another through ball sent Brian Stein clear and as Judge raced from his line Luton fans tumbled down the Cuckoo Lane terrace anticipating a goal, but the striker scuffed his shot narrowly wide.

Oxford's uncontrolled aggression conceded free kicks and territory, their defence becoming entrenched by a constant aerial barrage. If they dug themselves out, hopeful balls towards Saunders left him isolated and chasing shadows.

Unperturbed, Saunders worked with feverish industry, and with 15 minutes to go he pressured Donaghy to concede a throw on the right. Taking it quickly, Phillips and Rhoades-Brown exchanged passes before sending Saunders free to dart into the box, where Donaghy lunged desperately and Saunders crashed to the floor again. Penalty.

With the Luton players furiously surrounding Hackett, Saunders placed the ball and looked into Sealey's eyes. Suddenly, he was consumed with doubt. 'We'd agreed four months ago that if we had two penalties in a game Tommy Caton would take the second,' he said later. 'But I was buzzing and just picked the ball up and placed it on the spot.' Indecision seeped into his mind: go left again or blast the ball down the middle? His strike was neutered by uncertainty and Sealey saved comfortably.

As injury time approached, desperation grew, and Hill ferreted away on the edge of the box trying to carve one last chance, but in his eagerness he fluffed his shot. Saunders pounced as Sealey swung his arm at the ball, sweeping the striker's legs from under him. In the chaos, the London Road terrace screamed for another penalty, but the referee waved play on. The final whistle went. Oxford could have won but Luton had the advantage. 'We were frightened,' conceded Evans. 'In the first half we were just trying not to concede seven goals.'

Without a goal in five months, banned from driving and with a trail of drunken brawls in his wake, two days later Evans exacted a form of revenge on his old club when Billy Whitehurst ended his brief and eventful Oxford career by moving to Reading for £120,000.

The following Saturday Oxford welcomed mid-table Tottenham Hotspur to the Manor. Spurs manager Terry Venables' decision to go on a scouting mission in Scotland was vindicated when there was little to suggest either team could turn their fortunes around. In terrible conditions, Oxford had the better chances against former loanee Tony Parks with Saunders, Rhoades-Brown and Hill missing good chances as the game meandered to a goalless draw. Evans said his side had paralysed the visitors, although one reporter described it as a 'masterpiece of mediocrity' involving an 'overwhelming lack of invention'.

After the final whistle there was good news as Evans was cheered by the signing of Colin Greenall from Gillingham, who'd been watching in the stands, for a record £235,000. 'A leader,' Evans enthused. More significantly, Oxford fan Dean Golding woke from his coma after a month. 'When he heard the tape from the Oxford lads,' his mother said, 'he had tears in his eyes.'

A week later, honours were even as the Maxwell chairmen faced each other again. With Oxford and Derby separated by goal difference in the relegation zone, the tedious goalless draw did neither side any favours and was poor preparation for the second leg against Luton.

Evans was determined to go into the tie more prepared; despairing at the lack of local facilities, he had to take the team to train on synthetic pitches at High Wycombe, Bisham, Wokingham and, thanks to Jim Smith, Loftus Road.

But it came to nothing as Oxford looked defensively vulnerable from the opening moments at Kenilworth Road. Hebberd returned as sweeper, conceding the midfield and inviting Luton to attack. Harford's volley clipped the post early on and Phillips had to clear Foster's header off the line. After 33 minutes Caton misread the flight of a long free kick from Grimes. Harford's mis-control fell to Johnson, whose chip was picked up by Brian Stein to beat Bardsley and head home from eight yards; the stadium erupted.

Caton was at fault again when he fouled Harford nine minutes later, giving Grimes the opportunity to fire a majestic free kick beyond Judge from 25 yards for 2-0. Oxford's dream was over before half-time.

In desperation, Oxford speculated with a series of long shots, their hopes ebbing away with each wayward strike. Saunders' side-foot wide from two yards was the closest they came.

The misery was absolute, and at the final whistle Luton fans poured on to the pitch celebrating their first visit to Wembley for 29 years, 12 months after being banned from the competition. Evans walked into the bar to find his family talking with a group of supporters. The fans blanked him, like they didn't know who he was. For Oxford, it seemed to signal the beginning of the end. In the studio was the architect of it all, Jim Smith. He knew.

Chapter 26

Mark Lawrenson

MARK LAWRENSON'S control of space and place was a rare gift. Never hurried, rarely troubled, his deep intuition placed him at the heart of a club that dominated English and European football for a decade. In contrast to the one-dimensional defenders of the age he was quick, flexible and could pass, an archetype of a future time. Originally from Preston, he made his Republic of Ireland debut aged 19 before signing for Brighton in 1977. Four years later, Liverpool paid a club record £900,000 for his services. His versatility meant he played across the back four, before settling into a central partnership with Alan Hansen, winning five league titles and a European Cup in seven years.

By March 1987, Liverpool were on the verge of conceding the title to Everton. The visitors to Anfield were Wimbledon, the serial disruptors who relished the prospect of applying their dark craft at the home of more cultured football. Fearlessly, Wimbledon scored just before half-time through former Oxford trialist Nigel Winterburn, meaning the home side went into the break in the unfamiliar position of chasing the game.

The second half was moments old when Lawrenson fell to the floor with a searing pain in his ankle. Gripped by scything agony, he knew he was going to miss the following week's Littlewoods Cup Final, the rest of the season and most likely the European Championship finals the following year. He knew his career was over.

He didn't know how it happened; Wimbledon's John Fashanu was in his periphery, and Lawrenson wouldn't have been the first victim of the striker's brutish aggression. But Anfield was hushed and referee George Courtney confirmed Fashanu was nowhere near him. Quite simply, his Achilles tendon had ruptured. Coach Ronnie Moran helped Lawrenson off the pitch, his face etched with concern.

During Lawrenson's six-month absence Liverpool were transformed; John Barnes, Peter Beardsley, Ray Houghton and John Aldridge spearheaded an Anfield revolution designed to restore their domestic dominance.

Although he returned in 1987/88, a record-breaking unbeaten start to the season masked Lawrenson's limitations: his talent and experience got him through games and by the middle of January he was establishing himself back in the starting line-up. But the intense Christmas and new year schedule convinced him that he would never be the same again. Six minutes into the second half of a game against Arsenal the injury flared up again; Lawrenson launched the ball into the stand and walked off the pitch for the last time.

It took two months to confirm his career was over as scans revealed that he risked doing irreparable damage. At 31 he faced life outside the world he dominated. Republic of Ireland manager Jack Charlton was so surprised that even after his retirement was confirmed he still hoped to include Lawrenson in his squad for the European Championship.

Lawrenson's physical anguish was more than matched by Maurice Evans's mental torture. The illusion of the Littlewoods Cup run had gone, and relegation was now an all-consuming presence. Fans turned; the winless run, the loss of key players, the 11-goal debacle at Luton and now accusations of freezing in the competition that defined them was unforgivable.

Evans didn't need the boos cascading from the London Road terrace to understand the mood of the club. He was acutely aware he was the centre of an ecosystem that relied on him. He wanted to protect those he held dear and escape the pernicious forces staining the game.

A torrid winter turned to spring as Oxford travelled to mid-table West Ham. Despite an early scare, when David Bardsley headed Leroy Rosenior's looping header off the line, Oxford's display was more encouraging. Les Phillips went closest, bursting into the box only to see his shot parried by Tom McAlister.

After the break, Oxford remained resolute for an hour until Colin Greenall hobbled off on his debut. Despite the setback, 12 minutes later Phillips picked the ball up 25 yards out and jinked beyond the West Ham defence. McAlister parried Phillips's low drive, but the ricochet squirmed into the net. Evans's despair lifted; Oxford had 22 minutes to secure their first league win in 14 games.

Their resistance lasted a minute; Mark Ward pounced to drive through a crowd of players for the equaliser. The noise from Upton Park swamped the celebrating Oxford fans.

Maurice Evans knew it was over. The man who never wanted to be manager but had taken the club to Wembley resigned five days later after talking with Jim Hunt. He'd steered Oxford to glory because of and despite the owner. His spirit was broken by the battles on and off the pitch. Evans knew his decision would affect his staff. It was the only thing binding him to the job, but the impact his anguish had on his family life had broken him. 'I can't switch off every time we lose,' he said. 'I don't want my family to be burdened with my problems.'

There was no shortage of names linked with the vacancy: ex-Norwich City manager Ken Brown, former Gillingham boss Keith Peacock, Jim Smith's number two Peter Shreeve and ex-Spurs manager Keith Burkinshaw were all potential candidates.

The press speculated that Ron Atkinson may interest Kevin Maxwell. Since his dismissal from Manchester United, Atkinson had returned to West Bromwich Albion but couldn't rekindle his golden years of the 1970s. Despite the team slipping towards the Third Division, Atkinson was quick to quash the rumours, quipping that he didn't like boat races.

Fans campaigned for Billy Hamilton, after a year managing Limerick, but he wasn't ready to step up. Maurice Evans's mentee Steve Perryman also dismissed his prospects as did Trevor Francis, who Jim Smith wanted at QPR. Torquay manager Cyril Knowles was also an early favourite.

Despite the speculation, and 11 days between games due to Arsenal's FA Cup quarter-final against Nottingham Forest, Evans remained in charge as Oxford headed to in-form Norwich.

The visitors conceded an Andy Linighan goal after 11 minutes, before Les Phillips was sent off for dissent four minutes later. Despite the setback, Oxford persevered with Bryan Gunn saving from Martin Foyle and Gary Shelton.

After the break, Gunn fumbled Bardsley's fierce 30-yard shot for the equaliser, raising hopes of a vital point. Then just after the hour, Robert Fleck combined with Trevor Putney to put Norwich ahead before crossing for Kevin Drinkell to make it 3-1. Fleck headed the fourth nine minutes from time. Hebberd's late consolation couldn't stop Oxford dropping to 20th, four points from safety.

Evans craved a release from his purgatory, but as Kevin Maxwell searched for his replacement, his obligations remained. As 16th-placed Chelsea visited the Manor, Evans prepared to write his programme notes for the last time.

His column usually reflected his introverted character: short and benign, a stark contrast to Jim Hunt's two-page polemics directed at whoever had crossed his path that week. Evans's editorial was so short it was sometimes reproduced in a larger font to fill the space.

This time, he had something to say. He acknowledged the loyalty of his backroom staff Ray Graydon, David Fogg and chief scout Dave Coates who were 'football people', not the 'parasites' sucking enjoyment from the game. He lamented the loss of characters and the emergence of robotic footballers. His philosophy, inspired by his father, was to give players freedom to express themselves. His advice to fans was to 'live today like it's going to be your last because one day it will be'.

Evans was supportive of Chelsea manager John Hollins, whose own position was under threat. Chelsea were engulfed in a psychodrama; an injury crisis, a 17-game winless run, and the potential losses of Kerry Dixon to West Ham or Arsenal and Micky Hazard to QPR.

Their misfortune continued when defender Joe McLaughlin woke up at 3am on the day of the game hearing a tap dripping, and as he investigated he fell down the stairs, twisting his ankle.

Amid rictus grins, Hollins sat next to chairman Ken Bates in the Beech Road stand as the teams appeared from the tunnel below. The sense of chaos was reflected on the field from the opening minutes when Trevor Hebberd allowed a hopeful ball from Tony Dorigo through to Dixon, forcing the returning Greenall to scramble to cover. Moments later there was more suicidal defending; David Bardsley safely controlled a long punt from Perry Digweed but rolled the ball into the path of Kevin Wilson, forcing Alan Judge to clear.

Eventually, after 17 minutes, Dixon beat Judge to Colin Pates's cross, and Pat Nevin arrived at the back post to slam the ball into the roof of the net. Ten minutes later it was two when Dixon crossed for John Bumstead. A minute before half-time Dixon made it three. There was still time for him to narrowly miss a chance for a fourth, before taunts of 'what a load of rubbish' bellowed from all corners of the Manor at half-time. Evans hoped the ground might swallow him, or that Kevin Maxwell might give him his sweet release by deciding on his successor.

Hollins made his way down the touchline to join head coach Bobby Campbell, who many believed was recruited to replace the manager. With their elusive win now seemingly secure, Hollins wasn't going to allow Campbell the glory.

Chelsea had conceded three or more goals on seven occasions during their barren run including a two-goal lead to Coventry two weeks earlier. Oxford had one not so secret weapon, the Manor's slope.

Evans abandoned his hapless sweeper system, replacing the injured Tommy Caton with Sean Reck, bolstering the midfield and starving Chelsea's attack. Three minutes after the break, it paid dividends as Bardsley's cross was knocked down to Peter Rhoades-Brown, who scrambled a goal back.

For 15 minutes it looked like a consolation, until Rhoades-Brown played a long ball to the back post to Saunders to make it 3-2. A thundering roar cascaded from the London Road, willing each wave of attack to produce an equaliser. Chelsea disintegrated; every sortie seemed to result in a chance, and only Perry Digweed's heroics delayed the inevitable.

With 14 minutes to go, Saunders was pulled down and Bardsley's free kick was met with a diving header from Foyle for the equaliser. The Manor found its voice. Barrelled along by the avalanche of attacks, the supporters could forget their differences and be subsumed in the spectacle. It had been a remarkable turnaround, but Oxford had a thirst for more, surging to break the curse of the last few months. A near-post corner nearly brought the fourth, Robbie Mustoe's cross was nearly turned in and Saunders had a header saved.

Digweed despaired, and with four minutes to go he pounced on the ball, just happy to have it safely in his hands. He looked up towards the halfway line at the bewildered faces of his team-mates, lost deep in their thoughts. There was one hope, a player discovered by Maurice Evans as a teenager at Reading, who he'd nurtured and refined, who'd become an England international and one of the most sought-after strikers in the country, Kerry Dixon.

With Oxford jammed in a relentless forward gear, Digweed launched a long ball forward which landed at the feet of Nevin. The Scot cushioned his pass into the path of Dixon, who instinctively unleashed a drive beyond Alan Judge for 4-3. The Chelsea bench emptied; Hollins celebrated on the pitch, his damnation seemingly over.

Oxford were desolate; they'd pulled themselves back and then thrown it away. Disconsolate, they restarted, abandoning any sense of composure. Saunders rolled the ball to Rhoades-Brown, who launched another long clearance forward. Mustoe climbed to win the header, Chelsea scrambled, but the ball ran to Saunders, who crashed a half-volley into the back of the net. Chelsea's lead had lasted for 15 seconds.

The crowd dissolved into a collective madness, bodies collapsed on top of each other, players celebrated wildly. Then, slicing through the hysteria came the blast of a whistle. One by one, faces fell, eyes darted for confirmation – the referee had disallowed the goal for a foul by Mustoe.

The dejection was palpable, a deep cavern of injustice, and the debate raged as play restarted. It was hard to focus as the inquest began. More minutes passed, and just seconds remained; a hurried clearance from Judge landed at the feet of Hebberd, who charged into the box, checked his run like he did at Wembley and chipped the ball towards Saunders. The Welshman leapt into the air, twisting his torso, connecting with the cross and glancing his header beyond Digweed for 4-4.

The Manor had produced its magic again, one last shake of the tree before it returned to its quaint anonymity. In the final thrashings of a wild ride, bewildered by the modern game, Evans disappeared down the tunnel for the last time. John Hollins, who would last four more days in his job, gave a rueful smile: 'Well, you can't say it's not entertaining.'

A week after he retired, Mark Lawrenson received a call from deputy editor of the *Sunday People*, John Maddock, asking if he was interested in talking to Oxford United chairman Kevin Maxwell.

After the meeting in London, Lawrenson finalised insurance details in Liverpool before being helicoptered down to the Manor by his new boss. His first conversation with Ray Graydon was to tell him he was no longer needed. Graydon was preparing to leave anyway having put the cattery business he ran with his wife up for sale.

Lawrenson recalled Peter Hucker from his loan spell at West Brom and the following morning he boarded the team bus to Charlton to tell the players he was their new manager. He gave the team talk and sat in the stands with his chairman as Evans marshalled from the bench for the goalless draw. Lawrenson was agog, 'The game brought home to me the massive gulf in standards between the top three or four and the rest.'

The transition complete, Evans blended into the background, taking up his new scouting and youth development role. A new era under Lawrenson dawned. The youngest manager in the division and the youngest chairman; the club was being led by the postwar generation.

Despite his reputation, Lawrenson wasn't immune from prankster Terry Gordon, who burst into the manager's office accusing him of sleeping with his wife before chasing him around the pitch, only stopping after claiming he'd mistaken Lawrenson for David Fogg.

As accomplished as he was on the pitch, Lawrenson was overawed by the prospect of running a whole club, asking Maurice Evans to remain in his office as an advisor. Initially he wanted Frank Stapleton as his assistant, but would eventually appoint his old Brighton team-mate Brian Horton, who offered the experience he needed.

Despite Lawrenson's defiance, he found a club whose heart and commitment had gone, a lack of fight illustrated by the fact Tommy Caton hadn't been booked all season – a far cry from the days of Malcolm Shotton and Gary Briggs.

The renewal seemed to wash away much of the club's character. Arsenal were the first visitors but there was little to enjoy with debutant Brian Marwood occasionally threatening down the flank and Alan Smith keeping the Oxford back four busy.

Shelton and Saunders went close and Mustoe hit the inside of the post before Hucker saved from Nigel Winterburn and John Lukic denied Richard Hill. Bland and goalless, Lawrenson commended the effort but recognised there was work to do and little time to do it.

April opened with a trip to Coventry City. While boarding for travel, Martin Foyle fell up the steps of the team coach and injured his knee, meaning he only lasted until half-time.

The heavily sanded pitch offered little prospect of entertainment as both teams slogged their way through the 90 minutes. The home side seemed content with a point as the game drifted into the final minute. Oxford won a throw which Dean Saunders raced to take, hoping for a late chance.

In his eagerness, he conceded possession which led to a free kick. Dave Phillips's cross was met by Cyrille Regis to head home the winner. Lawrenson furiously branded Saunders 'unprofessional'.

Lawrenson, a self-declared winner, couldn't locate the bug in the system he'd inherited. On Easter Monday, before another goalless draw with Southampton, he finally found it. While giving his team talk, the dressing room door opened and in walked Robert Maxwell wearing a Derby County cap. Omnipresent yet absent, singular yet conflicted, distracted with a laser focus; everything Oxford United did and had done was inspired and tainted by Maxwell. He was the cog and the bug.

Five days later, Oxford headed to bottom-of-the-table Watford, the source of the mid-season turmoil which skittled their season and destroyed their spirit. Both sides, once underdog darlings of English football, were now its pariahs; Watford hadn't won for ten games, which was dwarfed by Oxford's run of 21.

Oxford conceded after four minutes, failing to clear Gary Porter's corner and allowing Rick Holden to fire home. Before the half-hour mark, Glyn Hodges made it two with Oxford barely raising a chance in response. Watford consolidated their lead, soaking up pressure before Hodges made it three eight minutes from time. Lawrenson admitted his players were resigned to their fate with many accepting life in the Second Division.

After seven and a half hours without a goal, the following Wednesday, just 5,727 fans trudged through the aged Manor turnstiles for the rearranged visit of Sheffield Wednesday. It was the lowest First Division attendance of the season, just ten more than had attended Ian Greaves's first game in 1980.

Briggs escaped a penalty after six minutes, fouling Lee Chapman just outside the box. Nine minutes later, Tony

Galvin beat Bardsley and crossed to David Hirst, whose cushioned header set up Chapman to open the scoring.

Nigel Worthington cleared Greenall's header off the line from Rhoades-Brown's cross before Chapman killed the brief revival with his second after 20 minutes. Ten minutes later Hucker's hesitancy allowed Galvin to shoot, but Briggs cleared his goalbound header.

After the break, Bardsley gave Pressman a scare from 30 yards, but Mel Sterland completed the thrashing with 17 minutes to go. Four games remained; Oxford were six points from safety and hadn't scored in nine hours of league football. The amiable Lawrenson snapped, cancelling their day off and a planned trip to Guernsey, demanding the players watch themselves on video. 'We're too nice,' he said. 'Too many players accept second best and allow the opposition to walk all over them.'

Ten days later, Oxford welcomed third-placed Everton to the Manor as a bright spring afternoon gave a sense of a new beginning after a harsh winter, but in many ways it was the end.

Sixteen points behind Liverpool, Everton's own golden era was over. Following his cathartic outburst after the Sheffield Wednesday game, Lawrenson was relaxed, his playing career behind him. With Liverpool set to confirm the title, he was due to pick up a winners' medal, while facing relegation in the same season. The contrast of Anfield and the Manor was not lost on him.

Despite the apathetic collapse in Oxford's form, Dean Saunders continued to show boundless enthusiasm, breaking through the ponderous Everton defence, but his meek shot was collected by Neville Southall.

This encouraged Rhoades-Brown to attack down the left. After 39 minutes, he cut inside Gary Stevens, giving the England defender little choice but to check his run. As soon as Rhoades-Brown hit the floor, the referee pointed to the spot. Finally, after nine hours without a goal, Saunders rolled the ball down the middle as Southall dived left. The Manor meekly acknowledged the feat as the ball hit the back of the net, a ripple of applause rolling around the ground.

The lead lasted until just before half-time when a simple ball found Graeme Sharp on the right. Sharp squared it to Wayne Clarke who equalised, leaving Oxford's defence trailing.

The point left Oxford eight points from safety with three games left. If they dropped points at Newcastle it would be over. Despite their youthful promise, on a pitch ravaged by the season, after five minutes Newcastle's veteran centre-back Glenn Roeder broke from defence, beating Foyle and Hebberd before releasing Darren Jackson.

Jackson found David McCreery, whose cross was intercepted but Bardsley's shambolic weak back-pass allowed McCreery to steal in and clip the ball to the back post for debutant Tony Lormor to head into the empty net.

Ten minutes after half-time, Roeder cut through the turgid midfield quagmire, combined with Jackson, and set up Michael O'Neill to clip in his 12th goal of the season.

Dispirited, broken, exhausted, Oxford accepted their fate as Newcastle fizzed with energy; a minute later, O'Neill clipped the ball to Paul Goddard, whose shot cannoned off the bar. Paul Gascoigne picked up the loose ball, waltzed round the Oxford defence and played it into the six-yard box for Goddard to make it three.

In the second half, a ghost from Oxford's past appeared on the touchline as Andy Thomas replaced Darren Jackson. With just three minutes remaining, Rhoades-Brown and Saunders combined to feed Les Phillips, whose one-two in the box with Mustoe gave him the space to curl in a quality consolation. It was never going to be enough. Relegation was confirmed and St James' Park rippled with sympathetic applause.

Obituaries were written, tributes to Oxford's resilience, their effort and their untapped quality, but Lawrenson took little comfort, announcing a summer clear-out. 'They seem to think you go down to the Second Division and go straight back up.'

For the final time, on bank holiday Monday, Oxford hosted top-flight football. Manchester United, who'd had a torrid history at the Manor, were fittingly the visitors.

Far from the epic Milk Cup tie in 1983, Alex Ferguson's debut in 1987 and the Littlewoods Cup win earlier in the year, Oxford were a husk of their former selves. After seven minutes Alan Judge flapped at a corner from Jesper Olsen, allowing Viv Anderson to head home. Judge redeemed himself, saving Peter Davenport's penalty after Colin Greenall was harshly penalised for handball. Gordon Strachan soloed his way to 2-0 three minutes before Greenall conceded a second spot kick only for Judge to deny Olsen again.

Relieved of their heavy burden, Oxford headed to Nottingham Forest for the last game of the season. Franz Carr ran at Oxford's brittle defence, helping Neil Webb open the scoring after five minutes. Undeterred, five minutes later Foyle headed in Rhoades-Brown's cross. In the 16th minute, Carr's deflected shot restored the lead and just before half-time, Nigel Clough grabbed two more. Oxford headed meekly into the break 4-1 down.

Just after the hour, captain Trevor Hebberd played in Foyle for 4-2; Hebberd then reduced the deficit further ten minutes later. The search for an unlikely though meaningless point was thwarted four minutes from time when Webb made it 5-3.

Oxford were relegated, bottom of the table and nine points from safety. They'd failed to score in 17 of their games and hadn't won in 25. As they slipped down the tunnel at the City Ground, the curtain finally fell on the glory years.

Chapter 27

Me (again)

THE BRUTAL angular features of the East and South stands frame a featureless grey sky which seems to stretch out beyond eternity; the expanse is only broken by the empty rows of blue plastic seats in the North Stand.

I stare out of my car window and question why I'm here at all. Apathy and a sense of hopelessness made me abandon my usual routine and drive into the expansive car park that encircles the current home of Oxford United, the Kassam Stadium.

Even in the bleakest times, the car park would be full long before kick-off, but today with 15 minutes to go, I'm directed to a spot outside Entrance 9, my turnstile. It seems I'm not the only one who is adrift with ennui; just 4,200 fans will watch today's game.

Nothing I see can muster any enthusiasm to head into the ground. A few people mill around, but like me they're there out of habit more than anticipation. The stadium, incomplete and crippled by a lack of ambition or vision offers no welcoming embrace; the club's now home is limp and lifeless, seemingly awaiting imminent death.

It's 21 January 2006, and in a few weeks the club will celebrate 20 years since the Milk Cup win. Oxford are preparing to host Darlington, hoping to arrest their slide towards relegation out of the Football League. Spiritually it feels like we've hit the bottom, but a quiet ghostly hand encourages me as I open the car door and head for the turnstile. Again, I will fulfil my obligations and again I will not be rewarded.

Relegation in 1988 brought little catharsis; there was no scent of Mark Lawrenson's summer clear-out or any great redemption. He was, at least, buoyed by Kevin Maxwell's commitment to retain Dean Saunders as the totem around whom Lawrenson could rebuild his battered squad.

That promise held until October 1988 when Robert Maxwell swooped in with a tissue-thin £1m to take Saunders to Derby. Maxwell's hostility towards Oxford was barely contained; it was like he'd been wronged and wanted revenge. Lawrenson was so incensed by the betrayal that he resigned, plunging Oxford into a deep fug. His assistant, Brian Horton, took over, adopting a pragmatism that arrested the slide as Oxford whimpered to a 17th-placed finish.

Horton took nearly two years to bring in a generation unbridled by the legacies of Wembley and the First Division. Finishing tenth in the Second Division in 1990 hinted at, if not a turnaround, some stability.

On 5 November 1991, news broke that Maxwell, on holiday in the Canary Islands, was missing, apparently having fallen off his yacht, the *Lady Ghislaine*, in the middle of the night. Drowning was the simplest explanation, but rumours circled as much as the controversies did when he was alive.

As his body was dragged from the sea, his business empire collapsed; his many misdemeanours and crimes, the subterfuge and deceit were no longer obscured by his eclipsing presence. The millions he claimed to have earned either didn't exist or weren't his. He'd stolen nearly half a billion pounds, most of which he plundered from the Mirror Group pension fund.

His remaining assets were sold, the lease of Headington Hill Hall handed over to Brookes University. In one tiny forgotten corner of his empire, Oxford United's financial lifeline was severed and they were plunged into an existential crisis which would last a generation.

Meanwhile, the wider fissures created through the wretched decade of the 1980s, fractures that Maxwell had helped lever open and profit from, finally split open. The lumbering, antiquated, exhausted Football League who'd spent a decade battling hooliganism and a hostile media collapsed.

The European ban, lifted in 1990, and a strong performance by England at that year's World Cup accelerated the appetite for change. Tired of living hand to mouth and having their dominance undermined by snotty upstarts like Oxford, the bigger clubs, who'd been humbled and threatened by smaller clubs, agreed to build a fortress around their dominance and broke away to form the Premier League.

Wantonly commercial, TV rights, an asset that Maxwell had vehemently complained were undersold, were auctioned off to his nemesis Rupert Murdoch and Sky TV. The Premier League began the process of insulating themselves from future financial problems.

Clubs scrambled to find safety as the chasm grew. Some would find themselves on the side of the haves – picking up the scraps of the big clubs' greed – grateful for the largesse of their captures. Oxford United, listless, directionless and unloved, drifted away with the have-nots just six years after they'd lifted the Milk Cup at Wembley.

A succession of owners dallied with bridging the widening financial gap until Robin Herd, an Oxford fan, Formula 1 entrepreneur and serial dreamer, achieved the goal Maxwell never had. In 1995 he finally gained planning permission to build the club a new stadium at Minchery Farm and leave the dilapidated Manor Ground with its fragments of memories still caught in the peeling paint and rusting girders.

Stadium construction started in 1996, but by the end of 1997, with only the steel carcass of three stands complete, it stopped; the money had gone. Herd had gambled on planning permission for a shopping centre adjacent to the ground, but when it was turned down, investors fled. The club was eventually bought by hotelier Firoz Kassam, who sold the Manor to his own company at a discount and forced through the completion of the three stands. The Kassam Stadium, with its gaping open end, opened in 2001.

In 2000 as the club imploded in rancour, Maurice Evans died of a heart attack aged 63. He'd spent a decade quietly maintaining stability as chief scout before returning to Reading after becoming disillusioned. In his wake were a slew of young players and hidden talents that kept Oxford in the Second Division, punching well above their weight.

Five years later, Ken Fish passed away aged 91 having returned to South Africa after his wife died. Seemingly immortal, Mr Fish battled through a double amputation before finally succumbing to his illnesses. The immaculate heart of the club had never dropped a stitch.

Kassam would remain owner for five more years, baulking at the investment needed to develop a sustainable football club. As each financial slingshot got bigger, the rewards seemed to get smaller.

Sitting in the car in 2006, looking out the window, steeling myself to walk the 20 feet to the turnstile, it felt like we'd finally become suffocated by the apathy.

Nine weeks later Oxford fans woke to the news that Kassam was no longer the owner. Having come under increasing pressure to move aside, he sold to Nick Merry, a former Oxford youth team player and entrepreneur. Alongside Merry was a familiar face: Jim Smith.

Smith took over as manager but failed to arrest the decline with relegation into non-league confirmed at the end of the season. He came close to returning the club to the Football League the following year, but after a play-off failure, he stood aside. Hope alone wasn't enough.

He remained, guiding the club, keeping it alive using his network of contacts to bring in players and coaches and arranging prestige friendlies including one against Sir Alex Ferguson's all-dominant Manchester United. He was part of the panel who appointed Chris Wilder in 2008; Wilder set about belligerently turning the club around, berating those who valued Oxford by their achievements 20 years earlier.

On 16 May 2010, Wilder returned Oxford to Wembley for the Conference National play-off final against York City. Having steered the club through some of its greatest days, Smith declared it the most important game in its history, a final roll of the dice before another financial crisis hit landfall. In front of 30,000 Oxford fans and a record Conference National final attendance they unleashed another barnstorming performance to win 3-1 and return to the Football League.

In the stands there were tears, on the pitch elation and in the boardroom relief. In the royal box was Jim Smith, finally a winner with Oxford at Wembley.

He would remain a constant presence around the club until he passed away in 2019 in Woodstock, where he'd lived since his arrival at the club nearly 40 years earlier.

Having been cast into a financial abyss by Maxwell's death and suffered a slow and painful decay in the years that followed, the club remained. The humiliating relegation into non-league, among the part-timers and rejects, can devour proud clubs. Many continue to slide, some disappear completely. Through it all Oxford's spirit remained.

Somewhere in the soul of a football club beats a heart that thrives on its memories, stories and legends. Without them the relegations, humiliations, food parcels and financial collapses chisel away until it collapses. For Oxford United, the triumphs of Jim Smith and Maurice Evans, the grit of Malcolm Shotton and Gary Briggs, the landmark achievements of Ray Houghton, John Aldridge and Dean Saunders, those years though brief and likely never to return, still resonate through the club, the generations and time. The Glory Years are why we stay.

Bibliography

Books:

Aldridge J., *My Story* (London: Hodder and Stoughton, 1999)

Brodetsky M., *Oxford United Miscellany* (Worthing: Pitch Publishing, 2010)

Brodetsky M., *The Complete Record 1893–2009* (Derby: Breedon Books, 2009)

Howland A., & Howland R., *Oxford United: A Complete Record 1893–1989* (Derby: Breedon Books Publishing, 1989)

Howland A., & Howland R., *The Headington Years* (Oxford: Perfitt-Bayliss, 2001)

Langan D., Keane T., & Conway A., *Running Through Walls: Dave Langan* (Derby: JMD Media, 2012)

Ley J., *Rags to Riches, The Rise and Rise of Oxford United* (Oxford: Queen Anne Press, 1985)

Morris D., *The Soccer Tribe* (London: Jonathan Cape, 1981)

Smith J., & Cass B., *Jim Smith: The Autobiography* (London: Andre Deutsch, 2000)

Swann G., & Ward A., *The Boys from Up the Hill: An Oral History of Oxford United* (London: Crowberry, 1996)

Bower T., *Maxwell, the Outsider* (New York: Viking, 1992)

Smith J., & Trelfer D., *Second Yellow: The Further Adventures of our Footballing Heroes* (Worthing: Pitch Publishing, 2020)

YouTube channels:
OUFC Archive: youtube.com/@OUFCArchive
Jim Hendo: youtube.com/@jimhendo8392
1980s Football Heaven: youtube.com/@sFootballHeaven

Podcasts:
Great British Scandal podcast – Maxwell
The Dub
The Fence End
The Manor Podcast
Behind the Badge
Oxford United Official Podcast

Websites:
rageonline.co.uk
oxfordkits.com
11v11.com
oxfordmail.co.uk

Newspapers:
Aldershot News
Birmingham Evening Mail
Birmingham Metro News
Black Country Evening Mail
Cambridge Evening News
Coventry Evening Telegraph
Daily Mirror
Daily Post
Daily Record
Daily Telegraph
Evening Chronicle
Evening Herald
Evening Post, Bristol
Evening Standard
Farnborough News

Huddersfield Daily Examiner
Leicester Mercury
Lincolnshire Echo
Liverpool Echo
Manchester Evening News
Oxford Mail
Reading Evening Post
Scunthorpe Evening Telegraph
Sports Argus
Stoke Evening Sentinel
Surrey Hants Star
The Guardian
The Independent
The Journal
The Observer
Sunday Mirror
Sunday People
Sunday Telegraph
Western Daily Press

Miscellaneous:
Oxford United programmes (various) 1980–1988